T0289702

Advanced Fixed Income Analysis

বিদ্যাসিন্ধুসাগর কুমানের চিন্তা

Advanced Fixed Income Analysis

2nd Edition

Moorad Choudhry

Michele Lizzio

AMSTERDAM • BOSTON • HEIDELBERG • LONDON
NEW YORK • OXFORD • PARIS • SAN DIEGO
SAN FRANCISCO • SINGAPORE • SYDNEY • TOKYO

Butterworth-Heinemann is an imprint of Elsevier

Butterworth Heinemann is an imprint of Elsevier
525 B Street, Suite 1800, San Diego, CA 92101, USA
The Boulevard, Langford Lane, Kidlington, Oxford OX5 1GB, UK
225 Wyman Street, Waltham, MA 02451, USA

Notices
Knowledge and best practice in this field are constantly changing. As new research and experience broaden our understanding, changes in research methods, professional practices, or medical treatment may become necessary.

Practitioners and researchers must always rely on their own experience and knowledge in evaluating and using any information, methods, compounds, or experiments described herein. In using such information or methods they should be mindful of their own safety and the safety of others, including parties for whom they have a professional responsibility.

To the fullest extent of the law, neither the Publisher nor the authors, contributors, or editors, assume any liability for any injury and/or damage to persons or property as a matter of products liability, negligence or otherwise, or from any use or operation of any methods, products, instructions, or ideas contained in the material herein.

British Library Cataloguing in Publication Data
A catalogue record for this book is available from the British Library

Library of Congress Cataloging-in-Publication Data
A catalog record for this book is available from the Library of Congress

ISBN: 978-0-08-099938-8

For information on all Butterworth Heinemann publications
visit our website at http://store.elsevier.com/

Printed and bound in the United States

Publisher: Nikki Levy
Acquisition Editor: Scott Bentley
Editorial Project Manager: Susan Ikeda
Production Project Manager: Jason Mitchell
Designer: Mark Rogers

Dedication

Moorad Choudhry
For my grandfather, Mr Abdul Hakim
(c. 1898–1983), Advocate
Citizen of Noakhali, Bangladesh

and

Michele Lizzio
For my mum and dad

Contents

About the Authors

Moorad Choudhry is CEO of Habib Bank Zurich plc in London, and Visiting Professor at the Department of Mathematical Sciences, Brunel University. He is Founder of The Certificate of Bank Treasury Risk Management (BTRM).

Moorad has over 25 years experience in banking in the City of London and was previsouly IPO Treasurer at the Royal Bank of Scotland, Head of Treasury at RBS Corporate Banking, Head of Treasury at Europe Arab Bank, Head of Treasury at KBC Financial Products and vice-president in structured finance services at JPMorgan Chase Bank.

Moorad is a Fellow of the Chartered Institute for Securities & Investment and a Fellow of IFS-University College. He is Editor of *Review of Financial Markets*, and the author of *The Principles of Banking* (John Wiley & Sons 2012).

Michele Lizzio is Senior Analyst at Deloitte Financial Advisory, Valuation Services in Milan. He has experience in equity valuation and is involved in the development and implementation of fixed income and derivate based models in Deloitte.

He graduated cum laude in MSc Corporate Finance from University of Brescia. He began his career collaborating with Alberto Falini, Professor of Corporate Finance at University of Brescia.

Preface

Everything in life is relative. One person's simple is another person's difficult. Comparisons are often problematic to undertake, because of the difficulties with ensuring that one is measuring like against like. So we begin the Second Edition of *Advanced Fixed Income Analysis* with the caveat that while it may be "advanced" to some it may well not be to others. But nevertheless it is worth updating the book simply to reflect changes in thinking and approach that have occurred since the First Edition was published.

What is worthy then of a further investment of cash to purchase this second edition? Hopefully the new chapters on asset swap spread relative value, convertible bonds, callable/putable bonds and floating-rate notes will be sufficient justification; additionally we have updated the previous chapters on inflation-linked bonds and risky corporate bonds valuation. We have also included Excel spreadsheets that enable the reader to apply the analysis described in the chapters right away to bonds that he or she selects.

We have deleted the chapters on cubic spline (a technique now very well known and with plenty of material about it out there on the internet) and Brady bonds. We have also removed the earlier edition's chapters on risk-free sovereign bonds trading, on the grounds that the logic of analysis employed for such investments has not changed since 2003, and also more indirectly because there are so few genuinely risk-free sovereign issuers left in the world!

I am grateful to my new co-author for this Second Edition, Michele Lizzio, for his tireless and energetic input.

As always readers are welcome to send feedback direct, please email me at mooradchoudhry@gmail.com

We hope you enjoy the book.

Moorad Choudhry
Surrey, England
February 2015

Michele Lizzio
Milan, Italy
February 2015

Preface to the First Edition (published 2004)

THE DYNAMICS OF THE YIELD CURVE

In chapter 2 of the companion volume to this book in the boxed-set library, *Corporate Bonds and Structured Financial Products*, we introduced the concept of the yield curve, and reviewed some preliminary issues concerning both the shape of the curve and to what extent the curve could be used to infer the shape and level of the yield curve in the future. We do not know what interest rates will be in the future, but given a set of zero-coupon (spot) rates today we can estimate the future level of forward rates using a yield curve model. In many cases however we do not have a zero-coupon curve to begin with, so it then becomes necessary to derive the spot yield curve from the yields of coupon bonds, which one can observe readily in the market. If a market only trades short-dated debt instruments, then it will be possible to construct a short-dated spot curve.

It is important for a zero-coupon yield curve to be constructed as accurately as possible. This because the curve is used in the valuation of a wide range of instruments, not only conventional cash market coupon bonds, which we can value using the appropriate spot rate for each cash flow, but other interest-rate products such as swaps.

If using a spot rate curve for valuation purposes, banks use what are known as *arbitrage-free* yield curve models, where the derived curve has been matched to the current spot yield curve. The concept of arbitrage-free, also known as no-arbitrage pricing or "the law of one price" is that if one is valuing the same product or cash flow in two different ways, the same result will be obtained from either method. So as we demonstrated in chapter 6, if one was valuing a two-year bond that was put-able by the holder at par in one year's time, it could be analysed as a one-year bond that entitled the holder to reinvest it for another year. The rule of no-arbitrage pricing states that an identical price will be obtained whichever way one chooses to analyse the bond. When matching derived yield curves therefore, correctly matched curves will generate the same price when valuing a bond, whether a derived spot curve is used or the current term structure of spot rates.

From our understanding of derivatives, we know that option pricing models such as Black-Scholes assume that asset price returns follow a lognormal distribution. The dynamics of interest rates and the term structure is the subject of some debate, and the main differences between the main interest-rate models is in the way that they choose to capture the change in rates over a time period. However although volatility of the yield curve is indeed the main area of difference, certain models are easier to implement than others, and this is a key factor a bank considers when deciding which model to use. The process of *calibrating* the model, that is, setting it up to estimate the spot and forward term structure using current interest rates that are input to the model, is almost as important as deriving the model itself. So the availability of data for a range of products, including cash money markets, cash bonds, futures and swaps, is vital to the successful implementation of the model.

As one might expect the yields on bonds are correlated, in most cases very closely positively correlated. This enables us to analyse interest-rate risk in a portfolio for example, but also to model the term structure in a systematic way. Much of the traditional approach to bond portfolio management assumed a parallel shift in the yield curve, so that if the 5-year bond yield moved upwards by 10 basis points, then the 30-year bond yield would also move up by 10 basis points. This underpins traditional duration and modified duration analysis, and the concept of immunisation. To analyse bonds in this way, we assume therefore that bond yield volatilities are identical and correlations are perfectly positive. Although both types of analysis are still common, it is clear that bond yields do not move in this fashion, and so we must enhance our approach in order to perform more accurate analysis.

FACTORS INFLUENCING THE YIELD CURVE

From the discussion in chapter we are aware that there are range of factors that impact on the shape and level of the yield curve. A combination of economic and non-economic factors are involved. A key factor is investor expectations, with respect to the level of inflation, and the level of real interest rates in the future. In the real world the market does not assume that either of these two factors is constant, however given that there is a high level uncertainty over anything longer than the short-term, generally there is an assumption about both inflation and interest rates to move towards some form of equilibrium in the long-term.

It is possible to infer market expectations about the level of real interest rates going forward by observing yields in government index-linked bonds, which trade in a number of countries including the US and UK. The market's view on the future level of interest rates may also be inferred from the shape and level of the current yield curve. Again from chapter 6, we saw that the slope of the yield curve also has an information content. There is more than one way to interpret any given slope however, and this debate is still open.

The fact that there are a number of factors that influence changes in interest rates and the shape of the yield curve means that it is not straightforward to model the curve itself. In the following chapter we consider some of the traditional and more recent approaches that have been developed.

APPROACHES TO MODELLING

The area of interest rate dynamics and yield curve modelling is one of the most heavily researched in financial economics. There are a number of models available in the market today, and generally it is possible to categorise them as following certain methodologies. By categorising them in this way, participants in the market can assess them for their suitability, as well as draw their own conclusions about how realistic they might be. Let us consider the main categories.

ONE-FACTOR, TWO-FACTOR AND MULTI-FACTOR MODELS

The key assumption that is made by an interest-rate model is whether it is one-factor, that is the dynamics of the yield change process is based on one factor, or multi-factor. From observation we know that in reality there are a number of factors that influence the price change process, and that if we are using a model to value an option product, the valuation of that product is dependent on more than one underlying factor. For example the payoff on a bond option is related to the underlying bond's cash flows as well as to the reinvestment rate that would be applied to each cash flow, in addition to certain other factors. Valuing an option therefore is a multi-factor issue. In many cases however there is a close degree of correlation between the different factors involved. If we are modelling the term structure, we can calculate the correlation between the different maturity spot rates by using a covariance matrix of changes each of the spot rates, and thus obtain a common factor that impacts all spot rates in the same direction. This factor can then be used to model the entire term structure in a one-factor model, and although two-factor and multi-factor models have been developed, the one-factor model is still commonly used. In principle it is relatively straightforward to move from a one-factor to a multi-factor model, but implementing and calibrating a multi-factor model is a more involved process. This is because the model requires the estimation of more volatility and correlation parameters, which slows down the process.

Readers will encounter the term *Gaussian* in reference to certain interest-rate models. Put simply a Gaussian process describes one that follows a normal distribution under a probability density function. The distribution of rates in this way for Gaussiam models implies that interest rates can attain negative values under positive probability, which makes the models undesirable for some market practitioners. Nevertheless such models are popular because they are relatively straightforward to implement and because the probability of the model generating negative rates is low and occurs only under certain extreme circumstances.

THE SHORT-TERM RATE AND THE YIELD CURVE

The application of risk-neutral valuation, which we discussed in chapter 45, requires that we know the sequence of short-term rates for each scenario, which is provided in some interest-rate models. For this reason, many yield curve models are essentially models of the stochastic evolution of the short-term rate. They assume that changes in the short-term interest-rate is a *Markov* process. (It is outside the scope of this book to review the mathematics of such processes, but references are provided in subsequent chapters.) This describes an evolution of short-term rates in which the evolution of the rate is a function only of its current level, and not the path by which it arrived there. The practical significance of this is that the valuation of interest-rate products can be reduced by the solution of a single partial differential equation.

Short-rate models are composed of two components. The first attempts to capture the average rate of change, also called the *drift*, of the short-term rate at each instant, while the second component measures this drift as a function of the volatility of the short-term rate. This is given by:

$$dr(t) = \mu(r,t)dt + \sigma(r,t)dW(t)$$

where $dr(t)$ is the instantaneous change in the short-term rate, and $W(t)$ is the stochastic process that describes the evolution in interest rates, known as a Brownian or Weiner process.

The term $\mu(r,t)$ is the value of the drift multiplied by the size of the time period. The term $\sigma(r,t)dW(t)$ is the volatility of the short-term rate multiplied by a random increment that is normally distributed. In most models the drift rate term is determined through a numerical technique that matches the initial spot rate yield curve, while in some models an analytical solution is available. Generally models assume an arbitrage-free relationship between the initial forward rate curve, the volatility $\sigma(r,t)$, the market price of interest-rate risk and the drift term $\mu(r,t)$.In models such as those presented by Vasicek (1977) and Cox-Ingersoll-Ross (1985), the initial spot rate yield curve is given by an analytical formula in terms of the model parameters, and they are known as *equilibrium* models, because they describe yield curves as being derived from an assumption of economic equilibrium, based on a given market interest rate. So the Vasicek and CIR models are models are models of the short-term rate, and both incorporate the same form for the drift term, which is a tendency for the short-term rate to rise when it is below the long-term mean interest rate, and to fall when it is below the long-term mean. This is known as *mean reversion*. Therefore we can describe the short-term rate drift in the form:

$$\mu = \kappa(\theta - r)$$

where r is the short-term rate as before and κ and θ are the mean reversion and long-term rate constants. In the Vasicek model, the rate dependence of the volatility is constant, in the CIR model it is proportional to the square-root of the short rate. In both models, because the dynamics of the short-rate cover all possible moves, it is possible to derive negative interest rates, although under most conditions of initial spot rate and volatility levels, this is quite rare. Essentially the Vasicek and CIR models express the complete forward rate curve as a function of the current short-term rate, which is why later models are sometimes preferred.

Other models that are similar in concept are the Black-Derman-Toy (1990) and Black-Karinski (1992) models, however these have different terms for the drift rate and require numerical fitting to the initial interest rate and volatility term structures. The drift rate term is not known analytically in these models. In the BDT model the short-term rate volatility is related to the strength of the mean reversion in a way that reduces the volatility over time.

ARBITRAGE-FREE AND EQUILIBRIUM MODELLING

In an arbitrage-free model, the initial term structure described by spot rates today is an input to the model. In fact such models could be described not as models per se, but essentially a description of an arbitrary process that governs changes in the yield curve, and projects a forward curve that results from the mean and volatility of the current short-term rate. An equilibrium term structure model is rather more a true model of the term structure process; in an equilibrium model the current term structure is an output from the model. An equilibrium model employs a statistical approach, assuming that market prices are observed with some statistical error, so that the term structure must be estimated, rather than taken as given.

RISK-NEUTRAL PROBABILITIES

When valuing an option written on say, an equity the price of the underlying asset is the current price of the equity. When pricing an interest-rate option the underlying is obtained via a random process that described the instantaneous risk-free zero-coupon rate, which is generally termed the short rate.

In the following chapters we explore the different models that may be used and their application.

MATHEMATICS PRIMER

The level of mathematics required for a full understanding of even intermediate concepts in finance is frighteningly high. To attempt to summarise even the basic concepts in just a few pages would be a futile task and might give the impression that the mathematics was being trivialised. Our intention is quite the opposite. As this is a financial markets book, and not a mathematics textbook, a certain level of knowledge has been assumed, and a formal or rigorous approach has not been adopted. Hence readers will find few derivations, and fewer proofs. What we provide here is a very brief introduction to some of the concepts; the aim of this is simply to provide a starting point for individual research. We assist this start by listing recommended texts in the bibliography.

RANDOM VARIABLES AND PROBABILITY DISTRIBUTIONS

In financial mathematics random variables are used to describe the movement of asset prices, and assuming certain properties about the process followed by asset prices allows us to state what the expected outcome of events are. A random variable may be any value from a specified *sample space*. The specification of the *probability distribution* that applies to the sample space will define the frequency of particular values taken by the random variable. The cumulative distribution function of a random variable X is defined using the distribution function $f()$ such that $Pr\{X \leq x\} = f()$. A discrete random variable is one that can assume a finite or *countable* set of values, usually assumed to be the set of positive integers. We define a discrete random variable X with its own probability function $p(i)$ such that $p(i) = Pr\{X = i\}$. In this case the probability distribution is

$$f(i) = Pr\{X \leq i\} = \sum_{n=0}^{i} p(n)$$

with $0 \leq p(i) \leq 1$ for all i. The sum of the probabilities is 1.

Discrete probability distributions include the Binomial distribution and the Poisson distribution.

Continuous random variables

The next step is to move to a continuous framework. A continuous random variable X may assume any real value and its probability density function $f(x)$ is defined as

$$f(x) = \lim_{dx \to 0} \frac{Pr\{x \leq X \leq x + dx\}}{dx}$$

$$= \frac{dF(x)}{dx}.$$

The probability distribution function is given as $F(x) = Pr\{X \leq x\} = \int_{s=-\infty}^{x} f(s)ds$.

Continuous distributions are commonly encountered in finance theory. The *normal* or Gaussian distribution is perhaps the most important. It is described by its mean μ and standard deviation σ, sometimes called the location and spread respectively. The probability density function is

$$f(x) = \frac{1}{\sqrt{2\pi\sigma^2}} e^{-\frac{1}{2}\left(\frac{x-\mu}{\sigma}\right)^2}$$

Where a random variable X is assumed to follow normal distribution it will be described in the form $X \sim N(\mu, \sigma^2)$ where $\sim$ means "is distributed according to". Examples of the graphical representation of the normal distribution are included in Chapter 37. The standard normal distribution is written as $N(0, 1)$ with $\mu = 0$ and $\sigma = 0$. The cumulative distribution function for the standard normal distribution is given by

$$\Phi(x) = N(x) = \int_{z=-\infty}^{x} \frac{1}{\sqrt{2\pi}} e^{-\frac{1}{2}z^2} \, dz$$

The key assumption in the derivation of the Black–Scholes option pricing model is that the asset price follows a *lognormal* distribution, so that if we assume the asset price is P we write

$$\log\left(\frac{P_t}{P_0}\right) \sim N\left(\left(r - \frac{1}{2}\sigma^2\right)t, \sigma^2 t\right)$$

Expected values

A probability distribution function describes the distribution of a random variable X. The expected value of X in a discrete environment is given by

$$E[X] = \bar{X} = \sum_{i=0}^{\infty} ip(i)$$

and the equivalent for a continuous random variable is

$$E[X] = \bar{X} = \int_{s=-\infty}^{x} sf(s) \, ds$$

The dispersion around the mean is given by the *variance* which is

$$Var[X] = E\left[(X - \bar{X})^2\right] = \sum_{i=0}^{\infty} (i - \bar{X})^2 pi$$

or

$$Var[X] = E\left[(X - \bar{X})^2\right] = \int_{s=-\infty}^{x} f(s) \, ds$$

in a continuous distribution. A squared measure has little application so commonly the square root of the variance, the standard deviation is used.

Regression analysis

A linear relationship between two variables, one of which is dependent, can be estimated using the least squares method. The relationship is

$$Y_i = \alpha + \beta X_i + \varepsilon_i$$

where X is the independent variable and ε is an error term capturing those explanatory factors not covered by the model. ε is described as $\varepsilon_i \sim N(0, \sigma^2)$. β is the slope of the linear regression line that describes the relationship, while α is the intercept of the y-axis. The sum of the squares of the form

$$SS = \sum_{i=1}^{n} (y_i - \hat{y}_i)^2$$

is minimised in order to calculate the parameters.

Where we believe the relationship is non-linear we can use a regression model of the form

$$Y_i = \alpha X_{1i}(1 + \beta X_{2i}) + \varepsilon_i$$

This can be transformed into a form that is linear and then fitted using least squares. This is carried out by minimising squares and is described by

$$SS = \sum_{i=1}^{n} \left(y_i - \alpha\left(1 - e^{-\beta x_i}\right)\right)^2.$$

Yield curve fitting techniques that use splines are often fitted using multiple regression methods.

Stochastic processes

This is perhaps the most difficult area of financial mathematics. Most references are also very technical and therefore difficult to access for the non-mathematician.

We begin with some definitions. A random process is usually referred to as a *stochastic* process. This is a collection of random variables $X(t)$ and the process may be either discrete or continuous. We write $\{X(t), t \in T\}$ and a sample $\{x(t), 0 \leq t \leq t_{\max}\}$ of the random process $\{X(t), t \geq 0\}$ is known as the *realisation* or *path* of the process.

A *Markov* process is one where the path is dependent on the present state of the process only, so that all historical data, including the path taken to arrive at the present state, is irrelevant. So in a Markov process, all data up to the present is contained in the present state. The dynamics of asset prices are frequently assumed to follow a Markov process, and in fact it represents a semi-strong form efficient market. It is written

$$Pr\{X(t) \leq y | X(u) = x(u), 0 \leq u \leq s\} = Pr\{X(t) \leq y | X(s) = x(s)\}$$

for $0 \leq s \leq t$.

A *Weiner process* or *Brownian motion* for $\{X(t), t \geq 0\}$ has the following properties:

- $X(0) = 0$;
- $\{X(t), t \geq 0\}$ has independent increments, so that $X(t+b) - X(t)$ and $X(t+2b) - X(t+b)$ are independent and follow the same distribution;
- the variable $X(t)$ has the property $X(t) \sim N(0, t)$ for all $t > 0$;
- $X(t) - X(s) \sim N(0, t-s)$ for $0 \leq s < t$.

Many interest rate models assume that the movement of interest rates over time follows a Weiner process.

Stochastic calculus

The Weiner process is usually denoted with W although Z and z are also used. For a Weiner process $\{W(t), t \geq 0\}$ it can be shown that after an infinitesimal time interval Δt we have

$$W(t+\Delta t) - W(t) \sim N(0, \Delta t).$$

If we also have $U \sim N(0, 1)$ then we may write

$$W(t+\Delta t) - W(t) = \sqrt{\Delta t}\, U$$

As the time interval decreases and approaches (but does not reach) 0, then the expression above may be written

$$dW(t) = \sqrt{\Delta t}\, U$$

A Weiner process is not differentiable but a generalised Weiner process termed an Itô process is differentiable and is described in the form

$$dX(t) = a(t, X)\, dt + b(t, X)\, dW$$

where a is the drift and b the noise or volatility of the stochastic process.

SELECTED BIBLIOGRAPHY

Baxter, A., Rennie, D., *Financial Calculus*, Cambridge University Press, 1996.

Gujarati, D., *Basic Econometrics*, AP, 1997.

Hogg, R., Craig, A., *An Introduction to Mathematical Statistics*, 5th edition, Prentice Hall, 1995.

Kreyszig, E., *Advanced Engineering Mathematics*, Wiley, 1993.

Ross, S., *An Introduction to Probability Models*, 5th edition, Academic Press, 1997.

Ross, S., *An Introduction to Mathematical Finance*, Cambridge University Press, 1999.

Chapter 1

Asset-Swap Spreads and Relative Value Analysis

Chapter Contents

Readers will be familiar with the basics of bond market instruments. We begin this book with a look at the use of asset swaps (ASW) and ASW spreads to determine relative value in a risky bond. Such analysis is a key part of the security selection decision. ASW spreads have been long in use in the market because the interest-rate swap (IRS) is an important reference for the bond market and is used to hedge the IR risk of bonds. This type of derivate contract typically exchanges a fixed rate interest payment to the floating one, and represents a fundamental tool in terms of hedging, speculation and managing risk. The spread between swap and bonds can be used to determine the relative value of the bond, but can be measured in several ways. It is, therefore, important to know which method is being used and quoted. Once known, the spread is taken to indicate the richness or cheapness of bonds with different features.

1.1 ASSET-SWAP SPREAD

The asset swap is an agreement that allows investors to exchange or swap future cash flows generated by an asset, usually fixed rates to floating rates. It is essentially a combination of a fixed coupon bond and an IRS. We define it thus:

An asset swap is a synthetically created structure combining a fixed coupon bond with a fixed-floating IRS, which then transforms the bond's swap fixed rate payments to floating rate. The investor retains the original credit exposure to the fixed rate bond. The pricing of asset swaps is therefore driven by the credit quality of the bond issuer and the size of any potential loss following issuer default.

A bond's swap spread is a measure of the credit risk of a bond relative to the interest-rate swap market. Because the swap is traded by banks, or interbank market, the credit risk of the bond over the interest-rate swap is given by its spread over the IRS. In essence, then the IRS represents the credit risk of the interbank market. If an issuer has a credit rating superior to that of the interbank market, the spread will be *below* the IRS level rather than above it.

The spread of the floating coupon over the bond's market price, that is the asset-swap value is the difference between the bond's market price and par. The package of the asset swap is structured in two phases:

- At issue, the investor pays the asset (cash bond) at par;
- At the same time, the investor enters in the swap contract, paying fixed cash flows equal to the coupon payment and receiving a fixed spread over the interbank rate, that is the asset-swap spread. Figure 1.1 shows the asset-swap mechanism.

The zero-coupon curve is used in the asset-swap analysis, in which the curve is derived from the swap curve. Then, the asset-swap spread is the spread that allows us to receive the equivalence between the present value of cash flows and the current market price of the bond.

In an asset-swap contract, the investor assumes the credit risk of the bond. In case the bond defaults, the investor will continue to pay the swap, without

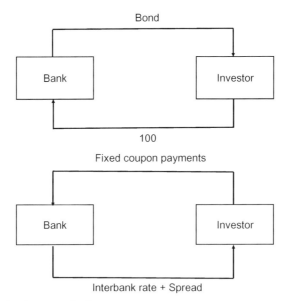

FIGURE 1.1   Asset-swap mechanism.

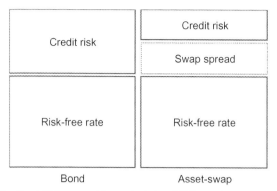

FIGURE 1.2   Bond's yield decomposition and relative ASW spread.

receiving the coupons and the redemption value at maturity. Therefore, the buyer of the bond takes the default exposure of the bonds. Figure 1.2 illustrates the bond's yield decomposition.

1.2   SWAP SPREAD FOR RICHNESS AND CHEAPNESS ANALYSIS

Making comparison between bonds could be difficult and several aspects must be considered. One of these is the bond's maturity. For instance, we know that the yield for a bond that matures in 10 years is not the same compared to the one that matures in 30 years. Therefore, it is important to have a reference yield curve and smooth that for comparison purposes. However, there are other features that affect the bond's comparison such as coupon size and structure, liquidity, embedded options and others. These other features increase the curve fitting and the bond's comparison analysis. In this case, the swap curve represents an objective tool to understand the richness and cheapness in bond market. According to O'Kane and Sen (2005), the asset-swap spread is calculated as the difference between the bond's value on the par swap curve and the bond's market value, divided by the sensitivity of 1 bp over the par swap.

$$\text{Parity} = \frac{P^{\text{Interbank rate}} - P^{\text{Full}}}{PV01}$$

where $P^{\text{Interbank rate}}$ is the bond's value discounted at interbank rate; P^{Full} is the market price of the bond and $PV01$ is the sensitivity of 1 bp on the coupon payment.

Let us now consider the following example of bonds issued by two companies operating in different industries. The first one is Hera S.p.A., an Italian company operating in the utility industry that issued the bond HERIM 3¼% 2021 (hereinafter HERIM); the second one is Telekom Finanzmanagement GmbH, a German company operating in the telecommunications industry that issued the bond TKAAV 3⅛% 2021 (hereinafter TKAAV). Therefore, both companies issued two bonds with similar features:

- The same time to maturity (8 years);
- Similar issue date (4 October 2013 for HERIM and 3 December 2013 for TKAAV);
- Similar maturity date (4 October 2021 for HERIM and 3 December 2021 for TKAAV);
- The same creditworthiness with a Bloomberg composite rating of BBB;
- The same currency (EUR);
- The same coupon payment (3.250% for HERIM and 3.125% for TKAAV, annual frequency payment);
- The same bond structure (bullet as maturity type, no embedded options).

Figures 1.4 and 1.5 show the Bloomberg screen for ASW analysis. To calculate the ASW spread, we use the bond's price, which is equal to 115.138 for HERIM and 114.592 for TKAAV. The swap structuring has been performed as follows:

- The same frequency payment as well as the bond's coupon structure, in this case annual;
- The same day count convention, in this case actual/actual;
- Euro swap curve as reference interbank curve, coherent with the bond's currency (EUR).

Depending on the reference yield curve selected and its currency denomination, the ASW spread changes. Figure 1.3 shows the ASW spread for different reference yield curves for TKAAV.

As shown in Figures 1.4 and 1.5, with this swap structuring, the asset-swap spread for HERIM is 39.5 bp and for TKAAV is 39.1 bp. These represent the spreads that will be received if each bond is purchased as an asset-swap package. In other words, the ASW spread provides a measure of the difference between the market price of the bond and the value of the cash flows evaluated using zero-coupon rates.

However, a critical issue on this spread measure is how the asset swap has been structured. ASW measure works very well when bond prices trade at or near to par. Most corporate bonds trade with price away from the par (as in this case), thus making the ASW an inaccurate spread measure. If the bond trades at premium, the ASW spread will overestimate the level of credit risk; conversely, if the bond trades at discount the ASW spread will underestimate the level of credit risk. Therefore, in the case of HERIM and TKAAV, the ASW spread overestimates the credit risk associated with the bonds because both trade significantly at premium.

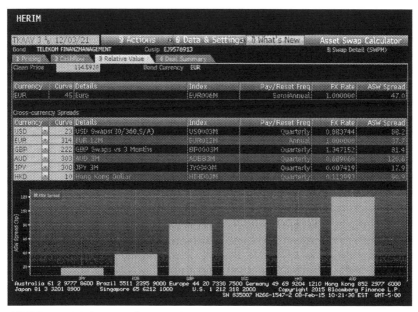

FIGURE 1.3   Relative value of TKAAV 3⅛% 2021, on ASW screen. *(Used with the permission of Bloomberg L.P. Copyright© 2014. All rights reserved.)*

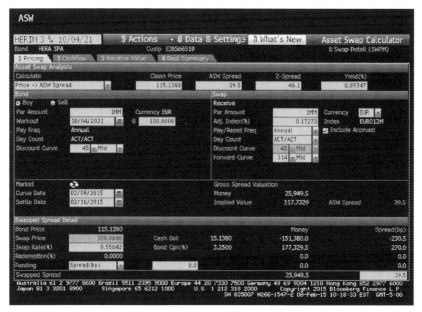

FIGURE 1.4   ASW screen for HERIM 3¼% 2021. *(Used with the permission of Bloomberg L.P. Copyright© 2014. All rights reserved.)*

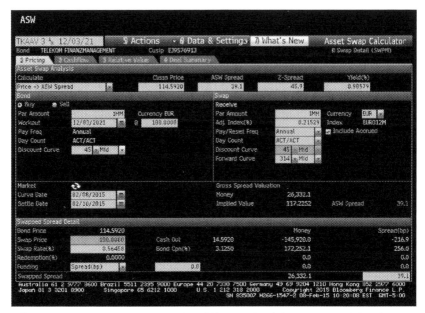

FIGURE 1.5   ASW screen for TKAAV 3⅛% 2021. *(Used with the permission of Bloomberg L.P. Copyright© 2014. All rights reserved.)*

1.3   Z-SPREAD MEASURE

Z-spread is an alternative spread measure to the ASW spread. This type of spread uses the zero-coupon yield curve to calculate the spread, in which in this case is assimilated to the interest-rate swap curve. Z-spread represents the spread needful in order to obtain the equivalence between the present value of the bond's cash flows and its current market price. However, conversely to the ASW spread, the Z-spread is a constant measure.

The Bloomberg ASW screen shows the Z-spread. It is 46.1 for HERIM and 45.9 for TKAAV. The Z-spread provides hence a better measure of spread, although giving a similar result in terms of investor's decision. However, being a constant measure, it does not consider the timing of default. In fact, each cash flow has a different level of credit risk. To overcome this limitation, the Z-spread spread could be adjusted by introducing a probability of default for each cash flow. This other spread is referred to adjusted Z-spread or C-spread.

1.4   THE CREDIT DEFAULT SWAP BASIS AND TRADING ISSUES

A credit default swap (CDS) price provides fundamental credit risk information of a specific reference entity or asset. As explained before, asset swaps are used to transform the cash flows of a corporate bond for interest rate hedging purpose. Since the asset swaps are priced at a spread over the interbank rate, the ASW spread is the credit risk of the same one. However, market evidence shows that credit default swaps trade at a different level to asset swaps due to technical

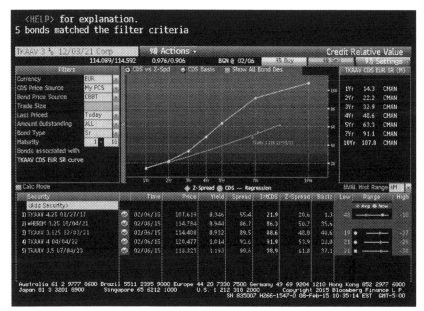

FIGURE 1.6 CRVD screen for TKAAV 3⅛% 2021 and HERIM 3¼% 2021. *(Used with the permission of Bloomberg L.P. Copyright© 2014. All rights reserved.)*

and market factors. Although the CDS and ASW spreads measure the credit risk of the reference name and they are driven by specific market factors, we assume that the comparison between them represents the reference credit risk. The difference between the CDS and the ASW is called the *basis* and is given by:

$$Basis = CDS\,spread - ASW\,spread$$

If this difference is positive we have a *positive basis*, and it happens when credit derivates trade at higher prices than asset swaps. Otherwise, if the difference is negative we have a *negative basis*. Consider the following example of a positive basis trade for HERIM and TKAAV. For both bonds, we calculate the CDS spread which is equal to 86.3 for HERIM and equal to 88.6 for TKAAV. The CDS basis over the ASW spread determined before is equal to 46.8 for HERIM and equal to 49.5 for TKAAV. However, the basis illustrated in Figure 1.6 is different because CRVD measures them relative to the Z-spread, which is 50.7 for HERIM and 48 for TKAAV.[1] The basis relative to the Z-spread is equal to 35.6 for HERIM and 40.6 for TKAAV. So, we note that either the ASW spread or the Z-spread can be used as the basis performance, giving a similar result and positive basis in both cases.

---

1. Note, these Z-spreads have been calculated with a different yield curve than the one used in Figures 1.4 and 1.5.

An important consequence of positive basis is that the trading strategy will be by selling the underlying asset (cash bond) and selling the CDS contract on the same name, with the goal to profit by higher CDS prices and a low spread of the bond. As explained before, the CDS basis above the spread depends on *technical* and *market* factors. Among *technical* factors we list the following:

- *CDS premiums are above zero*: As we know the CDS price represents a premium paid by the protection buyer to the protection seller. The protection seller, or the bank, will expect a premium, that is a positive CDS basis over the interbank curve;
- *Default protection*: The CDS size will be affected on the default event. Protection seller considers this risk on the CDS premium, increasing the basis;
- *Bonds trading above or below par*: Bonds that trade away from the par will affect the basis. In our example both bonds trade at premium, so, decreasing the loss in the case of default suffered by the protection seller in respect to one of the cash bondholder. This pushes down the basis.

The *market* factors that affect the basis are:

- *Market demand*: Strong market demand from the protection buyer will increase the basis and vice versa;
- *Liquidity demand*: The CDS for a cash bond may reflect a liquidity premium for that name. Therefore for illiquidity issue the protection requires a premium, increasing the CDS basis over the ASW spread. Note, the CDS price will be influenced also from the liquidity embedded in the synthetic instrument, which may be more or less liquid.

1.5 ANALYSIS USING MARKET OBSERVATION

We perform an analysis in which we compare bonds with similar characteristics within the same industry. This is a common analysis undertaken by bond portfolio managers looking to invest in a particular industry.

We selected five bonds rated BBB, similar maturity (around 6 years at maturity), trading in the European bond market. The bonds were issued by companies operating in the utility industry. The bonds are:

- SPPEUS 3¾% 2020, issued by SPP Infrastructure Financing BV;
- RWE 1⅞% 2020, issued by RWE Finance BV;
- ENEASA 3¼% 2020, issued by Energa Finance AB;
- IBESM 2⅞% 2020, issued by Iberdrola International BV;
- SRGIM 3⅜% 2021, issued by Snam S.p.A.

Figure 1.7 illustrates the historical trend of the ASW spread for each bond selected. Although the bonds are issued by companies operating in the same industry and have similar ratings, they each have a different ASW spread.

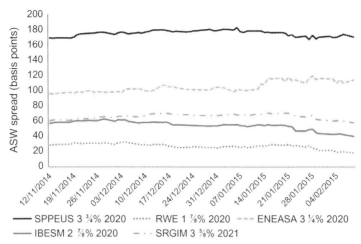

FIGURE 1.7   Historical asset-swap spread for bonds traded in the utility industry. *(Data Source: Bloomberg.)*

For instance, we can see that the ASW spread for SPPEUS 3¾% 2020 is around 170 basis, while the ASW spread for RWE 1⅞% 2020 is around 20 basis.

From Figure 1.7 we conclude that, if we assume the credit risk is virtually identical (from a rating agency and tenor perspective), the bond with the highest ASW spread will be the one we select.

However, it is worthwhile considering the CDS basis first, as that also gives an indication of richness or cheapness.

First we compare the basis between CDS and ASW spread (or Z-spread). In Figure 1.8, we can see that higher Z-spread pushes down the basis. For instance, SPPEUS 3¾% 2020 is the bond with the highest Z-spread compared to other bonds, but with negative basis. The negative basis is conventionally temporary, but it represents a good opportunity for arbitrageurs who can trade across cash and synthetic markets, reverting the current trend. In this case, there is a relatively lower spread in CDS market and higher spread for bond market, that is the bond is cheap. Conversely, RWE 1⅞% 2020 is the bond with the lowest Z-spread. Moreover, we can see from Figure 1.7 that the ASW spreads have low fluctuations, while the CDS spread changes overtime due to the credit market sentiment. For a worsening credit environment and deteriorating economic outlook, the basis can become positive quickly. Therefore, the basis will fluctuate in line with that.

However most investors do not enter into CDS basis trades to arbitrage, they simply wish to select a cash bond. From this analysis we see that the bond we would have selected first because of its value (to us) given by high ASW also looks to be trading at the 'right' level to the CDS, that is it is not 'expensive'. The two bonds with a positive basis would appear to be 'expensive' and so we would not, all else being equal, purchase them over the other securities.

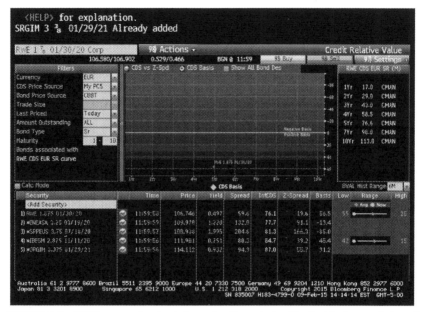

FIGURE 1.8 CRVD screen for the industry bond's analysis. *(Used with the permission of Bloomberg L.P. Copyright© 2014. All rights reserved.)*

APPENDIX 1   THE PAR ASSET-SWAP SPREAD

We assume we have constructed a market curve of Libor discount factors where $Df(t)$ is the price today of \$1 to be paid at time t. From the perspective of the asset swap seller, it sells the bond for par plus accrued interest. The net up-front payment has a value $100 - P$ where P is the market price of the bond. If we assume both parties to the swap are interbank credit quality, we can price the cash flows off the Libor curve.

For the calculation, we cancel out the principal payments of par at maturity. We assume that cash flows are annual and take place on the same coupon dates. The breakeven asset-swap spread A is calculated by setting the present value of all cash flows equal to 0. From the perspective of the asset swap seller, the present value is:

$$100 - P + C\sum_{i=1}Df(t_i) - \sum_{i=1}D_i(L_i + A)Df(t_i) = 0 \qquad (1.1)$$

There is a $100 - P$ up-front payment to purchase the asset in return for par. For the interest-rate swap, we have

$$C\sum_{i=1}Df(t_i) \qquad (1.2)$$

for the fixed payments and

$$\sum_{i=1} D_i(L_i + A)Df(t_i) \tag{1.3}$$

for the floating payments,

where C equals the bond annual coupon; L_i is the Libor rate set at time $t_i\text{-}l$ and paid at time t_i and D_i is the accrual factor in the corresponding basis (day-count adjustment). We then solve for the asset-swap spread A.

BIBLIOGRAPHY

Choudhry, M., 2005. An alternative bond relative value measure: determining a fair value of the swap spread using libor and gc repo rates. J. Asset Manag. 7 (1), 17–21.

Choudhry, M., 2006. The Credit Default Swap Basis. Bloomberg Press, New York.

Gale, G., May 2006. Using and trading asset-swaps: interest rate strategy. Morgan Stanley Fixed Income Research.

O'Kane, D., Sen, S., 2005. Credit spreads explained. J. Credit Risk 1 (2), 61–78.

Chapter 2

The Dynamics of Asset Prices

Chapter Contents

The modelling of the yield curve is a function of the movement in the price of the underlying asset, which in this case is the movement in interest rates. Both option valuation models and interest-rate models describe an environment where the price of an option (or the modelling of the yield curve) is related to the behaviour process of the variables that drive asset prices. This process is described as a *stochastic* process, and pricing models describe the stochastic dynamics of asset price changes, whether this is change in share prices, interest rates, foreign exchange rates or bond prices. To understand the mechanics of option pricing therefore, we must familiarise ourselves with the behaviour of functions of *stochastic variables*. The concept of a stochastic process is a vital concept in finance theory. It describes random phenomena that evolve over time, and these include asset prices. For this reason, an alternative title for this chapter could be *An Introduction to Stochastic Processes*.

     This is a book on bonds after all, not mathematics, and it is outside the scope of this book comprehensively to derive and prove the main components of

     13

dynamic asset pricing theory. There are a number of excellent textbooks that the reader is encouraged to read which provide the necessary detail, in particular Ingersoll (1987), Baxter and Rennie (1996), Neftci (1996) and James and Webber (2000). Another recommended text that deals with probability models in general, as well as their application in derivatives pricing, is Ross (2000). In this chapter, we review the basic principles of the dynamics of asset prices, which are required for an understanding of interest-rate modelling. The main principles are then considered again in the context of yield curve modelling, in the following chapters.

2.1   THE BEHAVIOUR OF ASSET PRICES

The first property that asset prices, which can be taken to include interest rates, are assumed to follow is that they are part of a *continuous* process. This means that the value of any asset can and does change at any time and from one point in time to another, and can assume any fraction of a unit of measurement. It is also assumed to pass through every value as it changes; so, for example, if the price of a bond moves from 92.00 to 94.00, it must also have passed through every point in between. This feature means that the asset price does not exhibit *jumps*, which in fact is not the case in many markets, where price processes do exhibit jump behaviour. For now, however, we may assume that the price process is continuous.

2.1.1   Stochastic Processes

Models that seek to value options or describe a yield curve also describe the dynamics of asset price changes. The same process is said to apply to changes in share prices, bond prices, interest rates and exchange rates. The process by which prices and interest rates evolve over time is known as a *stochastic process*, and this is a fundamental concept in finance theory.[1] Essentially, a stochastic process is a time series of random variables. Generally, the random variables in a stochastic process are related in a non-random manner, and so therefore we can capture them in a *probability density function*. A good introduction is given in Neftci (1996), and following his approach we very briefly summarise the main features here.

Consider the function $y = f(x)$; given the value of x, we can obtain the value of y. If we denote the set W as the state of the world, where $w \in W$, the function $f(x, w)$ has the property that given a value $w \in W$, it becomes a function of x only. If we say that x represents the passage of time, two functions $f(x, w_1)$ and $f(x, w_2)$ will be different because the second element w in each case is different. With x representing time, these two functions describe two different processes that are dependent on different states of the world W. The element w represents an

---

1. A formal definition of a stochastic process is given in Appendix **A**.

underlying random process, and so the function $f(x, w)$ is a *random function*. A random function is also called a *stochastic process*, one in which x represents time and $x \geq 0$. The random characteristic of the process refers to the entire process, not any particular value in that process at any particular point in time.

Examples of functions include the *exponential* function denoted by $y = e^x$ and the *logarithmic* function $\log_e(y) = x$.

The price processes of shares and bonds, as well as interest rate processes, are stochastic processes. That is, they exhibit a random change over time. For the purposes of modelling, the change in asset prices is divided into two components. These are the *drift* of the process, which is a *deterministic* element,[2] also called the mean, and the random component known as the *noise*, also called the volatility of the process.

We introduce the drift component briefly as follows. For an asset such as an ordinary share, which is expected to rise over time (at least in line with assumed growth in inflation), the drift can be modelled as a geometric growth progression. If the price process had no 'noise', the change in price of the stock over the time period dt can be given by

$$\frac{\mathrm{d}S_t}{\mathrm{d}t} = \mu S_t \qquad (2.1)$$

where the term μ describes the growth rate. Expression (2.1) can be rewritten in the form

$$\mathrm{d}S_t = \mu S_t \mathrm{d}t \qquad (2.2)$$

which can also be written in integral form. For interest rates, the movement process can be described in similar fashion, although as we shall see interest rate modelling often takes into account the tendency for rates to return to a mean level or range of levels, a process known as *mean reversion*. Without providing the derivation here, the equivalent expression for interest rates takes the form

$$\mathrm{d}r_t = \alpha(\mu - r_t)\mathrm{d}t \qquad (2.3)$$

where α is the mean reversion rate that determines the pace at which the interest rate reverts to its mean level. If the initial interest rate is less than the drift rate, the rate r will increase, while if the level is above the drift rate, it will tend to decrease.

For the purposes of employing option pricing models, the dynamic behaviour of asset prices is usually described as a function of what is known as a *Wiener process*, which is also known as *Brownian motion*. The noise or volatility component is described by an *adapted* Brownian or Wiener process, and involves introducing a random increment to the standard random process. This is described next.

---

2. There are two types of model: *deterministic*, which involves no randomness so the variables are determined exactly; and *stochastic*, which incorporates the random nature of the variables into the model.

2.1.2 Wiener Process or Brownian Motion

The stochastic process we have briefly discussed above is known as Brownian motion or a Wiener process. In fact, a Wiener process is only a process that has a mean of 0 and a variance of 1, but it is common to see these terms used synonymously. Wiener processes are a very important part of continuous-time finance theory, and interested readers can obtain more detailed and technical data on the subject in Neftci (1996) and Duffie (1996)[3] among others. It is a well-researched subject.

One of the properties of a Wiener process is that the sample pathway is continuous, that is, there are no *discontinuous* changes. An example of a discontinuous process is the Poisson process. Both are illustrated in Figures 2.1 and 2.2 below.

In the examples illustrated, both processes have an expected change of 0 and a variance of 1 per unit of time. There are no discontinuities in the Wiener process, which is a plot of many very tiny random changes. This is reflected in the 'fuzzy' nature of the sample path. However, the Poisson process has no fuzzy quality and appears to have a much smaller number of random changes. We can conclude that asset prices, and the dynamics of interest rates, are more akin to a Wiener process. This, therefore, is how asset prices are modelled. From observation, we know that

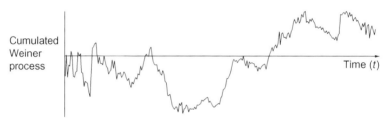

FIGURE 2.1   An example of a Wiener process.

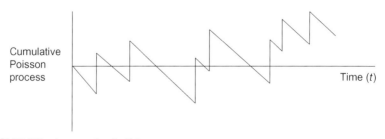

FIGURE 2.2   An example of a Poisson process.

---

3. Duffie's text requires a very good grounding in continuous-time mathematics.

in reality, asset prices and interest rates do exhibit discontinuities or *jumps*; however, there are other advantages to assuming a Wiener process, and in practice because continuous-time stochastic processes can be captured as a combination of Brownian motion and a Poisson process, analysts and researchers use the former as the basis of financial valuation models.

The first step in asset pricing theory builds on the assumption that prices follow a Brownian motion. The properties of Brownian motion W state that it is continuous, and the value of $W_t(t>0)$ is normally distributed under a probability measure P as a *random* variable with parameters $N(0, t)$. An incremental change in the asset value over time dt, which is a very small or *infinitesimal* change in the time, given by $W_{s+t} - W_s$, is also normally distributed with parameters $N(0, t)$ under P. Perhaps, the most significant feature is that the change in value is independent of whatever the history of the price process has been up to time s. If a process follows these conditions, it is Brownian motion. In fact, asset prices do not generally have a mean of 0 because over time we expect them to rise. Therefore, modelling asset prices incorporates a *drift* measure that better reflects asset price movement so that an asset movement described by

$$S_t = W_t + \mu t \tag{2.4}$$

would be a Brownian motion with a drift given by the constant μ. A second parameter is then added, a *noise* factor, which scales the Brownian motion by another constant measure, the standard deviation σ. The process is then described by

$$S_t = \sigma W_t + \mu t \tag{2.5}$$

which can be used to *simulate* the price path taken by an asset, as long as we specify the two parameters. An excellent and readable account of this is given in Baxter and Rennie (1996, Chapter 3), who also state that under Equation (2.5), there is a possibility of achieving negative values, which is not realistic for asset prices. However, using the exponential of the process given by Equation (2.5) is more accurate, and is given by Equation (2.6):

$$S_t = \exp(\sigma W_t + \mu t). \tag{2.6}$$

Brownian motion or the *Wiener process* is employed by virtually all option pricing models and we introduce it here with respect to a change in the variable W over an interval of time t. If W represents a variable following a Wiener process and ΔW is a change in value over a period of time t, the relationship between ΔW and Δt is given by Equation (2.7):

$$\Delta W = \varepsilon \sqrt{\Delta t} \tag{2.7}$$

where ε is a random sample from a normal distribution with a mean 0 and a standard deviation of 1. Over a short period of time, the values of ΔW are independent and therefore also follow a normal distribution with a mean of 0 and a standard deviation of $\sqrt{\Delta t}$. Over a longer time period, T made up of N periods of length Δt, the change in W over the period from time 0 to time T is given by Equation (2.8):

$$W(T) - W(0) = \sum_{i=1}^{N} \varepsilon_i \sqrt{\Delta t}. \tag{2.8}$$

The successive values assumed by W are serially independent; so from Equation (2.8), we conclude that changes in the variable W from time 0 to time T follow a normal distribution with mean 0 and a standard deviation of $\sqrt{T}$. This describes the Wiener process, with a mean of zero or a zero drift rate and a variance of T. This is an important result because a zero drift rate implies that the change in the variable (for which now read asset price) in the future is equal to the current change. This means that there is an equal chance of an asset return ending up 10% or down 10% over a long period of time.

The next step in the analysis involves using stochastic calculus. Without going into this field here, we summarise from Baxter and Rennie (1996) and state that a stochastic process X will incorporate a *Newtonian* term that is based on dt and a Brownian term based on the infinitesimal increment of W that is denoted by dW_t. The Brownian term has a 'noise' factor of σ_t. The infinitesimal change of X at X_t is given by the differential equation

$$dX_t = \sigma_t dW_t + \mu_t dt \tag{2.9}$$

where σ_t is the *volatility* of the process X at time t and μ_t is the drift of X at time t. For interest rates that are modelled on the basis of mean reversion, the process is given by

$$dr_t = \sigma_t dW_t + \alpha(u_t - r_t)dt \tag{2.10}$$

where the mean reverting element is as before. Without providing the supporting mathematics, which we have not covered here, the process described by Equation (2.10) is called an Ornstein-Uhlenbeck process and has been assumed by a number of interest rate models.

One other important point to introduce here is that a random process described by Equation (2.10) operates in a continuous environment. In continuous-time mathematics, the *integral* is the tool that is used to denote the sum of an infinite number of objects, that is, where the number of objects is *uncountable*. A formal definition of the integral is outside the scope of this book, but accessible accounts can be found in the texts referred to previously. A basic introduction is given in Appendix **D**. However, the continuous stochastic process X described by Equation (2.9) can be written as an integral equation in the form

$$X_t = X_0 + \int_0^t \sigma_s dW_s + \int_0^t \mu_s ds \tag{2.11}$$

where σ and μ are processes as before. The volatility and drift terms can not only be dependent on the time t but can also be dependent on X or W up to the point t.

This is a complex technical subject and readers are encouraged to review the main elements in the referred texts.

2.1.3   The Martingale Property

Continuous time asset pricing is an important part of finance theory and involves some quite advanced mathematics. An excellent introduction to this subject is given in Baxter and Rennie (1996) and Neftci (1996). A more technical account is given in Williams (1991). It is outside the scope of this book to derive, prove and detail the main elements. However, we wish to summarise the essential property, and begin by saying that in continuous time, asset prices can take on an unlimited number of values. Stochastic differential equations are used to capture the dynamics of asset prices in a generalised form. So for example, as we saw in the previous section, an incremental change in the price of an asset S at time t could be given by

$$dS = \mu S dt + \sigma S dW(t) \tag{2.12}$$

where

dS is an infinitesimal change in the price of asset S
$\mu S dt$ is the predicted movement during the infinitesimal time interval dt
$\sigma S dW(t)$ is an unpredictable random shock.

Martingale theory is a branch of mathematics that classifies the *trend* in an observed time series set of data. A stochastic process is said to behave like a martingale if there are no observable trends in its pattern. The martingale property is often used in conjunction with a Wiener process to describe asset price dynamics. The notion of the martingale property is that the best approximation of a set of integrable random variables M at the end of a time period t is M_0, which essentially states that the most accurate way to predict a future asset price is to use the price of the asset now. That is, using the price today is the same as using all available historical information, as only the newest information regarding the asset is relevant.

We do not describe or prove this property here, but the martingale property is used to derive Equation (2.13) the price of an asset at time t:

$$P_t = \exp\left(\sigma W_t - \frac{1}{2}\sigma^2 t\right). \tag{2.13}$$

A martingale is an important type of stochastic process and the concept of a martingale is fundamental to asset pricing theory. A process that is a martingale is one in which the expected future value, based on what is known up to now, is the same as today's value. That is, a martingale is a process in which the *conditional* expected future value, given current information, is equal to the current value. The martingale representation theorem states that given a Wiener process, and the fact that the path of the Wiener process up to that point is known, then any martingale is equal to a constant plus a stochastic integral, with respect to the Wiener process. This can be written as

$$E_t[S_T] = S_t \text{ for } t \leq T. \tag{2.14}$$

Therefore, a stochastic process that is a martingale has no observable *trend*. The price process described by Equation (2.9) is not a martingale unless the drift component μ is equal to zero; otherwise, a trend will be observed. A process that is observed to trend upwards is known as a *submartingale*, while a process that on average declines over time is known as a *supermartingale*.

What is the significance of this? Here we take it as given that because price processes can be described as *equivalent martingale measures* (which we do not go into here) they enable the practitioner to construct a risk-free hedge of a market instrument. By enabling a no-arbitrage portfolio to be described, a mathematical model can be set up and solved, including risk-free valuation models.

The background and mathematics to martingales can be found in Harrison and Kreps (1979) and Harrison and Pliska (1981) as well as Baxter and Rennie (1996). For a description of how, given that price processes are martingales, we are able to price derivative instruments, see James and Webber (2000, Chapter 3).

2.1.4   Generalised Wiener Process

The standard Wiener process is a close approximation of the behaviour of asset prices but does not account for some specific aspects of market behaviour. In the first instance, the prices of financial assets do not start at zero, and their price increments have positive mean. The variance of asset price moves is also not always unity. Therefore, the standard Wiener process is replaced by the generalised Wiener process, which describes a variable that may start at something other than zero, and also has incremental changes that have a mean other than zero as well as variances that are not unity. The mean and variance are still constant in a generalised process, which is the same as the standard process, and a different description must be used to describe processes that have variances that differ over time; these are known as stochastic integrals (Figure 2.3).

We now denote the variable as X and for this variable a generalised Wiener process is given by Equation (2.15):

$$\mathrm{d}X = a\mathrm{d}t + b\mathrm{d}W \tag{2.15}$$

where a and b are constants. This expression describes the dynamic process of the variable X as a function of time and $\mathrm{d}W$. The first term $a\mathrm{d}t$ is known as the deterministic term and states that the expected drift rate of X over time is a per unit of time; the second term $b\mathrm{d}W$ is the stochastic element and describes the variability of the move in X over time and is quantified by b multiplied by the Wiener process. When the stochastic element is zero, $\mathrm{d}X = a\mathrm{d}t$, or put another way

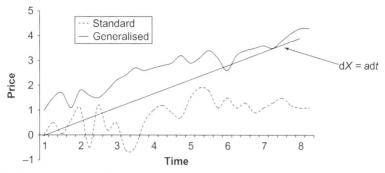

FIGURE 2.3   Standard and generalised Wiener processes.

$$\frac{dX}{dt} = a.$$

From this, we state that at time 0, $X = X_0 + at$. This enables us to describe the price of an asset, given its initial price, over a period of time. That is, the value of X at any time is given by its initial value at time 0, which is X_0, together with its drift multiplied by the length of the time period. We can restate Equation (2.15) to apply over a long time period Δt, shown as Equation (2.16):

$$\Delta X = a\Delta t + b\varepsilon\sqrt{dt}. \tag{2.16}$$

As with the standard Wiener process, ΔX has a normal distribution with mean $a\Delta t$ and standard deviation $b\sqrt{\Delta t}$.

The generalised Wiener process is more flexible than the standard one, but is still not completely accurate as a model of the behaviour of asset prices. It has normally distributed values, which means that there is a probability of observing negative prices. For assets such as equities, this is clearly unrealistic. In addition, the increments of a Wiener process are additive, whereas the increments of asset prices are more realistically multiplicative. In fact, as the increments of a Wiener process have constant expectation, this implies that the percentage incremental change in asset prices, or the percentage rate of return on the stock, would be declining as the stock price rises. This is also not realistic. For this reason, a geometric process or geometric Brownian motion has been introduced,[4] which is developed by an exponential transformation of the generalised process. From Equation (2.16), a one-dimensional process is a geometric Brownian motion if it has the form e^X, where X is a one-dimensional generalised Brownian motion with a deterministic initial value of $X(0)$.

---

4. See, for instance, Nielson (1999).

Another type of stochastic process is an Itô process. This a generalised Wiener process where the parameters a and b are functions of the value of the variable X and time t. An Itô process for X can be written as Equation (2.17):

$$dX = a(X, t)dt + b(X, t)dW. \qquad (2.17)$$

The expected drift rate and variance of an Itô process are liable to change over time; indeed the dependence of the expected drift rate and variance on X and t is the main difference between it and a generalised Wiener process. The derivation of Itô's formula is given in Appendix **C**.

2.1.5 A Model of the Dynamics of Asset Prices

The above discussion is used to derive a model of the behaviour of asset prices sometimes referred to as *geometric Brownian motion*. The dynamics of the asset price X are represented by the Itô process shown in Equation (2.18), where there is a drift rate of a and a variance rate of b^2X^2,

$$dX = aXdt + bXdW \qquad (2.18)$$

so that

$$\frac{dX}{X} = a + bdW.$$

The uncertainty element is described by the Wiener process element, with

$$dW = \varepsilon\sqrt{dt}$$

where ε is the error term, a random sample from the standardised normal distribution, so that $\varepsilon \sim N(0, 1)$. From this, and over a longer period of time Δt, we can write

$$\frac{\Delta X}{X} = a\Delta t + b\varepsilon\sqrt{\Delta t}.$$

Over this longer period of time, for application in a discrete-time environment, if we assume that volatility is zero, we have

$$\Delta X = a\Delta t + b\varepsilon\sqrt{\Delta t} \qquad (2.19)$$

and

$$dX = adt \quad \text{and} \quad \frac{dX}{dt} = a.$$

Return is given by $X = X_0 e^{at}$.

The discrete time version of the asset price model states that the proportional return on the asset price X over a short time period is given by an expected return of $a\Delta t$ and a stochastic return of $b\varepsilon\Delta t$. Therefore, the returns of asset price

EXAMPLE 2.1

A conventional bond has an expected return of 5.875% and a standard deviation of 12.50% per annum. The initial price of the bond is 100. From Equation (2.20), the dynamics of the bond price are given by:

$$dP/P = 0.05875dt + 0.125dW$$

and for a time period Δt by $dP/P = 0.05875\Delta t + 0.125\varepsilon\sqrt{\Delta t}$.

If the short time interval Δt is 4 weeks or 0.07692 years, assuming $\varepsilon = 1$, then the increase in price is given by:

$$\Delta P = 100(0.05875(0.07692) + 0.125\varepsilon\sqrt{0.07692}$$
$$= 100(0.00451905 + 0.0346681\varepsilon)$$

So, the price increase is described as a random sample from a normal distribution with a mean of 0.452 and a volatility of 3.467. Over a time interval of 4 weeks, $\Delta P/P$ is normal with:

$$\Delta P/P \sim N(0.00452, 0.001202).$$

changes $\Delta X/X$ are normally distributed with a mean of $a\Delta t$ and a standard deviation of $b\sqrt{\Delta t}$. This is the distribution of asset price returns and is given by Equation (2.20) (Example 2.1):

$$\frac{\Delta X}{X} \sim N\left(a\Delta t,\ b\sqrt{\Delta t}\right) \tag{2.20}$$

2.1.6 The Distribution of the Risk-Free Interest Rate

The continuously compounded rate of return is an important component of option pricing theory. If r is the continuously compounded rate of return, we can use the lognormal property to determine the distribution that this follows. At a future date T, the asset price S may be written as Equation (2.21):

$$S_T = S_t e^{r(T-t)} \tag{2.21}$$

and $r = \dfrac{1}{T-t} \ln\left(\dfrac{S_T}{S_t}\right)$.

Using the lognormal property, we can describe the distribution of the risk-free rate as:

$$r \sim N\left(\left(\mu - \frac{1}{2}\sigma^2\right), \frac{\sigma}{\sqrt{T-t}}\right). \tag{2.22}$$

2.2 STOCHASTIC CALCULUS MODELS: BROWNIAN MOTION AND ITÔ CALCULUS

We noted at the start of the chapter that the price of an option is a function of the price of the underlying stock and its behaviour over the life of the option. Therefore, this option price is determined by the variables that describe the process followed by the asset price over a continuous period of time. The behaviour of asset prices follows a stochastic process, and so option pricing models must capture the behaviour of stochastic variables behind the movement of asset prices. To accurately describe financial market processes, a financial model will depend on more than one variable. Generally, a model is constructed where a function is itself a function of more than one variable. Itô's lemma, the principal instrument in continuous time finance theory, is used to differentiate such functions. This was developed by a mathematician, Itô (1951). Here we simply state the theorem, as a proof and derivation are outside the scope of the book. Interested readers may wish to consult Briys et al. (1998) and Hull (1997) for a background on Itô's lemma; we also recommend Neftci (1996). Basic background on Itô's lemma is given in Appendices **B** and **C**.

2.2.1 Brownian Motion

Brownian motion is very similar to a Wiener process, which is why it is common to see the terms used interchangeably. Note that the properties of a Wiener process require that it be a martingale, while no such constraint is required for a Brownian process. A mathematical property known as the *Lévy's theorem* allows us to consider any Wiener process Z_t with respect to an information set F_t as a Brownian motion Z_t with respect to the same information set.

We can view Brownian motion as a continuous time *random walk*, visualised as a walk along a line, beginning at $X_0 = 0$ and moving at each incremental time interval dt either up or down by an amount $\sqrt{\mathrm{d}t}$. If we denote the position of the walk as X_n after the nth move, the position would be

$$X_n = X_{n-1} \pm \sqrt{\mathrm{d}t}, \quad n = 1, 2, 3 \ldots \tag{2.23}$$

where the $+$ and $-$ signs occur with an equal probability of 1/2. This is a simple random walk. We can transform this into a continuous path by applying linear interpolation between each move point so that

$$\bar{X}_t = X_n + (t - n\mathrm{d}t) \cdot (X_{n+1} - X_n), \quad n\mathrm{d}t \le t \le (n+1)\mathrm{d}t. \tag{2.24}$$

It can be shown (but not here) that the path described in Equation (2.24) has a number of properties, including that the incremental change in value each time it moves is independent of the behaviour leading up to the move, and that the mean value is 0 and variance is finite. The mean and variance of the set of moves are independent of dt.

What is the importance of this? Essentially this: the probability distribution of the motion can be shown, as dt approaches 0, to be normal or *Gaussian*.

2.2.2 Stochastic Calculus

Itô's theorem provides an analytical formula that simplifies the treatment of stochastic differential equations, which is why it is so valuable. It is an important rule in the application of stochastic calculus to the pricing of financial instruments. Here, we briefly describe the power of the theorem.

The standard stochastic differential equation for the process of an asset price S_t is given in the form

$$dS_t = a(S_t, t)dt + b(S_t, t)dW_t \tag{2.25}$$

where $a(S_t, t)$ is the drift coefficient and $b(S_t, t)$ is the volatility or *diffusion* coefficient. The Wiener process is denoted by dW_t and refers to the unpredictable events that occur at time intervals dt. This is sometimes denoted dZ or dz.

Consider a function $f(S_t, t)$ dependent on two variables S and t, where S follows a random process and varies with t. If S_t is a continuous-time process that follows a Wiener process W_t, then it directly influences the function $f(\ )$ through the variable t in $f(S_t, t)$. Over time, we observe new information about W_t as well as the movement in S over each time increment, given by dS_t. The sum of both these effects represents the *stochastic differential* and is given by the stochastic equivalent of the chain rule known as *Itô's lemma*. So, for example, if the price of a stock is 30 and an incremental time period later is 30½, the differential is ½.

If we apply a Taylor expansion in two variables to the function $f(S_t, t)$, we obtain

$$df_t = \frac{\partial f}{\partial S_t}dS_t + \frac{\partial f}{\partial t}dt + \frac{1}{2}\frac{\partial^2 f}{\partial S_t^2}b_t^2 dt. \tag{2.26}$$

Remember that ∂t is the partial derivative while dt is the derivative.

If we substitute the stochastic differential Equation (2.25) for S_t, we obtain *Itô's lemma* of the form

$$df_t = \left(\frac{\partial f}{\partial S_t}a_t + \frac{\partial f}{\partial t} + \frac{1}{2}\frac{\partial^2 f}{\partial S_t^2} \right)dt + \frac{\partial f}{\partial S_t}b_t dW_t. \tag{2.27}$$

What we have done is taken the stochastic differential equation (SDE) for S_t and transformed it so that we can determine the SDE for f_t. This is absolutely priceless, a valuable mechanism by which we can obtain an expression for pricing derivatives that are written on an underlying asset whose price can be determined using conventional analysis. In other words, using Itô's formula enables us to determine the SDE for the derivative once we have set up the SDE for the underlying asset. This is the value of Itô's lemma.

The SDE for the underlying asset S_t is written in most textbooks in the following form:

$$dS_t = \mu S_t dt + \sigma S_t dW_t \tag{2.28}$$

which has simply denoted the drift term $a(S_t, t)$ as μS_t and the diffusion term $b(S_t, t)$ as σS_t. In the same way, Itô's lemma is usually seen in the form

$$dF_t = \left[\frac{\partial F}{\partial S_t} \mu S_t + \frac{\partial F}{\partial t} + \frac{1}{2} \frac{\partial^2 F}{\partial S_t^2} \sigma^2 S_t^2 \right] dt + \frac{\partial F}{\partial S_t} \sigma S_t dW_t \tag{2.29}$$

although the noise term is sometimes denoted dZ. Further applications are illustrated in Example 2.2.

EXAMPLE 2.2

(i) Lognormal distribution
A variable (such as an asset price) may be assumed to have a *lognormal distribution* if the natural logarithm of the variable is normally distributed. So, if an asset price S follows a stochastic process described by

$$dS = \mu S dt + \sigma S dW \tag{2.30}$$

how would we determine the expression for $\ln S$? This can be achieved using Itô's lemma.
If we say that $F = \ln S$, then the first derivative $\frac{dF}{dS} = \frac{1}{S}$ and as there is no t, we have $\frac{dF}{dt} = 0$.
The second derivative is $\frac{d^2 F}{dS^2} = \frac{-1}{S^2}$.
We substitute these values into Itô's lemma given in Equation (2.29) and this gives us

$$d \ln S = \left(\mu - \frac{\sigma^2}{2} \right) dt + \sigma dW. \tag{2.31}$$

So, we have moved from dF to dS using Itô's lemma, and Equation (2.31) is a good representation of the asset price over time.
(ii) The bond price equation
The continuously compounded gross redemption yield at time t on a default-free zero-coupon bond that pays £1 at maturity date T is x. We assume that the movement in x is described by

$$dx = a(\alpha - x)dt + sx dZ$$

where a, α and s are positive constants. What is the expression for the process followed by the price P of the bond? Let us say that the price of the bond is given by

$$P = e^{-x(T-t)},$$

EXAMPLE 2.2—Cont'd

We have dx, and we require dP. This is done by applying Itô's lemma. We require

$$\frac{\partial P}{\partial x} = -(T-t)e^{-x(T-t)} = -(T-t)P$$

$$\frac{\partial^2 P}{\partial x^2} = -(T-t)e^{-x(T-t)} = -(T-t)^2 P \cdot$$

$$\frac{\partial P}{\partial t} = xe^{-x(T-t)} = xP$$

From Itô's lemma

$$dP = \left[\frac{\partial P}{\partial x}a(\alpha - x) + \frac{\partial P}{\partial t} + \frac{1}{2}\frac{\partial^2 P}{\partial x^2}s^2 x^2\right]dt + \frac{\partial P}{\partial x}sxdZ$$

which gives

$$dP = \left[-(T-t)Pa(\alpha - x) + xP + \frac{1}{2}(T-t)^2 Ps^2 x^2\right]dt - (T-t)psxdZ$$

which simplifies to

$$dP = \left[-a(\alpha - x)(T-t) + x + \frac{1}{2}s^2 x^2 (T-t)^2\right]Pdt - sx(T-t)PdZ.$$

So, using Itô's lemma, we have transformed the SDE for the bond yield into an expression for the bond price.

2.2.3   Stochastic Integrals

Although in no way wishing to trivialise the mathematical level, we will not consider the derivations here, we simply state that the observed values of the Brownian motion up to the point at time t determine the process immediately after, and that this process is Gaussian. Stochastic integrals are continuous path martingales. As described in Neftci (1996), the integral is used to calculate sums where we have an infinite or uncountable number of items, in contrast to the Σ sum operator which is used for a finite number of objects. In defining integrals, we begin with an approximation, where there is a countable number of items, and then set a limit and move to an uncountable number. A basic definition is given in Appendix **D**. Stochastic integration is an operation that is closely associated with Brownian paths; a path is partitioned into consecutive intervals or increments, and each increment is multiplied by a random variable. These values are then summed to create the stochastic integral. Therefore, the stochastic integral can be viewed as a random walk Brownian motion with increments that have varying values, a random walk with non-homogeneous movement.

2.2.4   Generalised Itô's Formula

It is possible to generalise Itô's formula in order to produce a multi-dimensional formula, which can then be used to construct a model to price interest-rate derivatives or other asset-class options where there is more than one variable. To do this, we generalise the formula to apply to situations where the dynamic function $f(\ )$ is dependent on more than one Itô process, each expressed as a standard Brownian motion.

Consider $W_T = \left(W_T^T, \ldots, W_T^n\right)$ where $\left(W_T^t\right)_{t\geq 0}$ are independent standard Brownian motions and W_T is an n-dimensional Brownian motion. We can express Itô's formula mathematically with respect to p Itô processes $(X_t^T, \ldots, X_T^t)$ as:

$$X_T^i = X_0^i + \int_0^t K_s^i \mathrm{d}s + \sum_{i=1}^n \int_0^t H_s^{ij} \mathrm{d}X_s^i. \tag{2.32}$$

Where the function $f(\ )$ contains second-order partial derivatives with respect to x and first-order partial derivatives with respect to t, which are a continuous function in (x, t), the generalised Itô's formula is given by

$$f\left(t, X_t^1, \ldots, X_T^p\right) = f\left(0, X_0^1, \ldots, X_0^p\right) + \int_0^t \left(\frac{\partial f}{\partial s}\right)(s, X_s^1, \ldots, X_s^p)\mathrm{d}s$$

$$+ \sum_{i=1}^p \int_0^t \left(\frac{\partial f}{\partial x_i}\right)(s, X_s^1, \ldots, X_s^p)\mathrm{d}X_s^i \tag{2.33}$$

$$+ \frac{1}{2}\sum_{i,j=1}^p \int_0^t \left(\frac{\partial^2 f}{\partial x_i \partial x_i}\right)(s, X_s^1, \ldots, X_s^p)\mathrm{d}\left(X^i, X^j\right)_s$$

with

$$\mathrm{d}X_s^i = K_s^i \mathrm{d}s + \sum_{j=1}^n H_s^{im}\mathrm{d}W_s^j$$

$$\mathrm{d}(X^i, X^j)_s = \sum_{m=1}^n H_s^{im} H_s^{jm}\mathrm{d}s \tag{2.34}$$

2.2.5   Information Structures

A key element of the description of a stochastic process is a specification of the level of information on the behaviour of prices that is available to an observer at each point in time. As with the martingale property, a calculation of the expected future values of a price process requires information on current prices. Generally, financial valuation models require data on both the current and the historical security prices, but investors are only able to deal on the basis of current known information and do not have access to future information. In a stochastic model, this concept is captured via the process known as *filtration*.

A filtration is a family $F = (F_t)$, $t \in T$ of variables $F_t \subset F$ which is increasing in level in the sense that $F_s \subset F_t$ whenever $s, t \in T$, $s \leq t$. Hence, a filtration can be viewed as a dynamic information structure, and F_t represents the information available to the investor at time t. The behaviour of the asset price is seen by the increase in filtration, which implies that more and more data are assimilated over time, and historical data is incorporated into the current price, rather than disregarded or forgotten. A filtration $F = (F_t)$ is said to be *augmented* if F_t is augmented for each time t. This means that only F_0 is augmented. A stochastic process W is described as being *adapted* to the filtration F if for each fixed $t \in T$, the random variable X:

$$X_t; \ w \mapsto X(w, \ t) = X_t(w) = X_t(w) : \Omega \to \mathrm{IR}^K$$

is measurable with respect to F_t.

This is an important description as it means that the value X_t of X at t is dependent only on information that is available at time t. It might also mean that an investor with access to the information level F is able to observe or make inferences on the value of X at each point in time. The augmented filtration generated by X is the filtration $F^\wedge = (F_t)$, $t \in T$. Any stochastic process X is adapted to the augmented filtration FX that it generates. If a stochastic process is measurable as a mapping or vector, then it is a measurable process; however, this does not impact significantly on finance theory so we shall ignore it.

2.3   PERFECT CAPITAL MARKETS

One of the assumptions of derivative pricing is that the financial markets are assumed to be near-perfect, for example, akin to Fama's semi-strong or strong-form market. The term *complete* market is also used. Essentially, the market is assumed to be a general stochastic economy where transactions may take place at any time, and interest rates behave under *Gaussian uncertainty*. We shall look at this briefly later in this section. Generally, pricing models assume that there is an almost infinite number of tradable assets in the market so that markets are assumed to be complete. This includes the assumptions that there is frictionless continuous trading, with no transaction costs or taxation.

Let us consider then the key assumptions that form part of the economy of, for example, the Black-Scholes option pricing model.

2.3.1   Stochastic Price Processes

The uncertainty in asset price dynamics is described as having two sources, both represented by independent standard Brownian motions. These are denoted

$$(W_1 t, W_2 t, t \in [0, T])$$

on a probability space denoted by (Ω, F, P).

The flow of information to investors is described by the filtration process. The two sources of risk in the Black-Scholes model are the risk-carrying underlying asset and the cash deposit which, though paying a riskless rate of interest, is at risk from the stochastic character of the interest rate itself.

2.3.2   Perfect Markets

The assumption of complete capital markets states that, as a result of arbitrage-free pricing, there is a unique probability measure Q, which is identical to the historical probability P, under which the continuously discounted price of any asset is a Q-martingale. This probability level Q then becomes the *risk-neutral* probability.

2.3.3   Uncertainty of Interest Rates

All derivative valuation models describe a process followed by market interest rates. As the future level of the yield curve or spot rate curve is uncertain, the key assumption is that interest rates follow a normal distribution and follow a Gaussian process. Thus, the interest rate is described as being a Gaussian interest rate uncertainty. Only the short-term risk-free interest rate, for which we read the T-bill rate or (in certain situations) the government bond repo rate, is captured in most models. Following Merton (1973), Vasicek (1977), Cox et al. (1985) and Jamshidian (1991), the short-dated risk-free interest r applicable to the period t is said to follow a Gaussian diffusion process under a constant volatility. The major drawback under this scenario is that under certain conditions it is possible to model a term structure that produces negative forward interest rates. However, in practice, this occurs only under certain limited conditions, so the validity of the models is not diminished. The future path followed by r_t is described by the following stochastic differential equation:

$$dr_t = a_t[b_t - r_t]dt + \sigma_t dW_t \qquad (2.35)$$

where a and b are constant deterministic functions and σ_t is the instantaneous standard deviation of r_t. Under Equation (2.35), the process describing the returns generated by a risk-free zero-coupon bond $P(t, T)$ that expires at time T and has a maturity of $T - t$ under the risk-neutral probability Q is given by Equation (2.36):

$$\frac{dP(t, T)}{P(t, T)} = r_t dt - \sigma_P(t, T)dW_t \qquad (2.36)$$

where σ_P is the standard deviation of the price returns of the $(T - t)$ bond and is a deterministic function defined by:

$$\sigma_P(t, T) = \sigma_t \cdot \int_t^T \exp\left(-\int_t^u a(s)ds\right) du.$$

In the Black-Scholes model, the value of a $1 (or £1) deposit invested at the risk-free zero-coupon interest rate r and continuously compounded over a period t will have grown to the value given by the expression below, where M_t is the value of the deposit at time t:

$$M_t = \exp\left(\int_0^t r(u)\mathrm{d}u\right).$$ (2.37)

2.3.4 Asset Price Processes

All valuation models must capture a process describing the dynamics of the asset price. This was discussed at the start of the chapter and is a central tenet of derivative valuation models. Under the Black-Scholes model for example, the price dynamics of a risk-bearing asset S_t under the risk-neutral probability function Q are given by

$$\frac{\mathrm{d}S_t}{S_t} = r_t\mathrm{d}t + \sigma_S\left(\rho\mathrm{d}W_t + \sqrt{1-\rho^2}\mathrm{d}W_2(t)\right)$$ (2.38)

where σ_S is the standard deviation of the asset price returns. The correlation between the price dynamics of the risk-bearing asset and the dynamics of interest-rate changes is given by ρ, $\rho \in [0, 1]$, while $W_2(t)$ is a standard Brownian motion that describes the dynamics of the asset price, and not that of the interest rates which are captured by W_t (and from which it is independent).

Under these four assumptions, the price of an asset can be described in present value terms relative to the value of the risk-free cash deposit M_t and, in fact, the price is described as a Q-martingale. A European-style contingent liability with maturity date t is therefore valued at time 0 under the risk-neutral probability as

$$V_0 = E^Q\left[\frac{h_t}{M_t}\right]$$

where

V_0 is the value of the asset at time 0

h_t is the stochastic payoff at maturity date t, where h is a measurable stochastic process and

$E^Q[]$ is the expectation of the value under probability function Q.

In the following chapter, we tie in the work on dynamics of asset prices to option valuation models.

APPENDIX A AN INTRODUCTION TO STOCHASTIC PROCESSES

A stochastic process can be described with respect to the notion of a vector of variables. If we set the following parameters

Ω is the set of all possible states ε

Ψ is a class of partitions of Ω

$X(\omega)$ is said to be a *random variable* when it is a measurable application from (Ω, ψ) to $\mathfrak{R}$. A vector of random variables $X(\omega) = [X_1(\omega), \ldots, X_n(\omega)]$ is an application that can be measured from (Ω, ψ) into $\mathfrak{R}^n$. Therefore, we have a vector of random variables that is similar to n ordinary variables defined under the same probability function.

A stochastic process is an extension of the notion of a vector of variables when the number of elements becomes infinite. It is described by

$$\{X_t(\omega)\}, t \in T$$

which is a set of random variables where the index varies in a finite or infinite group, and is denoted by $X(t)$.

APPENDIX B   ITÔ'S LEMMA

If f is a continuous and differentiable function of a variable x, and Δx is a small change in x, then using a Taylor expansion, the resulting change in f is given by Equation (2.39):

$$\Delta f = \left(\frac{\mathrm{d}f}{\mathrm{d}x}\right)\Delta x + \frac{1}{2}\left(\frac{\mathrm{d}^2 f}{\mathrm{d}x^2}\right)\Delta x^2 + \frac{1}{6}\left(\frac{\mathrm{d}^3 f}{\mathrm{d}x^3}\right)\Delta x^3 + \cdots. \quad (2.39)$$

If f is dependent on two variables x and y, then the Taylor expansion of Δf becomes Equation (2.40):

$$\Delta f \approx \left(\frac{\partial f}{\partial x}\right)\Delta x + \left(\frac{\partial f}{\partial y}\right)\Delta y + \frac{1}{2}\left(\frac{\partial^2 f}{\partial x^2}\right)\Delta x^2 + \frac{1}{2}\left(\frac{\partial^2 f}{\partial y^2}\right)\Delta y^2 + \left(\frac{\partial^2 f}{\partial x \partial y}\right)\Delta x \Delta y + \cdots.$$

$$(2.40)$$

The limiting case where Δx and Δy are close to zero will transform Equation (2.40) to Equation (2.41):

$$\partial f \approx \left(\frac{\partial f}{\partial x}\right)\mathrm{d}x + \left(\frac{\partial f}{\partial y}\right)\mathrm{d}y. \quad (2.41)$$

Consider now a derivative asset $f(x, \tau)$ whose value is dependent on time and on the asset price x. If we assume that x follows the general Itô process

$$\mathrm{d}x = a(x, t)\mathrm{d}t + b(x, t)\mathrm{d}W \quad (2.42)$$

where a and b are functions of x and t and $\mathrm{d}W$ is a Wiener process. The asset price x is described by a drift rate of x and a standard deviation of b. Using

Itô's lemma, it can be shown that a function f of x and t will follow the following process:

$$df = \left(\frac{\partial f}{\partial x}a + \frac{\partial f}{\partial t} + \frac{1}{2}\left(\frac{\partial^2 f}{\partial x^2}\right)b^2\right)dt + \frac{\partial f}{\partial x}bdW \qquad (2.43)$$

where dW is the Wiener process; therefore, f follows an Itô process and its drift and standard deviation are described by the expressions below:

$$\frac{\partial f}{\partial x}a + \frac{\partial f}{\partial t} + \frac{1}{2}\left(\frac{\partial^2 f}{\partial x^2}\right)b^2 \quad \text{and} \quad \left(\frac{\partial f}{\partial x}\right)b.$$

This may also be stated as:

$$\Delta x = a(x,\ t)\Delta t + b\varepsilon\sqrt{\Delta t}$$

where the term ε is normally distributed with a mean of 0, so that $E(\varepsilon)=0$, and a variance of 1, so that $E(\varepsilon^2)-E(\varepsilon)^2=1$. In the limit case Equation (2.40) becomes Equation (2.44), which is Itô's lemma:

$$df = \left(\frac{\partial f}{\partial x}\right)dx + \left(\frac{\partial f}{\partial t}\right)dt + \frac{1}{2}\left(\frac{\partial^2 f}{\partial x^2}\right)b^2 dt. \qquad (2.44)$$

The expression in Equation (2.44) is Itô's lemma and if we substitute Equation (2.42) for dx, it can be transformed to Equation (2.45):

$$df = \left[\left(\frac{\partial f}{\partial x}\right)a + \left(\frac{\partial f}{\partial t}\right) + \frac{1}{2}\left(\frac{\partial^2 f}{\partial x^2}\right)b^2\right]dt + \left(\frac{\partial f}{\partial x}\right)bdW. \qquad (2.45)$$

The derivation of Itô's formula is given in Appendix C.

APPENDIX C   DERIVATION OF ITÔ'S FORMULA

Let X_t be a *stochastic* process described by

$$dX_t = \mu_t dt + \sigma_t dW_t \qquad (2.46)$$

where W_t is a random variable and Brownian motion and dW_t is an incremental change in the Brownian motion W_t, equal to $Z_t\sqrt{dt}$, $Z_t \sim N(0,\ 1)$. Then suppose that we have a function $Y_t = f(X_t, t)$ and we require the differential dY_t. Applying a Taylor expansion of Y_t, we would obtain

$$dY_t = \frac{\partial f}{\partial X_t}dX_t + \frac{\partial f}{\partial t}dt + \frac{1}{2}\left[\frac{\partial^2 f}{\partial X_t^2}dX_t^2 + 2\frac{\partial^2 f}{\partial X \partial t}dX_t dt + \frac{\partial^2 f}{\partial t^2}dt^2\right] + \cdots. \qquad (2.47)$$

In Equation (2.46), if we square dX_t we obtain

$$dX_t^2 = \mu_t^2 dt^2 + 2\sigma_t\mu_t dW_t dt + \sigma_t^2 dW_t^2. \qquad (2.48)$$

The first two terms in Equation (2.48) are of a higher order and of minimal impact when dt is sufficiently small, and may be ignored. It can be shown that the variance of the $(dW_t)^2$ term will tend towards zero when the increment dt is sufficiently small. At this point, it no longer has the property of a random variable and becomes more a constant with expected value

$$E\left(Z^2 dt\right) = dt. \tag{2.49}$$

It can then be shown that for sufficiently small dt

$$dX_t^2 \Rightarrow \sigma_t^2 dW_t^2 \Rightarrow \sigma_t^2 dt.$$

The differential dY_t has an element that tends towards $\dfrac{1}{2}\dfrac{\partial^2 f}{\partial X_t^2}\sigma_t^2 dt$ for sufficiently small dt but cannot be dropped as were the higher-order terms of Equation (2.48) as it is of order dt. So the first-order differential of Y_t is

$$dY_t = \frac{\partial f}{\partial X_t}dX_t + \frac{\partial f}{\partial t}dt + \frac{1}{2}\sigma_t^2 \frac{\partial^2 f}{\partial X_t^2}dt \tag{2.50}$$

and now if we insert dX_t from Equation (2.46) into Equation (2.49), we will obtain

$$dY_t = \left(\mu_t\frac{\partial f}{\partial X_t} + \frac{\partial f}{\partial t} + \frac{1}{2}\sigma_t^2 \frac{\partial^2 f}{\partial X_t^2}\right)dt + \sigma_t\frac{\partial f}{\partial X_t}dW_t. \tag{2.51}$$

If the reader has followed this through, he or she has arrived at Itô's lemma. We can apply this immediately. Consider a process

$$X_t = X_0 + \int_0^t \mu_v\,dv + \int_0^t \sigma_s dW_s \tag{2.52}$$

for which the differential form is

$$dX_t = \mu_t dt + \sigma_t dW_t. \tag{2.53}$$

If we set the function $f(X)$ equal to X_t, the results of applying the Itô's lemma terms are

$$\frac{\partial f}{\partial X_t} = 1; \quad \frac{\partial f}{\partial t} = 0 \text{ and } \frac{\partial^2 f}{\partial X_t^2} = 0.$$

Therefore, using Itô's lemma we obtain

$$dX_t = \mu_t dt + \sigma_t dW_t \tag{2.54}$$

which is what we expect. What we have here is a stochastic differential equation at Equation (2.54) for which the solution is Equation (2.52).

APPENDIX D   THE INTEGRAL

Suppose we have a deterministic function $f(x)$ of time, with $x \in [0, T]$, that corresponds to a curve of $f(x)$ over the period from 0 to T, and we wish to calculate the area given by the function from time t_0 to t_T, this can be done by integrating the function over the time interval $[0, T]$, given by

$$\int_0^T f(s)\,\mathrm{d}s. \tag{2.55}$$

To calculate the integral, we split the area given by the function in the time period into a series of *partitions* or intervals, described by

$$t_0 = 0 < t_1 < t_2 < \ldots < t_n = T. \tag{2.56}$$

The approximate value of the area required is

$$\sum_{i=1}^{n} f\left(\frac{t_i + t_{i-1}}{2}\right)(t_i - t_{i-1}); \tag{2.57}$$

however, if we decrease the interval space such that it approaches 0, described by

$$\max_i \left| t_i - t_{i-1} \right| \to 0$$

the area under the space is given by the integral in Equation (2.49), as the approximating sum approaches the area defined by the limit

$$\sum_{i=1}^{n} f\left(\frac{t_i + t_{i-1}}{2}\right)(t_i - t_{i-1}) \to \int_0^T f(s)\,\mathrm{d}s. \tag{2.58}$$

SELECTED BIBLIOGRAPHY AND REFERENCES

Baxter, M., Rennie, A., 1996. Financial Calculus. Cambridge University Press, Cambridge.

Boyle, P., 1986. Option valuation using a three jump process. Int. Options J. 3, 7–12.

Briys, E., Bellalah, M., Mai, H., de Varenne, F., 1998. Options, Futures and Exotic Derivatives. Wiley, New York.

Cootner, P. (Ed.), 1964. The Random Character of Stock Market Prices. MIT Press, Cambridge.

Cox, D., Miller, H., 1965. The Theory of Stochastic Processes. Chapman & Hall, New York.

Cox, J., Ingersoll, J., Ross, S., 1985. A theory of the term structure of interest rates. Econometrica 53, 385–407.

Debreu, G., 1954. Representation of a preference ordering by a numerical function. In: Thrall, R., Coombs, C., Davis, R. (Eds.), Decision Processes. Wiley, New York.

Duffie, D., 1996. Dynamic Asset Pricing Theory. Princeton University Press, Princeton.

Fama, E., 1965. The behaviour of stock prices. J. Bus. 38, 34–105.

Feller, W., 1950. In: Probability Theory and Its Applications, vols. 1 and 2. Wiley, New York.

Harrison, J., Kreps, D., 1979. Martingales and arbitrage in multi-period securities markets. J. Econ. Theory 20, 381–408.

Harrison, J., Pliska, S., 1981. Martingales and stochastic integrals in the theory of continuous trading. Stochast. Proc. Appl. 11, 216–260.

Hull, J., 1997. Options, Futures and Other Derivatives. Wiley, New Jersey.

Ingersoll Jr., J., 1987. Theory of Financial Decision Making. Rowman & Littlefield, Totowa, New Jersey.

Itô, K., 1951. On stochastic differential equations. American Math. Soc. 4, 1–51.

James, J., Webber, N., 2000. Interest Rate Modelling. Wiley, Chichester, Chapters 3–5, 7–9, 15–16.

Jamshidian, F., 1991. Bond and option valuation in the Gaussian interest rate model. Res. Finance 9, 131–170.

Merton, R., 1973. Theory of rational option pricing. Bell J. Econ. Manag. Sci. 4, 141–183.

Neftci, S., 1996. An Introduction to the Mathematics of Financial Derivatives. Academic Press, San Diego.

Nielson, L.T., 1999. Pricing and Hedging of Derivative Securities. Oxford University Press, Oxford.

Rendleman, R., Bartter, B., 1979. Two state option pricing. J. Financ. 34, 1092–1110.

Ross, S., 2000. Introduction to Probability Models, seventh ed. Harcourt Academic Press, San Diego.

Vasicek, O., 1977. An equilibrium characterisation of the term structure. J. Financ. Econ. 5, 177–188.

Williams, D., 1991. Probability with Martingales. Cambridge University Press, Cambridge.

Chapter 3

Interest-Rate Models I

Chapter Contents

In Chapter 2, we introduced the concept of stochastic processes. Most but not all interest-rate models are essentially descriptions of the short-rate models in terms of stochastic process. Financial literature[1] has tended to categorise models into one of up to six different types, but for our purposes we can generalise them into two types. Thus, we introduce some of the main models, according to their categorisation as equilibrium or arbitrage-free models. This chapter looks at the earlier models, including the first ever term structure model presented by Vasicek (1977). The next chapter considers what have been termed 'whole yield curve' models, or the Heath-Jarrow-Morton family, while Chapter 5 reviews considerations in fitting the yield curve.

---

1. For example, see James and Webber (2000) or Van Deventer and Imai (1997).

3.1   INTRODUCTION

3.1.1   Bond Price and Yield

We first set the scene by introducing the interest-rate market. The price of a zero-coupon bond of maturity T at time t is denoted by $P(t, T)$ so that its price at time 0 is denoted by $P(0, T)$. The process followed by the bond price is a stochastic one and therefore can be modelled; equally, options that have been written on the bond can be hedged by it. If market interest rates are constant, the price of the bond at time t is given by $e^{-r(T-t)}$. This enables us to state that given a zero-coupon bond price $P(t, T)$ at time t, the yield $r(t, T)$ is given by Equation (3.1):

$$r(t, T) = -\frac{\log P(t, T)}{T - t}.$$ (3.1)

Of course, interest rates are not constant but Equation (3.1) is valuable as it is used later in constructing a model. By using Equation (3.1), we are able to produce a yield curve, given a set of zero-coupon bond prices. For modelling purposes, we require a definition of the *short rate*, or the current interest rate for borrowing a sum of money that is paid back a very short period later (in fact, almost instantaneously). This is the rate payable at time t for repayment at time $t + \Delta t$ where Δt is an incremental passage of time. This is given by

$$r(t, t + \Delta t) = -\frac{\log P(t, t + \Delta t)}{\Delta t}$$ (3.2)

and the incremental change can be steadily decreased to give the instantaneous rate, which is described by

$$r_t = -\frac{\partial}{\partial T} \log P(t, t)$$ (3.3)

and is identical to $r(t, t)$.

The instantaneous rate is an important mathematical construct that is widely used in the modelling process.

We can define forward rates in terms of the short rate. Again for infinitesimal change in time from a forward date T_1 to T_2 (for example, two bonds whose maturity dates are very close together), we can define a forward rate for instantaneous borrowing, given by

$$rf(t, T) = -\frac{\partial}{\partial T} \log P(t, T)$$ (3.4)

which is called the forward rate. We can also set

$$rf(t, t) = r_t$$ (3.5)

that is the forward rate for borrowing at the point $t = T$ which is identical to the short rate. The forward rate is valuable because, given the set of forward rates from t to T, we can calculate the bond price for a T-maturity date. This is presented in a number of texts, one of the best being Jarrow (1996). Given the expressions for the bond yield and the forward rate, the bond prices can be defined in terms of either the yield,

$$P(t, T) = \exp(-(T - t)r(t, T)) \tag{3.6}$$

or the forward rates, as a stochastic integral

$$P(t, T) = \exp\left(-\int_t^T rf(t, s)ds\right). \tag{3.7}$$

This is convenient because this means that the price at time t of a zero-coupon bond maturing at T is given by Equation (3.7), and forward rates can be calculated from the current term structure or vice versa.

For readers unfamiliar with the basic mathematics, an introductory primer is given in the Preface, which can be used to reference the relevant texts.

3.1.2   Interest-Rate Models

An interest-rate model provides a description of the dynamic process by which rates change over time, in terms of a statistical construct, as well as a means by which interest-rate derivatives such as options can be priced. It is often the practical implementation of the model that dictates which type is used, rather than mathematical neatness or more realistic assumptions. An excellent categorisation is given in James and Webber (2000), who list models as being one of the following types:

- The traditional one-, two- and multi-factor equilibrium models, known as *affine term structure* models (see James and Webber, 2000 or Duffie, 1996, p. 136).[2] These include Gaussian affine models such as Vasicek, Hull-White and Steeley, where the model describes a process with constant volatility; and models that have a square-root volatility such as Cox-Ingersoll-Ross (CIR);
- Whole yield curve models such as Heath-Jarrow-Morton;
- So-called market models such as Jamshidian;
- So-called consol models such as Brennan and Schwartz.
- There are also other types of models and we suggest that interested readers consult a specialist text; James and Webber is an excellent start, which also contains detailed sections on implementing models as well as a comparison of the different models themselves.

The most commonly used models are the Hull-White type models which are relatively straightforward to implement, although HJM models are also more

---

2. A function $\mathfrak{R} \to \mathfrak{R}$ is *affine* if there are constants a and b such that for all values of x, $H(x) = a + bx$. This describes certain term structure models' drift and diffusion functions.

commonly encountered. The Hull-White and *extended* CIR models incorporate a mean reversion feature that means that they can be fitted to the term structure in place at the time. The CIR model has a square-root factor in its volatility component, which prevents the short-term rate reaching negative values. What criteria are used by a bank in deciding which model to implement? Generally, a user will seek to implement a model that fits current market data, fits the process by which interest rates change over time and is *tractable*. This means that it should be computationally efficient, and provide explicit solutions when used for pricing bonds and vanilla options.

3.1.3   Introduction to Bond Analysis Using Spot Rates and Forward Rates in Continuous Time

This section analyses further the relationship between spot and forward rates and the yield curve.

3.1.3.1   The Spot and Forward Rate Relationship

In the discussion to date, we have assumed discrete time intervals and interest rates in discrete time. Here, we consider the relationship between spot and forward rates in continuous time. For this, we assume the mathematical convenience of a continuously compounded interest rate.

The rate r is compounded using e^r and an initial investment M earning $r(t, T)$ over the period $T - t$, initial investment at time t and for maturity at T, where $T > t$, would have a value of $Me^{r(t, T)(T-t)}$ on maturity.[3] If we denote the initial value M_t and the maturity value M_T, then we can state $M_t e^{r(t, T)(T-t)} = M_T$ and therefore the continuously compounded yield, defined as the continuously compounded interest rate $r(t, T)$, can be shown to be

$$r(t, T) = \frac{\log (M_T/M_t)}{T - t}. \tag{3.8}$$

We can then formulate a relationship between the continuously compounded interest rate and yield. It can be shown that

$$M_T = M_t e^{\int_t^T r(s)\,\mathrm{d}s} \tag{3.9}$$

where $r(s)$ is the instantaneous spot interest rate and is a function of time. It can further be shown that the continuously compounded yield is actually the equivalent of the average value of the continuously compounded interest rate. In addition, it can be shown that

---

3. e is the mathematical constant $2.7182818 \ldots$ and it can be shown that an investment of £1 at time t will have grown to e on maturity at time T (during the period $T - t$) if it is earning an interest rate of $1/(T - t)$ continuously compounded.

$$r(t, T) = \frac{\int_t^T r(s)ds}{T - t}. \tag{3.10}$$

In a continuous time environment we do not assume discrete time intervals over which interest rates are applicable, rather a period of time in which a borrowing of funds would be repaid instantaneously. So we define the forward rate $f(t, s)$ as the interest rate applicable for borrowing funds where the deal is struck at time t; the actual loan is made at s (with $s > t$) and repayable almost instantly. In mathematics the period $s - t$ is described as infinitesimally small. The spot interest rate is defined as the continuously compounded yield or interest rate $r(t, T)$. In an environment of no arbitrage, the return generated by investing at the forward rate $f(t, s)$ over the period $s - t$ must be equal to that generated by investing initially at the spot rate $r(t, T)$. So we may set

$$e^{\int_t^T f(t, s)ds} = e^{r(t)dt} \tag{3.11}$$

which enables us to derive an expression for the spot rate itself, which is

$$r(t, T) = \frac{\int_t^T f(t, s)ds}{T - t}. \tag{3.12}$$

The relationship described by Equation (3.12) states that the spot rate is given by the *arithmetic* average of the forward rates $f(t, s)$ where $t < s < T$. How does this differ from the relationship in a discrete time environment? We know that the spot rate in such a framework is the *geometric* average of the forward rates,[4] and this is the key difference in introducing the continuous time structure. Equation (3.12) can be rearranged to

$$r(t, T)(T - t) = \int_t^T f(t, s)ds \tag{3.13}$$

and this is used to show (by differentiation) the relationship between spot and forward rates, given below:

$$f(t, s) = r(t, T) + (T - t)\frac{dr(t, T)}{dT}. \tag{3.14}$$

If we assume we are dealing today (at time 0) for maturity at time T, then the expression for the spot rate becomes

---

4. To be precise, if we assume annual compounding, the relationship one plus the spot rate is equal to the geometric average of one plus the forward rates.

$$r(0,\ T) = \frac{\int_0^T f(0,s)\,ds}{T} \tag{3.15}$$

so we can write

$$r(0,\ T)\ \cdot\ T = \int_0^T f(0,\ s)\,ds. \tag{3.16}$$

This is illustrated in Figure 3.1 which is a diagrammatic representation showing that the spot rate $r(0,\ T)$ is the average of the forward rates from 0 to T, using the hypothetical value of 5% for $r(0,\ T)$. Figure 3.1 also shows the area represented by Equation (3.16).

What Equation (3.14) implies is that if the spot rate increases, then by definition the forward rate (or *marginal* rate as has been suggested that it may be called[5]) will be greater. From Equation (3.14), we deduce that the forward rate will be equal to the spot rate plus a value that is the product of the *rate* of increase of the spot rate and the time period $(T-t)$. In fact, the conclusions simply confirm that the forward rate for any period will lie above the spot rate if the spot rate term structure is increasing, and will lie below the spot rate if it is decreasing. In a constant spot rate environment, the forward rate will be equal to the spot rate.

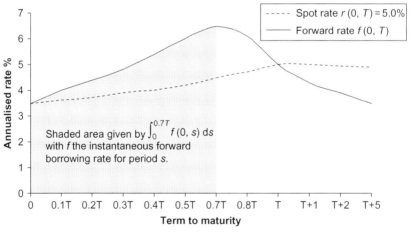

FIGURE 3.1   Diagrammatic representation of the relationship between spot and forward rate. The spot rate $r(t,\ T)$ is the average of the forward rates between t and T.

5. For example see Section 10.1 of Campbell, Lo and MacKinlay (1997), Chapter 10 of which is an excellent and accessible study of the term structure, and provides proofs of some of the results discussed here. This book is written in very readable style and is worth purchasing for Chapter 10 alone.

However, it is not as simple as that. An increasing spot rate term structure only implies that the forward rate lies above the spot rate, but not that the forward rate structure is itself also *increasing*. In fact one can observe the forward rate term structure to be increasing or decreasing while spot rates are increasing. As the spot rate is the average of the forward rates, it can be shown that in order to accommodate this, forward rates must in fact be *decreasing* before the point at which the spot rate reaches its highest point. This confirms market observation. An illustration of this property is given in the **Appendix**. As Campbell et al. (1997) state, this is a property of average and marginal cost curves in economics.

3.1.3.2   Bond Prices as a Function of Spot and Forward Rates

In this section, we describe the relationship between the price of a zero-coupon bond and spot and forward rates. We assume a risk-free zero-coupon bond of nominal value £1, priced at time t and maturing at time T. We also assume a money market bank account of initial value $P(t, T)$ invested at time t. The money market account is denoted M. The price of the bond at time t is denoted $P(t, T)$ and if today is time 0 (so that $t > 0$), then the bond price today is unknown and a random factor (similar to a future interest rate). The bond price can be related to the spot rate or forward rate that is in force at time t.

Consider the scenario below, used to derive the risk-free zero-coupon bond price.[6]

The continuously compounded *constant* spot rate is r as before. An investor has a choice of purchasing the zero-coupon bond at price $P(t, T)$, which will return the sum of £1 at time T, or of investing this same amount of cash in the money market account, and this sum would have grown to £1 at time T. We know that the value of the money market account is given by $Me^{r(t, T)(T-t)}$. If M must have a value of £1 at time T then the function $e^{-r(t, T)(T-t)}$ must give the present value of £1 at time t and therefore the value of the zero-coupon bond is given by

$$P(t, T) = e^{-r(t, T)(T-t)}. \tag{3.17}$$

If the same amount of cash that could be used to buy the bond at t, invested in the money market account, does *not* return £1 then arbitrage opportunities will result. If the price of the bond exceeded the discount function $e^{-r(t, T)(T-t)}$, then the investor could short sell the bond and invest the proceeds in the money market account. At time T, the bond position would result in a cash outflow of £1, while the money market account would be worth £1. However, the investor would gain because in the first place $P(t, T) - e^{-r(t, T)(T-t)} > 0$. Equally, if the price of the bond was below $e^{-r(t, T)(T-t)}$, then the investor would borrow

---

6. This approach is also used in Campbell et al. (q.v.).

$e^{-r(t, T)(T-t)}$ in cash and buy the bond at price $P(t, T)$. On maturity, the bond would return £1, which proceeds would be used to repay the loan. However, the investor would gain because $e^{-r(t, T)(T-t)} - P(t, T) > 0$. To avoid arbitrage opportunities, we must therefore have

$$P(t, T) = e^{-r(t, T)(T-t)}. \tag{3.18}$$

Following the relationship between spot and forward rates, it is also possible to describe the bond price in terms of forward rates.[7] We show the result here only. First we know that

$$P(t, T)e^{\int_t^T f(t, s)ds} = 1 \tag{3.19}$$

because the maturity value of the bond is £1, and we can rearrange Equation (3.19) to give

$$P(t, T) = e^{-\int_t^T f(t, s)ds}. \tag{3.20}$$

Expression (3.20) states that the bond price is a function of the range of forward rates that apply for all $f(t, s)$ that is, the forward rates for all time periods s from t to T (where $t < s < T$, and where s is infinitesimally small). The forward rate $f(t, s)$ that results for each s arises as a result of a random or *stochastic* process that is assumed to start today at time 0. Therefore, the bond price $P(t, T)$ also results from a random process, in this case all the random processes for all the forward rates $f(t, s)$.

The zero-coupon bond price may also be given in terms of the spot rate $r(t, T)$, as shown in Equation (3.18). From our earlier analysis, we know that

$$P(t, T)e^{r(t, T)(T-t)} = 1 \tag{3.21}$$

which is rearranged to give the zero-coupon bond price equation

$$P(t, T) = e^{-r(t, T)(T-t)} \tag{3.22}$$

as before.

Equation (3.22) describes the bond price as a function of the spot rate only, as opposed to the multiple processes that apply for all the forward rates from t to T. As the bond has a nominal value of £1, the value given by Equation (3.22) is the discount factor for that term; the range of zero-coupon bond prices would give us the discount function.

What is the importance of this result for our understanding of the term structure of interest rates? First, we see (again, but this time in continuous time) that spot rates, forward rates and the discount function are all closely related, and

---

7. For instance, see *ibid*, Section **3.2**.

given one we can calculate the remaining two. More significantly, we may model the term structure either as a function of the spot rate only, described as a stochastic process, or as a function of all of the forward rates $f(t, s)$ for each period s in the period $(T - t)$, described by multiple random processes. The first yield curve models adopted the first approach, while a later development described the second approach.

3.2   INTEREST-RATE PROCESSES

Term structure models are essentially models of the interest-rate process. The problem being posed is, what behaviour is exhibited by interest rates, and by the short-term interest rate in particular? An excellent description of the three most common processes that are used to describe the dynamics of the short-rate is given in Phoa (1998), who describes:

● the Gaussian or normal process: random shifts in forward rates are normally distributed and any given forward rate drifts upwards at a rate proportional to the initial time to the forward date. The interest-rate volatility is independent of the current interest rate, and the volatility term has the form $\sigma dW(t)$ where $W(t)$ is a generalised Weiner process or Brownian motion. An example of a Gaussian model is the Vasicek model;

● the square root or squared Gaussian process: the interest-rate volatility is proportional to the square root of the current interest rate, so the volatility term is given by $\sigma\sqrt{r}dW(t)$. An example of this is the Cox-Ingersoll-Ross model;

● the lognormal process: interest-rate volatility is proportional to the current interest rate, with the volatility term described by $\sigma r dW(t)$. An example of this is the Black-Derman-Toy model.

To illustrate the differences, this means that if the current short-rate is 8% and is assumed to have an annualised volatility of 100 basis points, and at some point in the future the short-rate moves to 4%, under the Gaussian process the volatility at the new rate will remain at 50 basis points, the square root process will assume a volatility of 82.8 basis points and the lognormal process will assume a volatility of 50 basis points.

The most straightforward models to implement are normal models, followed by square root models and then lognormal models. The process that is used will have an impact on the distribution of future interest rates predicted by the model. A generalised distribution is given in Figure 3.2.

Empirical studies have not pointed conclusively to one specific process as the most realistic. One study (Bank of England, 1999) states that observation of interest-rate behaviour in different markets suggests that when current interest-rate levels are low, at 4% or below, the rate process has tended to a Gaussian process, while when rates are relatively high the process is more akin to a lognormal process. At levels between these two, it would seem an 'intermediate'

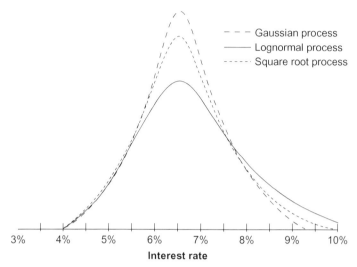

FIGURE 3.2   Distribution of future interest rates implied by different processes.

process is followed. These observations can be supported by economic argument, however. The nominal level of interest rates in an economy has two elements, a real interest rate and an inflation component. Thus, interest-rate volatility arises as a result of real interest-rate volatility and consumer prices volatility. When interest rates are low, the inflation component will be negligible, at which point only real rate volatility has an impact. However, as real rates are linked to the rate of growth, it is reasonable to assume that they follow a normal distribution. An extreme case has occurred in some markets where the real rates on index-linked bonds have occasionally been recorded as negative. When interest rates are at relatively high levels, the inflation component is more significant so that price volatility is important. However, economic rationale suggests that the price of traded goods follows a lognormal distribution.

Where does this leave the thinking on interest-rate models? As we demonstrate in the next section, one of the drawbacks of Gaussian interest-rate models is that they can result in negative forward rates. Although not impossible, this is an extremely unusual, not to say rare, situation and one that is unlikely in any environment bar one with very low current interest rates. However, such a phenomenon is not completely unheard of, and an environment of low interest rates is one that is best described by a Gaussian process. Negative interest rates have been recorded, for example, in the Japanese government bond repo market and certain other repo markets when bonds have gone very *special*, and bear in mind that rates in Japan have been very low for some time now. Essentially, then a model that permits negative interest rates is not necessarily unrealistic in an economic sense.

3.3 ONE-FACTOR MODELS

A short-rate model can be used to derive a complete term structure. We can illustrate this by showing how the model can be used to price discount bonds of any maturity. The derivation is not shown here. Let $P(t, T)$ be the price of a risk-free zero-coupon bond at time t maturing at time T that has a maturity value of 1. This price is a random process, although we know that the price at time T will be 1. Assume that an investor holds this bond, which has been financed by borrowing funds of value C_t. Therefore, at any time t the value of the short cash position must be $C_t = -P(t, T)$; otherwise, there would be an arbitrage position. The value of the short cash position is growing at a rate dictated by the short-term risk-free rate r, and this rate is given by

$$\frac{dC_t}{dt} = r(t)C_t.$$

By integrating this, we obtain $C_t = C_0 \cdot \exp\left(-\int_0^t r(s)ds\right)$ which can be rearranged to give

$$P(0, T)/P(t, T) = \exp\left(-\int_0^t r(s)ds\right)$$

so that the random process on both sides is the same, so that their expected values are the same. This can be used to show that the price of the zero-coupon bond at any point t is given by:

$$P(t, T) = E\left[\exp\left(-\int_t^T r(s)ds\right)\right].$$

Therefore, once we have a full description of the random behaviour of the short-rate r, we can calculate the price and yield of any zero-coupon bond at any time, by calculating this expected value. The implication is clear: specifying the process $r(t)$ determines the behaviour of the entire term structure; so, if we wish to build a term structure model, we need only (under these assumptions) specify the process for $r(t)$.

So, now we have determined that a short-rate model is related to the dynamics of bond yields and therefore may be used to derive a complete term structure. We also said that in the same way the model can be used to value bonds of any maturity. The original models were one-factor models, which describe the process for the short-rate r in terms of one source of uncertainty. This is used to capture the short-rate in the following form:

$$dr = \mu(r)dt + \sigma(r)dW \tag{3.23}$$

where μ is the instantaneous drift rate and σ is the standard deviation of the short-rate r. Both these terms are assumed to be functions of the short-rate and independent over time. The key assumption made in a one-factor model is that all interest rates move in the same direction.

3.3.1 The Vasicek Model

In the Vasicek (1977) model, the instantaneous short-rate r is assumed to follow a stochastic process known as the Ornstein-Uhlenbeck process, a form of Gaussian process, described by Equation (3.24):

$$dr = a(b - r)dt + \sigma dW. \tag{3.24}$$

This model incorporates *mean reversion*, which is not an unrealistic feature. Mean reversion is the process that describes that when the short-rate r is high, it will tend to be pulled back towards the long-term average level; when the rate is low, it will have an upward drift towards the average level. In Vasicek's model, the short-rate is pulled to a mean level b at a rate of a. The mean reversion is governed by the stochastic term σdW which is normally distributed. Using Equation (3.24), Vasicek shows that the price at time t of a zero-coupon bond of maturity T is given by:

$$P(t,\ T) = A(t,\ T)e^{-B(t,\ T)r(t)} \tag{3.25}$$

where $r(t)$ is the value of r at time t,

$$B(T,\ t) = \frac{1 - e^{-A(t-T)}}{a} \tag{3.26}$$

and

$$A(t,\ T) = \exp\left(\frac{B(t,\ T) - (T - t)(a^2 b - (\sigma^2/2))}{a^2} - \frac{\sigma^2 B(t,\ T)^2}{4a}\right) \tag{3.27}$$

It can be shown further that

$$r(t,\ T) = -\frac{1}{T - t}\ln A(t,\ T) + \frac{1}{T - t}B(t,\ T)r(T) \tag{3.28}$$

which describes the complete term structure as a function of $r(t)$ with parameters a, b and the standard deviation σ. The expression in Equation (3.28) states that $r(t, T)$ is a linear function of $r(t)$, and that the value of $r(t)$ will determine the level of the term structure at time t. Using the parameters described above, we can calculate the price function for a risk-free zero-coupon bond. Chan et al. (1992) used the following parameters: a long-run mean b of 0.07, drift rate a of 0.18 and standard deviation of 0.02. Using these parameters, Figure 3.3 shows two zero-coupon bond price curves that result from two different initial short rates, $r(t) = 4\%$ and $r(t) = 10\%$. The time to maturity T is measured on the x-axis, with the price of the zero-coupon bond with that time to maturity (a redemption value of 1) measured along the y-axis.

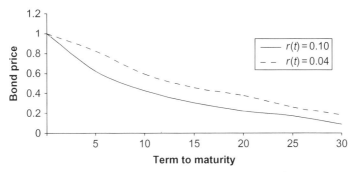

FIGURE 3.3 Zero-coupon bond price curves at $r(t)=0.04$ and $r(t)=0.10$.

For derived forward rates, the bond price function $P(t, T)$ is continuously differentiable with respect to t. Therefore, the model produces the following for the instantaneous forward rates:

$$f(t, T) = -\frac{\partial}{\partial t}\ln P(t, T)$$
$$= A'(T-t) + B'(T-t)r(t)$$
$$= \left(1 - e^{-a(T-t)}\right)b - \frac{1}{2}v(T-t) + e^{-a(T-t)r(t)}$$
$$= f(r(t), T-t)$$

(3.29)

where $f(r, T)$ is the function $f(r, T) = (1 - e^{-aT})b - \frac{1}{2}v(T) + e^{-aT}r$.

The forward rate is a function of the short-rate and is normally distributed. Figure 3.4 shows the forward rate curves that correspond to the price curves in Figure 3.3, under the same parameters.

An increase in the initial short-rate r will have the effect of raising forward rates, as will increasing the long-run mean value b. The effect of an increase in r is most pronounced at shorter maturities, whereas an increase in b has the greatest effect the longer the term to maturity. An equal increase or decrease in both

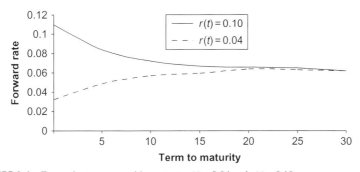

FIGURE 3.4 Forward rate curves with spot rate $r(t)=0.04$ and $r(t)=0.10$.

r and b will have the effect of moving all forward rates up or down by the same amount. With these changes, the forward curve moves up or down in a parallel fashion.

The derived forward rate is a decreasing function of the instantaneous standard deviation σ, one of the model parameters. The partial derivative of the forward rate with respect to the standard deviation is given in Equation (3.30):

$$\frac{\partial f(r,\,T)}{\partial \sigma} = -\sigma B(T-s)^2 = -\frac{\sigma}{a^2}\left(-2e^{-aT} + e^{-2aT} + 1\right). \qquad (3.30)$$

The expression in Equation (3.30) states that the forward rate is a decreasing function of T, that is, it becomes more negative as T becomes larger. The effect of the standard deviation on the forward rate is shown in Figure 3.5, which shows the two forward rate curves from Figure 3.4, with two additional forward rate curves where the standard deviation has been raised from 0.02 to 0.05.

In describing the dynamics of the yield curve, the Vasicek model only captures changes in the short-rate r, and not the long-run average rate b.

A key point about this model is that as the short-rate follows a normal distribution, it has a positive probability of becoming negative at any point in time. This is common to all models that assume a Gaussian interest-rate process, and although it might be considered a significant drawback, in fact it will only be exhibited under extreme parameter values. For instance, in the example in Figure 3.4, the forward rates are not unusual; however, if we increase the standard deviation, the effect will be to decrease forward rates, and this ultimately produces negative forward rates. For example, if we calculate the forward rates for a standard deviation $\sigma = 0.09$, the result will be to produce negative rates, as shown in Figure 3.6. A negative forward rate is equivalent to a zero-coupon bond price that increases over time, which is clearly unrealistic under all but the most unusual and rare conditions. The reason that Gaussian interest-rate

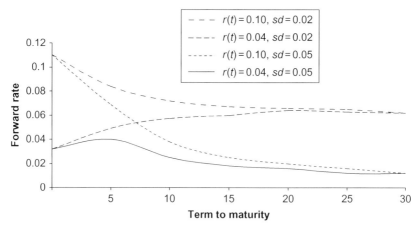

FIGURE 3.5   Forward rate curves with standard deviations of 0.02 and 0.05.

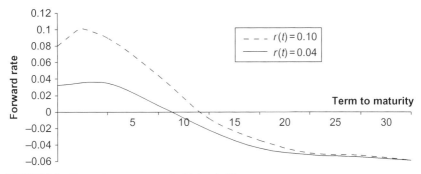

FIGURE 3.6 Forward rate curves under high volatility.

models can produce negative forward rates when the standard deviation is high is because the probability of achieving negative interest rates is high. Under certain parameter values, particularly under high values for the standard deviation, the probability of negative forward rates exists. However, we saw that this is only under certain parameters, and in fact the presence of mean reversion makes this a low possibility.

It might be considered to be more realistic to consider that there are no constant parameters for the drift rate and the standard deviation that would ensure that the price of a zero-coupon bond at any time is exactly the same as that suggested by observed market yields. For this reason, a modified version of the Vasicek model has been described by Hull and White (1990), known as the Hull-White or extended Vasicek model, which we will consider later.

3.3.2 The Merton Model

In Merton's (1971) model, the interest-rate process is assumed to be a generalised Weiner process, described by Equation (3.31):

$$r(t) = r_0 + \alpha t + \sigma W(t) \tag{3.31}$$

which in differential form is given by Equation (3.32):

$$dr = \alpha dt + \sigma dW. \tag{3.32}$$

For $0 \leq t \leq T$, it can be shown that

$$r(T) = r(t) + \alpha(T - t) + \sigma(W(T) - W(t)). \tag{3.33}$$

The distribution of $r(T)$ is normal with a mean of $r(t) + \alpha(T - t)$ and standard deviation of $\sigma\sqrt{T - t}$.

For a fixed term to maturity T, the forward rate $f(r(t), T - t)$ is an Itô process of the form:

$$\begin{aligned} dfr(r(t), T - t) &= dr - \alpha dt + \sigma^2(T - t)dt \\ &= \sigma^2(T - t)ds + \sigma dW \end{aligned} \tag{3.34}$$

The continuously compounded yield at time t of a risk-free zero-coupon bond paying 1 on maturity at time T is given by:

$$R(t, T) = \frac{1}{T-t} \ln \left(\frac{1}{P(r(t), T-t)} \right)$$

$$= \frac{1}{T-t} A(T-t) + R(t) \tag{3.35}$$

$$= R(r(t), T-t)$$

where R is the function

$$R(r, T) = \frac{1}{T} A(T) + r = \frac{1}{2}\alpha T - \frac{\sigma^2}{6} T^2 + r. \tag{3.36}$$

The average future interest rate over the time period (t, T) is given by Equation (3.37):

$$r_a = \frac{1}{T-t} \int_t^T r(s) \mathrm{d}s. \tag{3.37}$$

In the Merton model, forward rates will always be negative at long maturities, unlike the Vasicek model where there are a range of parameters under which the forward rates will be positive at all maturities. This is because although in both models the forward rate is negatively affected by the standard deviation of the future interest rate, which is an increasing function of the time to maturity, in the Merton model it changes in a linear fashion to infinity, whereas in the Vasicek model it grows to a finite limit. Therefore, the standard deviation is more powerful in the Merton model, and it results in the forward rates being negative at long maturities.

3.3.3 The Cox-Ingersoll-Ross Model

From the previous section, we see that under a model that assumes the short-rate to follow a normal distribution, there can arise instances of negative forward rates. The Cox et al. (1985) is a one-factor model and as originally presented removed the possibility of negative rates.[8] Under the CIR model, the dynamics of the short-rate are described by Equation (3.38):

$$\mathrm{d}r = a(b-r)\mathrm{d}t + \sigma\sqrt{r}\mathrm{d}W \tag{3.38}$$

which like Vasicek also captures a mean-reverting phenomenon. However, the stochastic term has a standard deviation that is proportional to $\sqrt{r}$. This is a significant difference because it states that as the short-rate increases, the standard

---

8. Although formally published in 1985, the Cox-Ingersoll-Ross model was being circulated in academic circles from the mid-1970s onwards, which would make it one of the earliest interest-rate models.

deviation will decrease. This means that forward rates will be positive. In the CIR model, the price of a risk-free zero-coupon bond is given by

$$P(t,T) = A(t,\ T)e^{-B(t,\ T)r} \qquad (3.39)$$

where

$$B(t,\ T) = \frac{2(e^{\gamma(T-t)} - 1}{(\gamma + a)(e^{\gamma(T-t)} - 1) + 2\gamma}$$

$$A(t,\ T) = \left(\frac{2\gamma e^{(a+\gamma)(T-t)/2}}{(\gamma + a)(e^{\lambda(T-t)} - 1) + 2\gamma} \right)^{2ab/\sigma^2}.$$

$$= \gamma = \sqrt{a^2 + 2\sigma^2}$$

The long-run interest rate $R(t, T)$ is a function of the short-rate $r(t)$ so that the short-rate only is all that is required to fit the entire term structure.

3.3.4   General Comment

The Gaussian models, also called affine models (see, for example, James and Webber, 2000), are popular because they are straightforward to implement and they provide explicit numerical solutions when used in instrument pricing. Although Gaussian models allow negative interest rates under certain conditions, this is not necessarily a completely unrealistic trait, although some academic opinion holds that any model that allows negative interest rates cannot be correct and should not be used. Negative interest rates will only result under very specific conditions, which have a low probability (see, for example, Rogers, 1995), and for this reason these models remain popular. However, in an environment of low interest rates for instance, the CIR type models, which do not permit negative interest rates, may be preferred.

3.4   ARBITRAGE-FREE MODELS

An equilibrium model of the term structure, of which we reviewed three in the previous section, is a model that is derived from (or consistent with) a general equilibrium model of the economy. They use generally constant parameters, including most crucially a constant volatility, and the actual parameters used are often calculated from historical time series data. Banks commonly also use parameters that are calculated from actual data and implied volatilities, which are obtained from the prices of exchange-traded option contracts.

An arbitrage-free model of the term structure on the other hand can be made to fit precisely with the current, observed term structure, so that observed bond yields are in fact equal to the bond yields calculated by the model. So, an arbitrage-free model is intended to be consistent with the currently observed zero-coupon yield curve, and the short-rate drift rate is dependent on time because the future average path taken by the short-rate is determined by the shape of the initial yield curve. This means that in a positively sloping yield curve environment, the short-rate r will be increasing, on average, while it will be decreasing in an initial inverted yield curve environment. In a humped initial yield curve environment, the expected short-rate path will also be humped. In an equilibrium model, the drift term for the short rate (that is, the coefficient of the d*t* term given above) is not dependent on time.

In theory, the price predicted by any model, were it to be observed in the market, would render that model to be an *arbitrage-free* one; however, arbitrage-free models are so-called because they compare the model-predicted price to the actual market price. In an equilibrium model, the initial term structure is a product of the model, while in an arbitrage-free model, the actual term structure is an input to the model in the first place. In practice, an equilibrium model may not be arbitrage-free under certain conditions; namely, it may show small errors at particular points along the curve, or it may feature a large error across the whole term structure. The most fundamental issue in this regard is that the concept of the risk-free short-term interest rate is difficult to identify as an actual interest rate in the money market. In practice, there may be more than one interest rate that presents itself, for example, the T-bill rate or the same maturity government bond repo rate, and this remains a current issue.

For these reasons, practitioners may prefer to use an arbitrage-free model if one can be successfully implemented and calibrated. This is not always straightforward, and under certain conditions, it is easier to implement an equilibrium multi-factor model (which we discuss in the next section) than it is to implement a multi-factor arbitrage-free model. Under one particular set of circumstances, however, it is always preferable to use an equilibrium model, and that is when reliable market data is not available. If modelling the term structure in a developing or 'emerging' bond market, it will be more efficient to use an equilibrium model.

Some texts have suggested that equilibrium models can be converted into arbitrage-free models by making the short-rate drift rate time dependent. However, this may change the whole nature of the model, presenting problems in calibration.

3.4.1 The Ho and Lee Model

The Ho-Lee (1986) model was one of the first arbitrage-free models and was presented using a binomial lattice approach, with two parameters: the standard deviation of the short-rate and the risk premium of the short-rate. We summarise it here. Following Ho and Lee, let $P_i^{(n)}(\cdot)$ be the equilibrium price of a zero-coupon bond maturing at time T under state i. That is $P_i^{(n)}(\cdot)$ is a discount function describing the entire term structure of interest rates, which will satisfy the following conditions:

$$P_i^{(n)}(0) = 1$$

$$\lim_{T \to \infty} P_i^{(n)}(T) = 0$$

To describe the binomial lattice, we denote the price at the initial time 0 as $P_0^{(0)}(\,\cdot\,) = 1$.

At time 1, the discount function is specified by two possible functions $P_1^{(1)}(0)$ and $P_0^{(1)}(0)$ which correspond respectively to the upside and the downside outcomes. Therefore, at time n, the binomial process is given by the discount function $P_i^{(n)}(\,\cdot\,)$ which can move upwards to a function $P_{i+1}^{(n+1)}(\,\cdot\,)$ and downwards to a function $P_i^{(n+1)}(\,\cdot\,)$ for $i = 0$ to n.

As described by Ho and Lee, there are two functions denoted $h(T)$ and $h^*(T)$ that describe the upstate and downstate as Equations (3.40) and (3.41) respectively, below,

$$P_{i+1}^{(n+1)}(T) = \left(\frac{P_i^{(n)}(T+1)}{P_i^{(n)}(1)} \right) h(T) \tag{3.40}$$

$$P_{i+1}^{(n+1)}(T) = \left(\frac{P_i^{(n)}(T+1)}{P_i^{(n)}(1)} \right) h*(T) \tag{3.41}$$

with $h(0) = h^*(0) = 1$.

The two functions specify the deviations of the discount functions from the implied forward functions. To satisfy arbitrage-free conditions, they define an implied binomial probability π that is independent of time T, while the initial discount function $P(T)$ is given by:

$$\pi h(T) + (1 - \pi)h*(T) = 1 \quad \text{for} \ \ n, \ i > 0 \tag{3.42}$$

and

$$P_i^{(n)}(T) = \left(\pi P_{i+1}^{(n+1)}(T-1) + (1 - \pi)P_i^{(n+1)}(T-1) \right) P_i^{(n)}(1). \tag{3.43}$$

Equation (3.43) shows that the bond price is equal to the expected value of the bond, discounted at the prevailing one-period rate. Therefore, π is the implied risk-neutral probability.

The assumption that the discount function evolves from one state to another as a function only of the number of upward and downward movements is equivalent to the assumption that a downward movement followed by an upward movement is equivalent to an upward movement followed by a downward movement. This produces the values for h and h^* given by Equation (3.44).

$$h(T) = \frac{1}{\pi + (1 - \pi)\delta^T} \quad \text{for } T \geq 0 \qquad (3.44)$$

$$h^*(T) = \frac{\delta^T}{\pi + (1 - \pi)\delta^T} \qquad (3.45)$$

where δ is the interest-rate spread.

It has been shown[9] that the model describes a continuous time process given by

$$dr = \theta(t)dt + \sigma dW(t) \qquad (3.46)$$

where σ is the constant instantaneous standard deviation of the short-rate and $\theta(t)$ is a time-dependent function that describes the short-rate process and fits the model to the current observed term structure. This term defines the average direction that the short-rate moves at time t, which is independent of the short-rate. The variable $\theta(t)$ is given by:

$$\theta(t) = f(0, t) + \sigma^2 t \qquad (3.47)$$

where $f(0, t)$ is the instantaneous forward rate for the period t at time 0. In fact, the term $\theta(t)$ approximates to $f(0, t)$ which states that the average direction of the short-rate in the future is given by the slope of the instantaneous forward curve.

The Ho and Lee model is straightforward to implement and is regarded by practitioners as convenient because it uses the information available from the current term structure so that it produces a model that precisely fits the current term structure. It also requires only two parameters. However, it assigns the same volatility to all spot and forward rates, so the volatility structure is restrictive for some market participants. In addition, the model does not incorporate mean reversion.

3.4.2   The Hull-White Model

The Hull-White (1990) model is an extension of the Vasicek model designed to produce a precise fit with the current term structure of rates. It is also known as the *extended Vasicek model*, with the interest rate following a process described by Equation (3.48):

$$dr = (\alpha - ar)dt + \sigma dW(t). \qquad (3.48)$$

It is also sometimes written as

$$dr = a\left(\frac{\alpha}{a} - r\right)dt + \sigma dW(t) \qquad (3.49)$$

---

9. For example, see Hull (1997).

where a is the mean reversion rate and a and σ are constants. It has been described as a Vasicek model with a time-dependent reversion level. The model is also called the *general Hull-White model*, while a special case where $a \neq 0$ is known as the simplified Hull-White model. In the Vasicek model, $a \neq 0$ and $\alpha = ab$ where b is constant.

The Hull-White model can be fitted to an initial term structure, and also a volatility term structure. A comprehensive analysis is given in Pelsser (1996) as well as James and Webber (2000).

It can be shown that

$$r(t) = e^{-K(t)} \left(r_0 + \int_t^T e^K \alpha dt + \int_t^T e^K \sigma dW(t) \right) \tag{3.50}$$

where the process K is given by $K(t) = \int_t^T adt$.

To calculate the price of a zero-coupon bond, the first step is to calculate the integral $I(t, T) = \int_t^T rds$ which follows a normal distribution with mean $m(r(t), t; T)$ and standard deviation $\sqrt{v(t; T)}$. The price of a bond is given by Equation (3.51):

$$P(t, T) = E_Q[\exp[-I(t, T)]|F_t]$$
$$= \exp\left(-m(r(t), t;T) + \frac{1}{2}v(t;T) \right) \tag{3.51}$$
$$= P(r(t), t;T)$$

where $P(r, t; T)$ is the function

$$P(r(t),t;T) = \exp\left(-m(r, t; T) + \frac{1}{2}v(t; T) \right). \tag{3.52}$$

The price of a zero-coupon discount at time t is defined in terms of the short-rate r at time t and the current term structure. The price function is not static, and the price of a bond at time t that matures at time T is a function of the short-rate, as we have noted, and separately of the time t.

The volatility of the bond price is given by the function $B(t; T)\sigma(t)$ where B is defined as

$$B(t, T) = \int_t^T e^{K(u) + K(t)} du = e^{K(t)} \int_t^T e^{-K} du. \tag{3.53}$$

The bond price volatility is a deterministic function of t. The 'pull to par' of the zero-coupon bond is captured by the fact that the volatility reduces to zero as t approaches T, as long as σ is continuous at t. As the mean m is normally distributed, it follows that the bond price is log-normally distributed, so therefore we have the function

$$\ln P(t, T) = -A(t, T) - B(t, T)r(t)$$

where $A(t, T)$ is defined by $A(t, T) = \displaystyle\int_t^T e^{-K(u)} \int_t^u e^K \, \alpha dx du - \frac{1}{2}\nu(t, T)$.

The price function above can be continuously differentiated as a function of t. The forward rate is given by Equation (3.54):

$$
\begin{aligned}
f(t, T) &= -\frac{\partial}{\partial T} \ln P(t, T) \\
&= A_T(t, T) + B_T(t, T)r(t) \\
&= e^{-K(T)} \int_t^T \alpha dx - \frac{1}{2}\nu_T(t, T) + e^{-K(T)+K(t)} r(t) \\
&= f(r(t);t, T)
\end{aligned}
\tag{3.54}
$$

where $f(r(t); t, T)$ is defined by the function below:

$$f(r(t);t, T) = e^{-K(T)} \int_t^T \alpha dx - \frac{1}{2}\nu_T(t, T) + e^{-K(T)+K(t)} r. \tag{3.55}$$

The forward rate function f at time t is not static and is a function of the short-rate r at time t, the time t and the time to maturity T. The Hull-White model can be calibrated in terms of the forward rate f. That is, at time t the information (parameters) required to implement this are the short-rate $r(t)$, the standard deviation σ of the short-rate, the forward rate f and the standard deviations $B_T(t, T)\sigma(t)$ of the forward rates at time t. If the forward rates are known in a form that allows their first differential to be calculated with respect to t, using the other information, it is possible to calculate the function B_T, the derivative of this function and thereby the value for $a(t)$, using the relationship in Equation (3.56):

$$a(t) = -\frac{B_T'(t, T)}{B_T(t, T)} \tag{3.56}$$

which describes the volatility of the bond price as a function of the maturity date T.

The continuously compounded yield of a zero-coupon bond at time t that matures at time T is shown to be

$$
\begin{aligned}
R(t, T) &= \frac{1}{T-t}\left(m(r(t), t;T) - \frac{1}{2}\nu(t,T)\right) \\
&= \frac{1}{T-t} \ln\left(\frac{1}{P(t, T)}\right) \\
&= \frac{1}{T-t}(A(t, T) + B(t, T)r(t)) \\
&= R(r(t), t, T)
\end{aligned}
\tag{3.57}
$$

where R is given by the function shown in Equation (3.58):

$$R(r,\ t,\ T) = \frac{1}{T-t}(A(t,\ T) + B(t,\ T)r).\tag{3.58}$$

Like the bond price function, the yield on a zero-coupon bond is a function of the short-rate r and follows a normal distribution; the yield curve is a function of the short-rate r, the time t and the time to maturity T. The long-run average future interest over the time to maturity $(t,\ T)$ is normally distributed and given by:

$$r_a = \frac{1}{T-t}\int_t^T r(s)\mathrm{d}s = \frac{1}{T-t}I(t,\ T).\tag{3.59}$$

3.4.3   The Black-Derman-Toy Model

In the models we have reviewed in this chapter, there has only been one function of time, the parameter a. In certain models, either or both of the parameters a and σ are also made to be functions of time. In their 1990 paper Black, Derman and Toy (BDT) proposed a binomial lattice model described by Equation (3.60),

$$\mathrm{d}\ln\ r = \left(\alpha + \frac{\sigma'(t)}{\sigma(t)}\ln(r)\right)\mathrm{d}t + \sigma(t)\mathrm{d}W\tag{3.60}$$

where $\sigma'(t)$ is the partial derivative of σ with respect to time t. The BDT model is a lognormal model, which means that the short-rate volatility is proportional to the instantaneous short-rate so that the ratio of the volatility to the rate level is constant. The drift term is more complex than that described in the earlier models, and so the BDT model requires numerical fitting to the observed current interest-rate and volatility term structures. That is, the drift term is not calculated analytically. The short-rate volatility is also linked to the mean reversion such that where long-term rates are less volatile than the short-term rates, the short-rate volatility will decrease in the long-term. A later model developed by Black and Karasinski (1991) removed the relationship between mean reversion and the volatility level. This is given in Equation (3.61):

$$\mathrm{d}\ln\ r = (\theta(t) - a(t)\ln(r))\mathrm{d}t + \sigma(t)\mathrm{d}W(t).\tag{3.61}$$

As with the previous models, the key factor is the short-rate. Using the binomial tree approach, a one-step tree is used to derive the current short-rate to the short-rates one period in the future. These derived rates are then used to derive rates two periods away, and so on.

3.5   FITTING THE MODEL

Implementing an interest-rate model requires the input of the term structure yields and volatility parameters, which are used in the process of calibrating the model. The process of fitting the model is called *calibration*. This can be done in at least three ways, which are:

- Calibration to the current spot rate yield curve, using a pre-specified volatility level and not the volatility values given by the prices of exchange-traded options. This may result in mispriced bonds and options if the selected volatilities are not accurate;
- Calibration to the current spot rate curve, using the volatilities implied by the prices of exchange-traded options; therefore, the model would be implemented using volatility parameters that were exactly similar to those implied by the traded option prices. In practice, this can be a lengthy process;
- Calibrating the model to the current spot rate curve, using volatility parameters that are approximately close enough to result in prices that are near to those of observed exchange-traded options. This is usually the method that is adopted.

Generally, volatility values for the different period interest rates are taken from the volatilities of exchange-traded options. However, where great accuracy is not required, for example, for regulatory capital purposes, practitioners may use the first method, while for the purposes of fixed income research, the third method is suitable. In both the second and third methods, there is the danger that calibrating the model to option prices will result in error simply because the options are mispriced. This is quite possible if using long-dated and/or OTC options, which frequently differ in price according to which bank is pricing them.

In any case a model will usually therefore use volatility inputs from option prices for a range of options that range in maturity from the shortest period to the longest in the term structure. To test the accuracy of the model, one can use the expression in Equation (3.62):

$$\sum_{n=1}^{N} (p_n - P_n)^2 \qquad (3.62)$$

where p_n is the observed price of the nth option and P_n is the price of the option as calculated by the model, and N options have been used to calibrate the model. A model that has the lowest value given by Equation (3.62) can be considered to be the most accurate. In deciding which option products should be used to calibrate the model, care should be taken to use instruments that are most similar to the instrument that is being priced by the model.

The different models can lend themselves to a particular calibration method. In the Ho-Lee model, only parallel yield curve shifts are captured and the current yield curve is a direct input; therefore, a constant volatility parameter is used. This implies that all the forward rate implied volatilities are identical. In practice, this is not necessarily realistic, as long-dated bond prices often experience lower volatility than short-dated bond prices. The model also assumes that volatility is a decreasing function of the time to maturity, which may also be unrealistic. Models that incorporate mean reversion can be implemented with more realistic volatility parameters, as it is the mean reversion effect that results in long-dated bonds having lower volatilities. Therefore, a mean-reverting model can be implemented more accurately using the second or third methods described above.

To recap on the issues involved in fitting the extended Vasicek model or Hull-White model; this describes the short-rate process as following the form

$$dr = (\alpha - ar)dt + \sigma dW(t). \tag{3.63}$$

In implementing this model, there are three possible approaches. The model could be calibrated by keeping α and a constant and calibrating the standard deviation parameter. This means that the model is fitted to the current yield curve and the volatility value is adjusted to that required to produce the observed curve. However, this may result in high volatility values, which rise by a squared function, and therefore will not be realistic. The second method is to calibrate α, keeping the other two parameters constant. This is adjusting the mean reversion rate in order to fit the derived curve with the observed curve. The resulting derived yield curve will be a function of the current short-rate and the mean reversion rate. This method is sometimes applied in practice, although it can result in inaccurate volatility levels for long-dated bonds because large adjustments in the mean reversion rate are needed to fit the derived curve to the long-dated part of the observed curve. The third approach would be to calibrate ar, keeping the other parameters constant. This produces a stable yield curve and is most commonly followed by practitioners in the market.

3.6   SUMMARY

In this chapter, we have considered both equilibrium and arbitrage-free interest-rate models. These are one-factor Gaussian models of the term structure of interest rates. We saw that in order to specify a term structure model, the respective authors described the dynamics of the price process, and that this was then used to price a zero-coupon bond. The short-rate that is modelled is assumed to be a risk-free interest rate, and once this is modelled, we can derive the forward rate and the yield of a zero-coupon bond, as well as its price. So, it is possible to model the entire forward rate curve as a function of the current short-rate only, in the Vasicek and Cox-Ingersoll-Ross models, among others. Both the Vasicek and Merton models assume constant parameters, and because of equal probabilities of forward rates and the assumption of a normal distribution, they can, under certain conditions relating to the level of the standard deviation, produce negative forward rates.

The models are based on the fact that the price of a bond, which exhibits a pull-to-par effect, and the forward rate, are both Itô processes. For the bond price, the relative drift is the interest rate, and is deterministic, as is the forward rate. The bond price, yield and forward rate are functions of the current short-rate, and follow a normal distribution. An increase in the short-rate will result in a rise in the forward rates, and this is more pronounced for the shortest maturity rates. The instantaneous volatility of the forward rates decreases with decreasing time to maturity, and approaches the volatility of the current short-rate at time t.

The Vasicek, Cox-Ingersoll-Ross, Hull-White and other models incorporate mean reversion. As the time to maturity increases and as it approaches infinity, the forward rates converge to a point at the long-run mean reversion level of the current short-rate. This is the limiting level of the forward rate and is a function of the volatility of the current short-rate. As the time to maturity approaches zero, the short-term forward rate converges to the same level as the instantaneous short-rate. In the Merton and Vasicek models, the mean of the short-rate over the maturity period T is assumed to be constant. The same constant for the mean, or the *drift* of the interest rate, is described in the Ho-Lee model, but not the extended Vasicek or Hull-White model.

We also noted that the efficacy of a model was not necessarily solely related to how realistic its assumptions might be, but how straightforward it was to implement in practice, that is, the ease with which it could be calibrated.

3.7   WEBSITE MODELS

The Web site associated with this book contains an Excel spreadsheet demonstrating the following two term structure models:

- Vasicek model
- Cox-Ingersoll-Ross model

Both of these models were described in this chapter. The reader may use the spreadsheet to construct term structure curves using his or her own parameter inputs.

Details of how to access the Web site are contained in the Preface.

APPENDIX   ILLUSTRATION OF FORWARD RATE STRUCTURE WHEN SPOT RATE STRUCTURE IS INCREASING

We assume the spot rate $r(0, T)$ is a function of time and is increasing to a high point at $\overline{T}$. It is given by

$$r(0, T) = \frac{\int_0^T f(0, s)\mathrm{d}s}{T}. \tag{3.64}$$

At its high point, the function is neither increasing nor decreasing; so, we may write

$$\frac{\mathrm{d}r\left(0,\,\overline{T}\right)}{\mathrm{d}T} = 0 \tag{3.65}$$

and therefore the second derivative with respect to T will be

$$\frac{\mathrm{d}^2 r\left(0,\,\overline{T}\right)}{\mathrm{d}T^2} < 0 \tag{3.66}$$

From Equations (3.14) and (3.65), we may state

$$f\left(0,\,\overline{T}\right) = r\left(0,\,\overline{T}\right) \tag{3.67}$$

and from Equations (3.66) and (3.67), the second derivative of the spot rate is

$$\frac{\mathrm{d}^2 r\left(0,\,\overline{T}\right)}{\mathrm{d}T^2} = \left[\frac{\mathrm{d}f\left(0,\,\overline{T}\right)}{\mathrm{d}T} - \frac{\mathrm{d}r\left(0,\,\overline{T}\right)}{\mathrm{d}T}\right]\frac{1}{\overline{T}} < 0. \tag{3.68}$$

From Equation (3.65), we know the spot rate function is zero at $\overline{T}$; so, the derivative of the forward rate with respect to T would therefore be

$$\frac{\mathrm{d}f\left(0,\,\overline{T}\right)}{\mathrm{d}T} < 0. \tag{3.69}$$

So, in this case the forward rate is decreasing at the point $\overline{T}$ when the spot rate is at its maximum value. This is illustrated hypothetically in Figure 3.1 and it is common to observe the forward rate curve decreasing as the spot rate is increasing.

SELECTED BIBLIOGRAPHY AND REFERENCES

Bank of England, 1999. Quarterly Bulletin.

Baxter, M., Rennie, A., 1996. Financial Calculus. Cambridge University Press, Cambridge.

Black, F., Karasinski, P., 1991. Bond and option prices when short rates are lognormal. Financ. Anal. J. 47, 52–59.

Black, F., Derman, E., Toy, W., 1990. A one-factor model of interest rates and its application to Treasury bond options. Financ. Anal. J. 46, 33–39.

Brennan, M., Schwartz, E., 1979. A continuous time approach to the pricing of bonds. J. Bank. Financ. 3, 134.

Brennan, M., Schwartz, E., 1980. Conditional predictions of bond prices and returns. J. Financ. 35, 405.

Campbell, J., Lo, A., Lo, A., MacKinlay, A., 1997. The Econometrics of Financial Markets. Princeton University Press, Princeton, NJ.

Chan, K., et al., 1992. An empirical comparison of alternative models of the short-term interest rate. J. Financ. 47, 1209–1227.

Choudhry, M., 2001. Bond Market Securities. FT Prentice Hall, London.

Cox, J., Ingersoll, J., Ross, S., 1985. A theory of the term structure of interest rates. Econometrica 53, 385–407.

Duffie, D., 1996. Dynamic Asset Pricing Theory, second ed. Princeton University Press, Princeton, NJ.

The Economist, Out of Debt, 2000. The Economist, 12 February.

Fisher, L., Leibowitz, M., 1983. Effects of alternative anticipations of yield curve behaviour on the composition of immunized portfolios and on their target returns. In: Kaufmann, G. et al. (Ed.), Innovations in Bond Portfolio Management. Jai Press.

Ho, T., Lee, S., 1986. Term structure movements and pricing interest rate contingent claims. J. Financ. 41, 1011–1029.

Hull, J., 1997. Options, Futures and Other Derivatives. Wiley, New Jersey.

Hull, J., White, A., 1990. Pricing interest-rate derivative securities. Rev. Financ. Stud. 3, 573–592.

James, J., Webber, N., 2000. Interest Rate Modelling. Wiley, Chichester.

Jamshidian, F., 1996. Bond, futures and option valuation in the quadratic interest rate model. Appl. Math. Finance 3, 93–115.

Jarrow, R., 1996. Modelling Fixed Income Securities and Interest Rate Options. McGraw-Hill, New York.

Merton, R., 1971. Optimum consumption and portfolio rules in a continuous time model. J. Econ. Theory 3, 373–413.

Merton, R., 1973. Theory of option pricing. Bell. J. Econ. Manag. Sci 4, 141–183.

Neftci, S., 2000. An Introduction to the Mathematics of Financial Derivatives, second ed. Academic Press, San Diego.

Pelsser, A., 1996. Efficient methods for valuing and managing interest rate and other derivative securities. PhD thesis, Erasmus University, Rotterdam.

Phoa, W., 1998. Advanced Fixed Income Analytics. FJF Associates.

Pliska, S., 1986. A stochastic calculus model of continuous trading: optimal portfolios. Math. Oper. Res. 11, 371–382.

Rebonato, R., 1998. Interest Rate Option Models, second ed. Wiley, Chichester.

Rogers, L., 1995. Which model for the term-structure of interest rates should one use? In: Davis, M., et al. (Ed.), Mathematical Finance. Springer-Verlag, Berlin, pp. 93–115.

Steeley, J., 1991. Estimating the gilt-edged term structure: basis splines and confidence intervals. J Bus. Finan. Account 18, 513–530.

Van Deventer, J., Imai, K., 1997. Financial Risk Analytics. McGraw-Hill, New York.

Vasicek, O., 1977. An equilibrium characterization of the term structure. J. Financ. Econ. 5, 177–188.

Chapter 4

Interest-Rate Models II

Chapter Contents

In this chapter we consider multi-factor and whole yield curve models. As we noted in the previous chapter, short-rate models have certain drawbacks, which, though not necessarily limiting their usefulness, do leave room for further development. The drawback is that as the single short-rate is used to derive the complete term structure, in practice, this can be unsuitable for the calculation of bond yields. When this happens, it becomes difficult to visualise the actual dynamics of the yield curve, and the model no longer fits observed changes in the curve. This means that the accuracy of the model cannot be observed. Another drawback is that in certain equilibrium model cases, the model cannot be fitted precisely to the observed yield curve, as they have constant parameters. In these cases, calibration of the model is on a 'goodness of fit' or best fit approach.

In response to these issues, interest-rate models have been developed that model the entire yield curve. In a whole yield curve, the dynamics of the entire term structure are modelled. The Ho-Lee model is a simple type of whole curve model, which allows random parallel shifts in the yield curve. More advanced models, the Heath-Jarrow-Morton (HJM) family of models, are discussed in this chapter, as are factors involved in their implementation.

4.1   INTRODUCTION

A landmark development in interest-rate modelling has been the specification of the dynamics of the complete term structure. In this case, the volatility of the term structure is given by a specified function, which may be a function of time, term to maturity or zero-coupon rates. A simple approach is described in the Ho-Lee model, in which the volatility of the term structure is a parallel shift in the yield curve, the extent of which is independent of the current time and the level of current interest rates. The Ho-Lee model is not widely used, although it was the basis for the HJM model, which *is* widely used. The HJM model describes a process whereby the whole yield curve evolves simultaneously, in accordance with a set of volatility term structures. The model is usually described as being one that describes the evolution of the forward rate; however, it can also be expressed in terms of the spot rate or of bond prices (see, e.g., James and Webber (1997), Chapter 8). For a more detailed description of the HJM framework refer to Baxter and Rennie (1996), Hull (1997), Rebonato (1998), Bjork (1996) and James and Webber (1997). Baxter and Rennie is very accessible, while Neftci (1996) is an excellent introduction to the mathematical background.

In seeking to develop a model for the entire term structure, the requirement is to model the behaviour of the entire forward yield curve, that is, the behaviour of the forward short-rate $f(t, T)$ for all forward dates T. Therefore, we require the random process $f(T)$ for all forward dates T. Given this, it can be shown that the yield R on a T-maturity zero-coupon bond at time t is the average of the forward rates at that time on all the forward dates s between t and T, given by Equation (4.1):

$$R(t, T) = \frac{1}{T-t} \int_t^T f_t(s)\mathrm{d}s. \tag{4.1}$$

To model the complete curve, it is necessary to specify a drift rate and volatility level for $f(t, T)$ for each T.

4.2   THE HJM MODEL

A landmark development in the longstanding research into yield curve modelling was presented by David Heath, Robert Jarrow and Andrew Morton in their 1989 paper, which formally appeared in volume 60 of *Econometrica* (1992). The paper considered interest-rate modelling as a stochastic process, but applied to the entire term structure rather than only the short-rate. The importance of the HJM presentation is this: in a market that permits no arbitrage, where interest rates including forward rates are assumed to follow a Wiener process, the drift term and the volatility term in the model's stochastic differential equation are not independent from each other, and in fact the drift term is a deterministic function of the volatility term. This has significant practical implications for the pricing and hedging of interest-rate options.

The general form of the HJM model is very complex, not surprisingly as it is a multi-factor model. We begin by describing the single-factor HJM model. This section is based on Chapter 5 of Baxter and Rennie, *Financial Calculus*, Cambridge University Press (1996), and follows their approach with permission. This work is an accessible and excellent text and is highly recommended.

4.2.1   The Single-Factor HJM Model

In the previous chapter, and indeed in previous analysis, we have defined the *forward rate* as the interest rate applicable to a loan made at a future point in time and repayable instantaneously. We assume that the dynamics of the forward rate follow a Wiener process. The *spot rate* is the rate for borrowing undertaken now and maturing at T, and we know from previous analysis that it is the geometric average of the forward rates from 0 to T that is

$$r(0,\ T) = T^{-1} \int_t^T f(0,\ t)\,\mathrm{d}t. \tag{4.2}$$

We also specify a money market account that accumulates interest at the continuously compounded spot rate r.

A default-free zero-coupon bond can be defined in terms of its current value under an *initial probability measure*, which is the Wiener process that describes the forward rate dynamics, and its price or present value under this probability measure. This leads us to the HJM model, in that we are required to determine what is termed a 'change in probability measure', such that the dynamics of the zero-coupon bond price are transformed into a *martingale*. This is carried out using Itô's lemma and a transformation of the differential equation of the bond price process. It can then be shown that in order to prevent arbitrage, there would have to be a relationship between drift rate of the forward rate and its volatility coefficient.

First, we look at the forward rate process. We know from the previous chapter for $[0,\ T]$ at time t that the stochastic evolution of the forward rate $f(t,\ T)$ can be described as

$$\mathrm{d}f(t,\ T) = a(t,\ T)\mathrm{d}t + \sigma(t,T)\mathrm{d}W_t \tag{4.3}$$

or alternatively in integral form as

$$f(t,\ T) = f(0,\ T) + \int_0^t a(s,\ T)\mathrm{d}s + \int_0^t \sigma(s,\ T)\mathrm{d}W_s \tag{4.4}$$

where a is the drift parameter, σ is the volatility coefficient and W_t is the Wiener process or Brownian motion. The terms dz and dZ are sometimes used to denote the Wiener process.

In Equation (4.3), the drift and volatility coefficients are functions of time t and T. For all forward rates $f(t, T)$ in the period $[0, T]$, the only source of uncertainty is the Brownian motion. In practice, this would mean that all forward rates would be perfectly positively correlated, irrespective of their terms to maturity. However, if we introduce the feature that there is more than one source of uncertainty in the evolution of interest rates, it would result in less than perfect correlation of interest rates, which is what is described by the HJM model.

Before we come to that, however, we wish to describe the spot rate and the money market account processes. In Equation (4.4), under the particular condition of the maturity point T as it tends towards t (that is $T \to t$), the forward rate tends to approach the value of the short rate (spot rate), so we have

$$\lim_{T \to t} f(t, T) = f(t, t) = r(t)$$

so that it can be shown that

$$r(t) = f(0, t) + \int_0^t a(s, t)ds + \int_0^t \sigma(s, t)dW_s. \tag{4.5}$$

The money market account is also described as a Wiener process. We denote by $M(t, t) = M(t)$ the value of the money market account at time t, which has an initial value of 1 at time 0 so that $M(0, 0) = 1$. This account earns interest at the spot rate $r(t)$ which means that at time t the value of the account is given by

$$M(t) = e^{\int_0^t r(s)ds} \tag{4.6}$$

that is, the interest accumulated at the continuously compounded spot rate $r(t)$. It can be shown by substituting Equation (4.5) into Equation (4.6) so that

$$M(t) = \exp\left(\int_0^t f(0, s)ds + \int_0^t \int_0^s a(u, s)duds + \int_0^t \int_0^s \sigma(u, s)dW_u ds \right). \tag{4.7}$$

To simplify the description, we write the double integrals in Equation (4.7) in the form given below, which is

$$\int_0^t \int_s^t a(s, u)duds + \int_0^t \int_s^t \sigma(s, u)dudW_s.$$

For reasons of space, the description of the process by which this simplification is achieved is not shown here.

Using the simplification above, it can be shown that the value of the money market account, which is growing by an amount generated by the continuously compounded spot rate $r(t)$, is given by

$$M(t) = \exp\left(\int_0^t f(0,\ u)\mathrm{d}u + \int_0^t \int_s^t a(s,\ u) + \int_0^t \int_s^t \sigma(s,\ u)\mathrm{d}u\mathrm{d}W_s \right). \qquad (4.8)$$

The expression for the value of the money market account can be used to determine the expression for the zero-coupon bond price, which we denote as $P(t, T)$. The money market account earns interest at the spot rate $r(t)$, while the bond price is the present value of 1 discounted at this rate. Therefore, the inverse of Equation (4.8) is required, which is

$$M^{-1}(t) = \mathrm{e}^{-\int_0^t r(u)\mathrm{d}u}. \qquad (4.9)$$

Hence, the present value at time 0 of the bond $P(t, T)$ is

$$P(t,\ T) = \mathrm{e}^{-\int_0^t r(u)\mathrm{d}u} P(t,\ T)$$

and it can be shown that as a Wiener process the present value is given by

$$P(t,\ T) = \exp\left(-\int_0^T f(0,\ u)\mathrm{d}u - \int_0^t \int_s^t \sigma(s,\ u)\mathrm{d}u\mathrm{d}W_s - \int_0^t \int_s^t a(s,\ u)\mathrm{d}u\mathrm{d}s \right).$$

$$(4.10)$$

4.2.2   Transforming the Probability Measure

Since the pioneering work of Harrison and Pliska (1981), which recognised that the absence of arbitrage was linked to the existence of a martingale probability measure, the valuation of derivatives has been deemed to require a probability measure that would transform the underlying security process into a martingale. This is the case here; what is required is a change in probability measure such that $P(t, T)$ becomes a martingale.

This is done by using Itô's lemma[1] to transform the stochastic differential equation of the price process and then determine the change in the Brownian differential $\mathrm{d}W$ so that there remains no drift term. The first step is to consider the differential of $P(t, T)$. We express this in the form

$$P(t,\ T) = \mathrm{e}^{-X_t} \qquad (4.11)$$

where X_t is a Wiener process described by

---

1. See Appendices B and C (Chapter 2).

$$X_t = \int_0^T f(0,\, u)du + \int_0^t \int_s^T \sigma(s,\, u)dudW_s + \int_0^t \int_s^T a(s,\, u)dudt. \qquad (4.12)$$

The differential of X_t is written as

$$dX_t = \int_t^T \sigma(t,\, u)dudW_t + \int_t^T a(t,\, u)dudt$$
$$= \nu(t,\, T)dW_t + \int_t^T a(t,\, u)dudt \qquad (4.13)$$

where $\nu(t, T) \equiv \int_t^T \sigma(t,\, u)du$ represents the volatility element of the X_t stochastic process. It can be shown by applying Itô's lemma to Equation (4.11) so that

$$dP(t,\, T) = P(t,\, T)\left(-\nu(t,\, T)dW_t - \int_t^T a(t,\, u)dudt + \frac{\nu^2}{2}(t,\, T)dt\right). \qquad (4.14)$$

To obtain a new probability measure such that $P(t, T)$ is transformed into a martingale, following Baxter and Rennie, we effect a change in dW_t such that Equation (4.14) may be expressed as

$$dP(t,\, T) = -P(t,\, T)\nu(t,\, T)d\widetilde{W}_t. \qquad (4.15)$$

It can then be shown that the solution of Equation (4.15) under such conditions is indeed a martingale, described by

$$P(t) = P_0 \exp\left(\int_0^t \nu(\tau,\, T)d\widetilde{W}_\tau - \frac{1}{2}\int_0^t \nu^2(\tau,\, T)d\tau\right). \qquad (4.16)$$

To reiterate, then, we require a transformation of Equation (4.14) so that it becomes a Wiener process with no drift term, in other words a relationship between $d\widetilde{W}_t$ and dW_t. It has been shown that this exists in the form

$$d\widetilde{W}_t = dW_t + \frac{1}{\nu(t,\, T)}\int_t^T a(t,\, u)dudt - \frac{\nu(t,\, T)}{2}dt \equiv dW_t + \gamma_t dt \qquad (4.17)$$

where the change of measure γ_t is given by

$$\gamma_t = \frac{1}{\nu(t,\, T)}\int_t^T a(t,\, u)du - \frac{\nu(t,\, T)}{2}. \qquad (4.18)$$

4.2.3   The Principle of No-Arbitrage

The demonstration of the no-arbitrage condition in the evolution of the HJM model is perhaps its most significant aspect, as it demonstrates that for arbitrage to be avoided, the volatility function must be related to the drift parameter. This is effected through a constraint that is the change of measure element we introduced just now: again, following Baxter and Rennie and to summarise the original paper, in order to prevent arbitrage, a bond of maturity less than T must have the same change of measure γ_t. The change of measure must, by implication, therefore not be a function of and be independent from T. It can be shown that if we multiply Equation (4.18) by $\nu(t, T)$ and then differentiate it with respect to T we obtain Equation (4.19):

$$
\begin{aligned}
a(t, T) &= \frac{\partial \nu(t, T)}{\partial T}(\nu(t, T) + \gamma_t) \\
&= \sigma(t, T)(\nu(t, T) + \gamma_t)
\end{aligned}
\tag{4.19}
$$

The expressions (4.18) and (4.19) represent the two fundamental constraints of the single-factor HJM model. Equation (4.18) is the result of the change in the drift term required by the transformation of $P(t, T)$ into a martingale, while Equation (4.19) comes from the need to incorporate a no-arbitrage condition. This is the model in essence, an expression for the value of the drift parameter for $f(t, T)$ in the context of the W_t Brownian motion. This impacts as follows: in Equation (4.3), the Brownian motion term dW_t is replaced by $d\widetilde{W}_t - \gamma_t dt$ and $a(t, T)$ is replaced with the constraint given by Equation (4.19). This results in

$$
\begin{aligned}
df(t, T) &= \sigma(t, T)\left(d\widetilde{W}_t - \gamma_t dt\right) + \sigma(t, T)(\nu(t, T) + \gamma_t)dt \\
&= \sigma(t, T)d\widetilde{W}_t + \sigma(t, T)\nu(t, T)dt
\end{aligned}
\tag{4.20}
$$

In conclusion, then, in the single-factor HJM model under the martingale measure, the coefficient of the drift must be equal to Equation (4.21):

$$
\sigma(t, T)\nu(t, T) = \sigma(t, T)\int_t^T \sigma(t, u)du.
\tag{4.21}
$$

In an important application of the HJM model, Jarrow and Turnbull (1996) express the price of a zero-coupon risk-free bond as a function of the spot rate $r(t)$, given by

$$
P(t, T) = \frac{P(0, T)}{P(0, T)}\exp\left(-(r(t) - f(0, t))X(t, T) - \frac{\sigma^2}{4\lambda}X^2(t, T)\left(1 - e^{-2\lambda t}\right)\right)
\tag{4.22}
$$

where $X(t, T) \equiv (1 - e^{T-t})/\lambda$ and σ and λ are positive constants of the volatility coefficient $\sigma(t, T)$ which is of the form, $\sigma \exp(-\lambda(T-t))$.

Thus, at time t the price of any bond of maturity T is given by the ratio of prices of bonds of maturity t and T, which are the first part of Equation (4.22) and which are observed in the market, and the random variable given by the exponential element of Equation (4.22). If we express the latter as $A(t, T)$, we have

$$
P(t, T) = \frac{P(0, T)}{P(0, T)}A(t, T)
\tag{4.23}
$$

and under conditions of zero volatility where $\sigma(t, T) = 0$, it can be shown that this element disappears and

$$P(t,\ T) = \frac{P(0,\ T)}{P(0,\ t)} = \frac{e^{-rT}}{e^{-rt}}$$
$$= e^{-r(T-t)}$$

(4.24)

which is exactly what we expect.

4.3 MULTI-FACTOR TERM STRUCTURE MODELS

Previously, we considered one-factor models used to varying degrees in the market; these describe only a single kind of change in the yield curve, the parallel shift. In practice, there are a range of changes that may occur to the curve, including non-parallel (pivotal) shifts and changes in the slope of the curve. Certain two-factor and multi-factor models have been developed that seek to describe the different type of yield curve shifts. An early two-factor model was that presented by Brennan and Schwartz (1982), which described the stochastic process of the short-rate r and the yield of the long-dated government bond R. In this model, these two factors move independently of each other, thus permitting both parallel and pivotal changes in the yield curve. The Brennan-Schwartz model is categorised as a *consol* model in James and Webber (1997). A modified version of the Brennan-Schwartz model[2] has been developed in which the two variable factors are the price of the long bond $P = 1/R$ and the spread between the long-dated yield and the short-rate, which is $S = R - r$. Both factors are assumed to follow a random stochastic process described by Equation (4.25):

$$dP = \mu_P P dt + \sigma_P P dW_t^{(1)}$$
$$dS = \mu_S dt + \sigma_S W_t^{(2)}$$

(4.25)

where $E\left[dW_t^{(1)}\ dW_t^{(2)}\right] = pdt$, and the values of μ_P and μ_S are set to be arbitrage-free in terms of the price of bonds of different maturities. So, the price of the long-dated bond follows a lognormal process, while the spread S follows a Gaussian process. This means that the spread can be either positive or negative, which permits both a positive sloping and an inverted yield curve.

The modified Brennan-Schwartz model is used in the markets which describes a realistic process for changes in the yield curve and is relatively straightforward to implement; only two variables are required to model the entire term structure.

The HJM model (1992) is a general approach which is a multi-factor whole yield curve model, where arbitrary changes in the entire term structure can be one of the factors. In practice, because of the mass of data that is required to derive the yield curve, the HJM model is usually implemented by means of Monte Carlo simulation, and requires powerful computing systems. The model is described in the next section.

---

2. See Rebonato and Cooper (1996).

4.3.1   The Multi-Factor HJM Model

A multi-factor model of the whole yield curve has been presented by Heath et al. (1992). This is a seminal work and a ground-breaking piece of research. The approach models the forward curve as a process arising from the entire initial yield curve, rather than the short-rate only. The spot rate is a stochastic process and the derived yield curve is a function of a number of stochastic factors. The HJM model uses the current yield curve and forward rate curve, and then specifies a continuous time stochastic process to describe the evolution of the yield curve over a specified time period.

The model is summarised here only; readers interested in the derivation of the model are directed to the original paper or a discussion of it in Baxter and Rennie (1996), Hull (1997) or James and Webber (1997). To describe the model, we use the following notation:

(t, T) is the trading interval for a fixed period from t to T, where $t > 0$

$W(t)$ is the independent Brownian motion or Wiener process that describes the interest rate process

(Ω, F, Q) is the probability space where F is the σ-algebra representing measurable events and Q is the measure of probability

$P(t, T)$ is the price at time t of a zero-coupon bond that matures at time T.

The bond has a redemption value of 1 at time T.

The instantaneous forward rate $f(t, T)$ at time t is given by Equation (4.26):

$$f(t, T) = \frac{-\partial \ln P(t, T)}{\partial T} \tag{4.26}$$

and describes the interest rate that is applicable on a default-free loan at time t for the period from T to a point one instant later. In their paper, Heath, Jarrow and Morton state that the solution to the differential Equation (4.26) results in the expression for the price of the bond, shown in Equation (4.27):

$$P(t, T) = \exp\left(-\int_t^T f(t, s) ds\right) \tag{4.27}$$

while the spot interest rate at time t is the instantaneous forward rate at time t for maturity date t, shown by:

$$r(t) = f(t, t).$$

We now describe the model's exposition of movements in the term structure.

The HJM model describes the evolution of forward rates given an initial forward rate curve, which is taken as given. For the period $T \in [0, t]$, the forward rate $f(t, T)$ satisfies the Equation (4.28):

$$f(t, T) - f(0, T) = \int_0^t \alpha(\nu, T, \omega) d\nu + \sum_{i=1}^n \int_0^t \sigma_i(\nu, T, \omega) dW(t). \tag{4.28}$$

The expression describes a stochastic process composed of n independent Wiener processes, from which the whole forward rate curve, from the initial curve at time 0, is derived. Each individual forward rate maturity is a function of a specific volatility coefficient. The volatility values (σ_i (t, T, ω)) are not specified in the model and are dependent on historical Wiener processes. From Equation (4.28) following the HJM model, the spot rate stochastic process is given by Equation (4.29):

$$r(t) = f(0, t) + \int_0^t \alpha(v, t, \omega)dv + \sum_{i=1}^n \int_0^t \sigma_i(v, t, \omega)dW(t) \qquad (4.29)$$

for the period $t \in (0, T)$.

The model then goes on to show that the process of changes in the bond price is given by:

$$\ln P(t, T) = \ln P(0, T) + \int_0^t (r(v) + b(v, T))dv - \frac{1}{2}\sum_{i=1}^n \int_0^t a_i(v, T)^2 dv$$

$$+ \sum_{i=1}^n \int_0^t a(v, T)dW(t) \qquad (4.30)$$

where $\qquad a_i(t, T, \omega) \equiv -\int_t^T \sigma_i(t, v, \omega)dv$ for $i = 1, 2, \ldots, n \qquad$ and

$$b(t, T, \omega) \equiv -\int_t^T \alpha(t, v, \omega)dv + \frac{1}{2}\sum_{i=1}^n a_i(t, T, \omega)^2.$$

The expression in Equation (4.30) describes the dynamics of the bond price as a continuous stochastic process with a drift of $(r, (t, \omega)) + b(t, T, \omega)$ and a volatility value of $a_i(t, T, \omega)$.

The no-arbitrage condition is set by defining the price of a zero-coupon bond that matures at time T in terms of an 'accumulation factor' $B(t)$ which is the value of a money market account that is invested at time 0 and reinvested at time t at an interest rate of $r(t)$. This accumulation factor is defined as Equation (4.31):

$$B(t) = \exp\left(\int_0^t r(y)dy\right) \qquad (4.31)$$

and the value of the zero-coupon bond in terms of this accumulation factor is $Z(t, T) = P(t, T)/B(t)$ for the period $T \in (0, t)$ and $t \in (0, T)$.

Following HJM, by applying Itô's lemma, the model obtains the following result for $Z(t, T)$, shown in Equation (4.32):

$$\ln Z(t, T) = \ln Z(0, T) + \int_0^t b(v, T)dv - \frac{1}{2}\sum_{i=1}^n \int_0^t a_i(v, T)^2 dv + \sum_{i=1}^n \int_0^t a_1(v, T)dW(t).$$

$$(4.32)$$

In the HJM model, the processes for the bond price and the spot rate are not independent of each other. As an arbitrage-free pricing model, it differs in crucial respects from the equilibrium models presented in the previous chapter. The core of the HJM model is that given a current forward rate curve, and a function capturing the dynamics of the forward rate process, it models the entire term structure.

A drawback of the model is that it requires the input of instantaneous forward rates, which cannot necessarily be observed directly in the market. Models have been developed that are in the HJM approach that take this factor into account, including those presented by Brace et al. (1997) and Jamshidian (1997). This family of models is known as the LIBOR market model or the BGM model. In the BGM model, there is initially one factor, the forward rate $f(t)$ which is the rate applicable from time t_κ to time $t_{\kappa+1}$ at time t. The forward rate is described by Equation (4.33):

$$\mathrm{d}f(t) = \theta(t)f(t)\mathrm{d}W \tag{4.33}$$

where the market is assumed to be forward risk-neutral.

The relationship between forward rates and the price of a zero-coupon bond at time t is given by Equation (4.34):

$$\frac{P(t, t_i)}{P(t, t_{i+1})} = 1 + \delta_i f_i(t) \tag{4.34}$$

where δ_i is the compounding period between t and t_{i+1}.

To determine the volatility of the zero-coupon bond price $v(t)$ at time t, it can be shown that applying Itô's lemma to Equation (4.34), we obtain

$$\nu_i(t) - \nu_{i+1}(t) = \frac{\delta_i f_i(t)\theta_i(t)}{1 + \delta_i f_i(t)}. \tag{4.35}$$

It is possible to extend the BGM model to incorporate more independent factors.

4.3.2   Jump-Augmented Models

Further research has produced a category of models that attempt to describe the jump feature of asset prices and interest rates. Observation of the markets confirms that many asset price patterns and interest rate changes do not move continuously from one price (rate) to another, but sometimes follow a series of jumps. A good example of a jump movement is when a central bank changes the base interest rate; when this happens, the entire yield curve shifts to incorporate the effect of the new base rate. There is a considerable body of literature on the subject, and we only refer to a small number of texts here.

One type of jump model is the jump-augmented HJM model, described in Jarrow and Madan (1991), Bjork (1996) and Das (1997). This is not described here because we have not covered the necessary technical background. Another is the jump-augmented Vasicek model described by Das and Foresi (1996) and Baz and Das (1996). In this, the short rate process is captured by

$$dr_t = \alpha(\mu - r_t)dt + \sigma dW_t + J dN_t \qquad (4.36)$$

where N_t is a Poisson process with a constant intensity λ and J is a random jump size.

Other jump models have been described by Attari (1996), Das and Foresi (1996) and Honore (1998).

4.4   ASSESSING ONE-FACTOR AND MULTI-FACTOR MODELS

In assessing the value of the different models that have been developed and the efficacy of each, what is important is how they can be applied in the market, rather than any notion that multi-factor models are necessarily 'better' than one-factor models because they are somehow more 'real-world'. What is required is a mechanism that efficiently prices bonds and interest-rate options; a term structure model attempts to accomplish this by describing the dynamics of the interest rate process and generating random interest-rate paths. The generated paths are then used to discount the cash flows from the fixed income instrument, having initially been used to generate the cash flows in the first place. In practice, a one-factor model that has been accurately calibrated will value fixed income instruments efficiently. This is because of the determinants of bond pricing; to illustrate, consider a fixed income instrument with a fixed maturity date. To value such a bond at a particular time, we need only know the bond yield at that time, and this is essentially a one-factor process. Similarly for a callable bond, when generating its cash flow, we will know whether it will be called by knowing its price at a future date. Generating this cash flow from the interest-rate model is again a one-factor process. Therefore, if we are pricing a bond, the dynamics of the price process can usually be adequately described by Equation (4.37):

$$dP = \mu_P P dt + \sigma_P P dW(t) \qquad (4.37)$$

which is the process followed by, for example, the Black-Scholes option model when used to price an interest-rate option. This model does not discount the forward price of the option, which is the second part of the B-S approach: that of assuming a single continuously compounded short-term risk-free interest-rate.

While this approach would work in practice, this would only be for a single security portfolio; it would be unwieldy and inaccurate for valuing a number of securities. As banks and market makers must value many hundreds of cash and off-balance sheet instruments, another approach is required. This other approach was considered in this chapter and involves describing the dynamics of the bond price process in the form of a term structure model. Under this situation, a multi-factor model may be more suitable, particularly when used to value options.

To consider one-factor models then, we know that the yield of a bond at a future date is essentially a one-factor process; so, a one-factor model may well be accurate. A one-factor model describes only parallel shift yield changes, and it assumes that bond yields and discount rates are perfectly correlated, so that it will not generate all the possible paths of the future discount rate. In practice, however, much yield curve movement is close to a parallel shift; so, this may not be as much of a problem for the majority of situations. If a term structure model accurately reflects the random evolution of the price of a bond, and the actual current rate and forward rate volatilities of the bond are as generated by the model, then the model can be considered effective, and it will generate reasonable cash flow scenarios and with accurate probabilities. It is possible to achieve this with one-factor models. Essentially then, a bank can use a one-factor model when conditions are appropriate, and need only use a multi-factor model where the one-factor model cannot be expected to be accurate. That said, why not simply use a multi-factor model at all times? The main reason is because generating forward rates and valuations from a multi-factor model is a time-consuming process, employing considerable computing power, and as rapidity of analysis and response is of the essence in the markets, it is logical to use a slower model only when it is significantly more accurate than the one-factor model.

It is generally accepted that one-factor models can be used for most bond applications; where multi-factor models are more appropriate may be in the following situations:

- where the instrument being valued is linked to two different interest rates, for example, an interest-rate quanto option, or an option with a payoff profile that is a function of the spread between two different reference rates;
- for the valuation of long-dated options or deeply in-the-money or out-of-the-money options, which are affected by the volatility smile. As a stochastic volatility factor will impact the price, a model that assumes constant volatilities would be inaccurate;
- for the valuation of securities that to some extent reflect the slope of the yield curve, such as certain mortgage-backed bonds whose level of prepayment is sometimes a function of the slope of the yield curve;
- for the valuation of very long-dated options, where all possible paths of the future discount rate may be required.

The optimum approach would appear to be a combination of a one-factor model and a multi-factor model to suit individual requirements. However, this may not be practical; it might not be ideal to have different parts of a bank using different models (although this does happen, desks across the larger investment banks sometimes use different models) and valuing instruments using different models. The key factors to focus on are accessibility, accuracy, appropriateness and speed of computation.

4.4.1 Choosing the Model

There are essentially two approaches to modelling the term structure that we have discussed in this and the previous chapter. The Ho-Lee and HJM models begin with the evolution of the whole yield curve, while the BDT, Hull-White and other models specify the dynamics of the short rate, and determine the parameters so that the model itself corresponds to the current term structure. We have also discussed the relative merits of the equilibrium model approach and the no-arbitrage approach. In this final section, we discuss the different issues that apply in each case.

Essentially, there are two dimensions to consider: risk-neutral versus realistic and equilibrium versus no-arbitrage. There are situations under which each approach may be applied with validity.

4.4.1.1   No-Arbitrage, Risk-Neutral Approach

A commonly encountered approach is the risk-neutral, no-arbitrage model. This is a no-arbitrage model used frequently to value interest-rate options, using parameters that have been interpolated from a set of current market prices rather than estimated from actual historical data. This approach is valid when there is a reliable set of observable market prices and rates. Note that two different no-arbitrage models that are applied in a risk-neutral framework will only generate identical term structures and valuations if exactly identical input parameters have been used. The actual type of model used will have a significant effect on the valuation that is achieved. If however market data is not readily observable, or not reliable, this approach can lead to inaccuracies. This can be expected in illiquid markets such as that for certain long-dated exotic options; where this occurs, there is no way to estimate a correlation term structure that allows the model to interpolate between the option prices because there are two of them or their reliability is not accepted. In this scenario, a multi-factor model that captures the correlations between interest rates of different maturities, as well as the impact of the shape of the yield curve on these correlations, may be more valid. A model with a good statistical fit to the historical correlations recorded by the option product may therefore produce more robust prices. We hesitate to say 'accurate' because, in an illiquid market with only a small number of market makers, who is to say which price is the most accurate? For certain exotic options, the valuation depends on each market making bank's valuation model, and how effectively the model has been calibrated.

4.4.1.2   No-Arbitrage, Realistic Approach

A no-arbitrage model that is implemented in a realistic approach matches precisely the term structure of interest rates that are implied by the current (or initial) observed market yields. It then derives a forward curve for the future that is dependent on the way it has modelled the dynamics of the interest-rate process, which is a measure of probability. This approach is valid when it is important that the initial yield curve must be identical to the current observed yield curve, and is often used for analysing hedging strategy or portfolio strategies. In implementing this method, it is sometimes difficult to evaluate the efficacy of the model because of problems in discriminating between model error and exogenous effects. In this approach, the model parameters are set to match precisely observed market yields, with no regard to historical data, and there is little degree of freedom by which one can evaluate the model results. Only in a situation where the model generated an identical true term structure, so that the time-dependent parameters resulted in no pricing error at all points along the term structure, and for all dates past and forward, could the model be described for certainty as accurate. Otherwise, the difficulty in assessing the effectiveness of this approach means that it is rarely used in practice.

4.4.1.3   Equilibrium, Risk-Neutral Approach

The second approach is an equilibrium model under risk-neutral conditions. This is also valid under certain conditions. Remember that a no-arbitrage model uses input parameters that are based on observed prices and yields. However, observed bond yields reflect a number of factors that frequently distort them away from 'fair value', resulting in a discount function that is also distorted. For instance, we saw in our discussions in Part I that bond prices reflect liquidity, benchmark effects, supply and demand and other factors, which can include taxation, coupon size, convexity effect and so on. The same applies in the government zero-coupon bond market. Therefore, a no-arbitrage model will use parameters that have been distorted by these factors. However, equilibrium models are able to capture the global behaviour of the term structure over a long-term period, which has the effect of stripping out the market distortions (they are treated as 'noise'). Therefore, risk-neutral equilibrium models have an advantage over no-arbitrage models as they are not as sensitive to external market factors. In addition, when used to price bonds today, equilibrium models can be estimated from historical data when market-observed current prices are unavailable or unreliable. So, we conclude that one of the most appropriate times to adopt the risk-neutral equilibrium approach is when observed market yields are not available or subject to excessive distortions. This brings us to the subject of *horizon pricing*, which is the estimation of prices for a bond or other instrument under some expected future market state. While parameters are usually available, and reasonably reliable (in developed markets) for use in current pricing, they will not be available for a scenario-type valuation. In this situation, no-arbitrage models cannot be used at all because they require the input of a set of market yields, which would not be available for horizon pricing as they would be unknown. Therefore, in this case we use an equilibrium model; otherwise, no analysis would be possible.

4.4.1.4 Equilibrium, Realistic Approach

In fact, the inappropriateness of the no-arbitrage realistic approach means that only the equilibrium realistic approach is available. This methodology is used where speed of computation and accuracy of term structure generation and valuation are not of prime importance. It is used most frequently for risk management, regulatory and testing purposes; this includes value-at-risk calculations, VaR stress testing, capital adequacy calculations and other scenario purposes. In this approach and with equilibrium models, the derived current term structure that is generated will not match the actual current term structure precisely. This has led to some analysts suggesting that any testing performed with the model will not be perfectly realistic. However, the main purpose behind scenario analysis is to assess the impact of different situations; there is nothing illogical about comparing the effect of a theoretical future yield curve on an asset book held today and valued using today's actual yield curve. An equilibrium model is a statistical model of the behaviour of the term structure of rates; therefore, using it implies an acceptance that its derived curve will differ from the observed curve. Using a no-arbitrage model would imply that the current term structure model was completely accurate. Therefore, for risk management and capital purposes, it is common to encounter the equilibrium model, realistic approach.

4.4.2 Choosing the Model: Second-Time Around

It is important to remain focused on the practical requirements of interest-rate modelling. Market participants are more concerned with the ease with which a model can be implemented, and its accuracy with regard to pricing. In practice, different models are suited to different applications; so, the range of products traded by a market practitioner will also influence the model that is chosen. For instance, the extended Vasicek model can be fitted very accurately to the initial term structure, and its implementation is relatively straightforward, being based on a lattice structure. It is also able to accurately price most products; however, like all one-factor models, it is not a valid model to use when pricing instruments are sensitive to two or more risk factors, for example, quanto options. The extended CIR model is also tractable, although it has a more restricted set of term structures compared to the extended Vasicek model, as a result of the limitations imposed by the $\sqrt{r_t}$ term on the volatility parameter. Both types of models are unable to capture the dynamics of the whole yield curve, for which HJM models must be used.

A drawback of these models is that although they fit the initial term structure, due to their structure they may not continue to calculate prices as the term structure evolves. In practice, the models must be re-calibrated frequently to ensure that they continue to describe term structure volatilities that exist in the market.

In selecting the model, a practitioner will select the market variables that are incorporated in the model; these can be directly observed such as zero-coupon rates or forward rates, or swap rates, or they can be indeterminate such as the mean of the short rate. The practitioner will then decide the dynamics of these market or *state variables*; so, for example, the short rate may be assumed to be mean reverting. Finally, the model must be calibrated to market prices; so, the model parameter values input must be those that produce market prices as accurately as possible. There are a number of ways that parameters can be estimated; the most common techniques of calibrating time series data such as interest rate data are *general method of moments* and the *maximum likelihood* method. For information on these estimation methods, refer to the bibliography.

Models exhibit different levels of sensitivity to changes in market prices and rates. The extent of a model's sensitivity will also influence the frequency with which the model must be re-calibrated. For example, the Black-Derman-Toy model is very sensitive to changes in market prices; because it is a log-r model, changes in the process of the underlying variable are larger as they are log-r, than those in the process for rt itself. Some practitioners believe that as they take bond prices and the term structure as given, arbitrage models suffer from an inherent weakness. Liquidity and other considerations frequently result in discrepancies between market yields and theoretical value, and such discrepancies would feed through into an arbitrage model. This drawback of arbitrage models means that users must take care about term structure inputs, and the curve fitting techniques and *smoothing* techniques that are used become critical to model effectiveness. This is discussed in the next chapter.

Other considerations are detailed below.

- *Model inputs*: Arbitrage models use the term structure of spot rate as an input, and this data is straightforward to obtain. Equilibrium models require a measure of the investor's market risk premium, which is rather more problematic. Practitioners analyse historical data on interest rate movements, which is considered less desirable.

- *Using models as part of bond trading strategy*: A key element of market makers' and proprietary traders' strategy is relative value trading, which includes simultaneous buying and selling of certain bonds against others, or classes of bonds against other classes. A yield curve spread trade is a typical relative value trade. How does one determine relative value?[3] Using an interest-rate model is the answer. For such purposes though, only equilibrium models can be used. By definition, since arbitrage models take bond prices and the current term structure as given, they clearly cannot be used to assess relative value. This is because the current price structure would be assumed to be correct. If one were to use such a model for a yield curve

3. Some traders determine relative value by conducting the analysis inside their head! Nowadays, one needs to back up one's gut feeling with formal analysis. A term structure model will assist.

trade, it would imply a zero profit potential. Therefore, only equilibrium models can be used for such purposes.

- *Model consistency*: As we have noted elsewhere, using models requires their constant calibration and re-calibration over time. For instance, an arbitrage model makes a number of assumptions about the interest rate drift rate and volatility, and in some cases, the mean reversion of the dynamics of the rate process. Of course, these values will fluctuate constantly over time so that the estimate of these model parameters used one day will not remain the same over time. So, the model will be inconsistent over time and must be re-calibrated to the market. Equilibrium models use parameters that are estimated from historical data, and so there is no unused daily change. Model parameters remain stable. Over time therefore these models remain consistent, at least with themselves. However, given the points we have noted above, market participants usually prefer to use arbitrage models and re-calibrate them frequently.

We have only touched on the range of considerations that must be followed when evaluating and implementing an interest-rate model. This is a complex subject with a number of factors to consider, and ongoing research in the area serves to reinforce the fact that it is an important and very current topic.

SELECTED BIBLIOGRAPHY AND REFERENCES

Attari, M., 1996. Discontinuous Interest Rate Processes: An Equilibrium Model for Bond Option Prices: Working Paper. University of Iowa, Iowa City, pp. 1–32.

Baxter, M., Rennie, A., 1996. Financial Calculus. Cambridge University Press, Cambridge.

Baxter, M., Rennie, A., 1998. An Introduction to Derivative Pricing. Cambridge University Press, Cambridge (Chapter 5).

Baz, J., Das, S., 1996. Analytical approximations of the term structure for jump diffusion processes: a numerical analysis. J. Fixed Income 6 (1), 78–86.

Bjork, T., 1996. Interest Rate Theory: CIME Lectures, Working Paper. Stockholm School of Economics, Stockholm, Sweden, pp. 1–90.

Black, F., Karasinski, P., 1991. Bond and option pricing when short rates are lognormal. Financ. Anal. J. 47 (4), 52–59.

Brace, A., Gatarek, D., Musiela, M., 1997. The market model of interest-rate dynamics. Math. Financ. 7 (2), 127–155.

Brennan, M., Schwartz, E., 1982. An equilibrium model of bond pricing and a test of market efficiency. J. Financ. Quant. Anal. 17 (3), 301–329.

Cheyette, O., 1992. Term structure dynamics and mortgage valuation. J. Fixed Income 1 (4), 28–41.

Das, S., 1997. A Direct Discrete-Time Approach to Poisson-Gaussian Bond Option Pricing in the Heath–Jarrow–Morton Model: Working Paper. Harvard Business School, Boston, MA, pp. 1–44.

Das, S., Foresi, S., 1996. Exact solutions for bond and option prices with systematic jump risk. Rev. Deriv. Res. 1, 1–24.

Duffie, D., Kan, R., 1996. A yield-factor model of interest rates. Math. Financ. 6 (4), 379–406.

Fitton, P., McNatt, J., 1997. The four faces of an interest rate model. In: Fabozzi, F. (Ed.), Advances in Fixed Income Valuation Modelling and Risk Management. FJF Associates, New Hope, PA.

Harrison, M., Pliska, S., 1981. Martingales and stochastic integrals in the theory of continuous trading. Stochastic Process. Appl. 11, 215–260.

Heath, D., Jarrow, R., Morton, A., 1990. Bond pricing and the term structure of interest rates: a discrete time approximation. J. Financ. Quant. Anal. 25 (4), 419–440.

Heath, D., Jarrow, R., Morton, A., 1992. Bond pricing and the term structure of interest rates: a new methodology. Econometrica 60 (1), 77–105.

Ho, T.S.Y., Lee, S.-B., 1986. Term structure movements and pricing interest rate contingent claims. J. Financ. 41, 1011–1029.

Honore, P., 1998. Five essays on financial econometrics in continuous-time models. PhD Thesis, Aarhus School of Business.

Hughston, L. (Ed.), 1996. Vasicek and Beyond: Approaches to Building and Applying Interest Rate Models. Risk Publications, London.

Hull, J., 1997. Options, Futures and Other Derivatives. Wiley, New Jersey.

Hull, J., White, A., 1993. Bond option pricing based on a model for the evolution of bond prices. Adv. Fut. Opt. Res. 6, 1–13.

Hull, J., White, A., 1994. Numerical procedures for implementing term structure models II: two-factor models. J. Deriv. 2 (2), 37–48.

James, J., Webber, N., 1997. Interest Rate Modelling. Wiley, Chichester.

Jamshidian, F., 1997. LIBOR and swap market models and measures. Finance Stochast. 1, 293–330.

Jarrow, R., Madan, D., 1991. Option Pricing Using the Term Structure of Interest Rates to Hedge Systematic Discontinuities in Asset Returns: Working Paper. Cornell University, Ithaca, NY, pp. 1–47.

Jarrow, R., Turnbull, S., 1996. Derivative Securities. South-Western Publishing, Cincinnati.

Rebonato, R., 1998. Interest Rate Option Models, second ed. Wiley, Chichester.

Rebonato, R., Cooper, I., 1996. The limitations of simple two-factor interest-rate models. J. Financ. Eng. 5 (1), 1–16.

Ritchken, P., Sankarasubramanian, L., 1995. Volatility structures of forward rates and the dynamics of the term structure. Math. Financ. 5, 55–72.

Uhrig, M., Walter, U., 1996. A new numerical approach for fitting the initial yield curve. J. Fixed Income 5 (4), 82–90.

REFERENCES ON ESTIMATION METHODS

Andersen, T., Lund, J., 1997. Estimating continuous-time stochastic volatility models of the short-term interest rate. J. Econometrics 77, 343–377.

Brown, R., Schaefer, S., 1994. The term structure of real interest rates and the Cox, Ingersoll and Ross model. J. Financ. Econ. 35, 2–42.

Campbell, J., Lo, A., MacKinlay, C., 1997. The Econometrics of Financial Markets. Princeton University Press, New Jersey, USA.

Davidson, R., MacKinnon, J., 1993. Estimation and Inference in Econometrics. Oxford University Press, Oxford.

Duffie, D., Singleton, K., 1993. Simulated moments estimation of Markov models of asset prices. Econometrica 61, 929–952.

Hansen, L., 1982. Large sample properties of generalized method of moments estimators. Econometrica 50, 1029–1055.

Lo, A., 1986. Statistical tests of contingent claims asset pricing models. J. Financ. Econ. 17, 143–173.

Longstaff, F., Schwartz, E., 1992. Interest rate volatility and the term structure: a two-factor general equilibrium model. J. Finance 47, 1259–1282.

Chapter 5

Fitting the Term Structure

Chapter Contents

The two previous chapters introduced and described a fraction of the most important research into interest-rate models that has been carried out since the first model, presented by Oldrich Vasicek, appeared in 1977. These models can be used to price derivative securities, and equilibrium models can be used to assess fair value in the bond market. Before this can take place; however, a model must be fitted to the yield curve, or *calibrated*.[1] In practice, this is carried out in two ways; the most popular approach involves calibrating the model against market interest rates given by instruments such as cash Libor deposits, futures, swaps and bonds. The alternative method is to model the yield curve from the market rates and then calibrate the model to this fitted yield curve. The first approach is common when using, for example extended Vasicek

---

1. In fact, a model needs to be calibrated to the market, but the most important item against which it must be calibrated is the current term structure.

85

models, while the second technique is more useful with whole yield curve models such as the Heath-Jarrow-Morton model.

There are a number of techniques that can be used to fit the yield curve. These include regression methods and *spline* techniques. More recent methods such as *kernel approximations* and *linear programming* are also beginning to be used by practitioners. In this chapter, we provide an introduction to some of these; however, a detailed exposition would warrant a book in its own right. We discuss fitting the spot and forward yield curve and review the methods used to estimate spot and forward yield curves. We then illustrate the cubic spline method for fitting a yield curve from observed government bond yields. There is a large body of literature on this subject. For further information, readers are recommended to review Anderson et al. (1996) and James and Webber (2000) for the most important research, and interested readers may also wish to consider Bliss (1997), Dahlquist and Svensson (1996) and Waggoner (1997). Alternative approaches are given in Kim (1993) and Zheng (1994).

For a number of reasons practitioners, investors, central banks and government authorities are interested in fitting the zero-coupon yield curve, or the true term structure of interest rates. The use of yield curves is standard in monetary policy analysis, and central banks are increasingly making use of forward interest rates for this purpose as well. Forward rates must be estimated from the yield curve that has been constructed from current market yields, generally T-bill and government bond yields. Particularly useful information that can be derived from government bond prices includes the yield curve for implied forward rates, as these reflect the market's expectations of the future path of interest rates.[2] They are also used by the market to price bonds and determine the extent of the credit spread applicable to corporate bonds. The requirements of the monetary authorities, however, are slightly different to those of market practitioners: central bankers and the government are not so concerned with the accuracy of the spot curve with regard to pricing securities; rather, they are interested in the information content of the fitted curve, particularly concerning implied forward rates and the market expectations of future interest rates and levels of inflation.

5.1 INTRODUCTION

From an elementary understanding of the markets, we know that there is a relationship between a set of discount factors, and the discount function, the par yield curve, the zero-coupon yield curve and the forward yield curve. If we know one of these functions, we may readily compute the other three. In practice, although the zero-coupon yield curve is directly observable from the yields of zero-coupon

---

2. Remember of course that the forward rate is derived from the current spot rate term structure, and therefore although it is an expectation based on all currently known information, it is not a prediction of the term structure in the future. Nevertheless the forward rate is important because it enables market makers to price and hedge financial instruments, most especially contracts with a forward starting date.

government bonds, liquidity and investor preferences usually mean that a theoretical set of all these curves is derived from the yields of coupon government bonds in the market. There are a number of ways that the zero-coupon curve can be fitted, using either a discount function or the par yield curve.

The pricing of financial instruments in the debt market revolves around the yield curve. The use in the market and by the central authorities of the government term structure to ascertain the market's expectation of future interest rates is well established. This reflects the fact that the spot yield curve is the geometric average of the same maturity structure implied forward rates. Here we discuss the information content of the yield curve, and how the zero-coupon curve may be best fitted to enable analysts to extract information from the implied forward rate yield curve. This is used for a number of purposes by central government monetary authorities and by analysts and economists. In the United Kingdom, for example the yield on government bonds is used as the benchmark for interest charges to local authorities and public sector bodies. Yield curve data may also be used as one of the parameters for a general interest-rate model (e.g. see Cox et al. (1985) for a one-factor model and Heath et al. (1992) for a multifactor model).

Although the use of yield curves is quite common as part of monetary policy analysis, central banks such as the US Federal Reserve and the Bank of England have only recently begun to use *forward* interest rates as an indicator for monetary policy purposes. We know that a forward rate is an interest rate applicable to a debt instrument whose term begins at a future date, and ends at a date beyond that. Although there is a market in forward rates, the prices at which forward instruments are quoted are derived from spot interest rates. That is, *implied* forward rates are calculated from the spot yield curve, which is in turn modelled from the prices of instruments in the market, usually government bills and bonds. This implies that the shape and position of the spot curve reflects market belief on future interest rates, which is why it is used to calculate forward rates. The information content and predictive power of a spot term structure is based on this belief. Forward rates may be estimated using any one of a number of models. They can be interpreted as reflecting the market's expectations of future *short-term* interest rates, which in turn are indicators of expected inflation levels. The same information is contained in the spot yield curve; however, monetary authorities often prefer to use forward rates as they are better applied to policy analysis. Whereas the spot yield curve is the expected average of forward rates, the forward rate curve reflects the expected future time period of one short-term forward rate. This means that the forward curve can be split into short- and long-term segments in a more straightforward fashion than the spot curve.

As it is used as a predictive indicator, the spot yield curve needs to be fitted as accurately as possible. This is an area that has been extensively researched (see McCulloch, 1975; Deacon and Derry, 1994; Schaefer, 1981; Waggoner, 1997; Nelson and Siegel, 1987; Svensson, 1994, 1995 *inter alia*). Invariably researchers use the government debt market as the basis for modelling the term structure. This is because the government market is the most liquid debt market in any country, and also because (in a developed economy) government securities are default free, so that government borrowing rates are considered risk free. Whatever method is used to fit the term structure, it should aim to meet the following criteria when the main use is for government policy, rather than the pricing of financial instruments:

- The method should attempt to fit implied forward rates, because the primary objective is to derive the forward curve and not market spot yields;
- The resulting derived forward curve should be as smooth as possible, again because the aim is to provide information on the future level and direction of interest rates, and expectations on central bank monetary policy, rather than an accurate valuation of financial instruments along the maturity term structure;
- It should have as few market assumptions as possible.

There are a number of curve-fitting methods that may be employed. In the United Kingdom gilt market, the Bank of England previously used an in-house model,[3] but has since adopted a modified technique proposed by Svensson (1995) and subsequently Fisher et al. (1995), Waggoner (1997) and Anderson and Sleath (1999). The Waggoner method is discussed in a later section. In the United Kingdom, the introduction of a market in government zero-coupon bonds has enabled the accuracy of a fitted spot term structure to be compared to actual market spot rates; there is also useful information to be gleaned from using data from the gilt repo market when comparing the accuracy of the short end of the fitted curve, as discussed by Anderson and Sleath (1999). We set the scene below.

5.2   BOND MARKET INFORMATION

5.2.1   Basic Concepts

Central banks and market practitioners use interest rates prevailing in the government bond market to extract certain information, the most important of which is implied forward rates. These are an estimate of the market's expectations about the future direction of short-term interest rates. They are important because they signify the market's expectations about the future path of interest rates; however, they are also used in derivative pricing and to create synthetic bond prices from the extent of credit spreads of corporate bonds.

Forward rates may be calculated using the discount function or spot interest rates. If spot interest rates are known, then the bond price equation can be set as:

$$P = \frac{C}{(1+rs_1)} + \frac{C}{(1+rs_2)^2} + \cdots + \frac{C+M}{(1+rs_n)^n} \qquad (5.1)$$

---

3. See Mastronikola (1991).

where C is the coupon; M is the redemption payment on maturity (par) and rs_t is the *spot interest rate* applicable to the cash flow in period t $(t=1,\ldots, n)$.

The bond price equation is usually given in terms of *discount factors*, with the present value of each coupon payment and the maturity payment being the product of multiplying them by their relevant discount factors. This allows us to set the price equation as shown by Equation (5.2),

$$P = \sum_{t=1}^{n} C df_t + M df_n \qquad (5.2)$$

where df_t is the *t*-period discount factor $(t=1, \ldots, m)$ given by Equation (5.3):

$$df_t = \frac{1}{(1+rs_t)^t}, \quad t=1,\ldots,m. \qquad (5.3)$$

A discount factor is a value for a discrete point in time, whereas markets often prefer to think of a continuous value of discount factors that applies a specific discount factor to any time t. This is known as the *discount function*, which is the continuous set of discrete discount factors and is indicated by $df_t = \delta(t_t)$.

The discount function relates the current cash bond yield curve with the spot yield curve and the implied forward rate yield curve. From Equation (5.3) we can set:

$$df_t = (1+rs_t)^{-t}.$$

As the spot rate rs is the average of the implied short-term forward rates rf_1, $rf_2, \ldots, rf_t$ we state

$$\begin{aligned}
1/df_1 &= (1+rs_1) = (1+rf_1) \\
1/df_2 &= (1+rs_2)^2 = (1+rf_1)(1+rf_2) \\
1/df_t &= (1+rs_t)^t = (1+rf_1)(1+rf_2)\cdots(1+rf_t)
\end{aligned} \qquad (5.4)$$

From Equation (5.4) we see that $1+rs_t$ is the geometric mean of $(1+rf_1)$, $(1+rf_2), \ldots, (1+rf_t)$.

Implied forward rates indicate the expected short-term (one-period) future interest rate for a specific point along the term structure; they reflect the spread on the marginal rate of return that the market requires if it is investing in debt instruments of longer and longer maturities.

In order to calculate the range of implied forward rates, we require the term structure of spot rates for all periods along the continuous discount function. This is not possible in practice, because a bond market will only contain a finite number of coupon-bearing bonds maturing on discrete dates. While the coupon yield curve can be observed, we are then required to 'fit' the observed curve to a continuous term structure. Note that in the United Kingdom gilt market, for example there is a zero-coupon bond market, so that it is possible to observe spot rates directly, but for reasons of liquidity, analysts prefer to use a fitted yield curve (the *theoretical* curve) and compare this to the observed curve.

5.2.2   Estimating Yield Curve Functions

The traditional approach to yield curve fitting involves the calculation of a set of discount factors from market interest rates. From this, a spot yield curve can be estimated. The market data can be money market interest rates, futures and swap rates and bond yields. In general, though this approach tends to produce 'ragged' spot rates and a forward rate curve with pronounced jagged knot points, due to the scarcity of data along the maturity structure.[4] A refinement of this technique is to use polynomial approximation to the yield curve.

The McCulloch (1971, 1975) method describes the discount function as a linear combination of a specified number of approximating functions, so for example, if there are k such functions on which j coefficients are estimated, the discount function that is generated by the set of approximations is a k-th degree polynomial. The drawback of this approach is that unless the market observations are spaced at equal intervals through the maturity range, such a polynomial will fit the long end of the curve fairly inaccurately. To account for this, McCulloch proposed using piecewise polynomial functions or splines to approximate the discount function. A polynomial spline can be thought of as a number of separate polynomial functions, joined smoothly at a number of join, break or *knot* points. In mathematics, the term 'smooth' has a precise meaning, but in the context of a piecewise r-degree spline it is generally taken to mean that the $(r-1)$th derivative of the functions either side of each knot point are continuous. McCulloch originally used a quadratic spline to estimate the discount function. This results, however, in extreme bumps or 'knuckles' in the corresponding forward rate curve, which makes the curve unsuitable for policy analysis. To avoid this effect, it is necessary to increase the number of estimating functions and to use a *cubic spline*. This was presented by McCulloch in his second paper, and his specification is summarised in Appendix A.

One of the main criticisms of cubic and polynomial functions is that they produce forward rate curves that exhibit unrealistic properties at the long end, usually a steep fall or rise in the curve. A method proposed by Vasicek and Fong (1982) avoids this feature, and produces smoother forward curves. Their approach characterises the discount function as exponential in shape, which is why splines, being polynomials, do not provide a good fit to the discount function, as they have a different curvature to exponential functions. Vasicek and Fong instead propose a transform to the argument T of the discount function $v(T)$. This transform is given by

$$T = -(1/\alpha)\ln(1-x), \quad \text{where } 0 \le x \le 1 \tag{5.5}$$

and has the effect of transforming the discount function from an approximately exponential function of T to an approximately linear function of x. Polynomial

---

4. For a good account of why this approach is not satisfactory see James and Webber (2000, Chapter 15).

splines can then be employed to estimate this transformed discount function. Using this transform, it is straightforward to impose additional constraints on the discount function. The parameter α constitutes the limiting value of the forward rates, and can be fitted to the date as part of the estimation. Vasicek and Fong use a cubic spline to estimate the transformed discount function. In terms of the original variable T, this is equivalent to estimating the discount function by a third-order exponential spline, that is between each pair of knot points $\nu(T)$ takes the form:

$$\nu(T) = b_0 + b_1 e^{-2\alpha T} + b_3 e^{3\alpha T}. \qquad (5.6)$$

However, Shea (1985) has indicated that in practice exponential splines do not produce more stable estimates of the term structure than polynomial splines. He also recommended using basis splines or *B-splines*, functions that are identically 0 over most of the approximation space, to prevent loss of accuracy due to the lack of observations at the long end of the curve.

5.3   CURVE-FITTING TECHNIQUES: PARAMETRIC

There are a number of models that one may use to fit the spot rate term structure. One-factor models (see Vasicek, 1977; Dothan, 1978; Cox et al., 1985) model the one-period short rate to obtain a forward yield curve. The simplest method uses a binomial model of probabilities to model the forward rate. Multifactor models (see Heath et al., 1992) express analytically the entire yield curve in terms of two forward rates (or 'spanning' rates). For an analysis of the information content of both methodologies see Edmister and Madan (1993), who conclude that the multifactor models provide more accurate results. Essentially the information content of the yield curve is best estimated using a multifactor model, and is more accurate at the longer end of the curve whatever methodology is used. Edmister and Madan also conclude that modelling the short end of the curve suffers from distortions resulting from government intervention in short-term interest rates.

The Bank of England uses a variation of the Svensson yield curve model, a one-dimensional *parametric* yield curve model. This is similar to the Nelson and Siegel model and defines the forward rate curve *f(m)* as a function of a set of unknown parameters, which are related to the short-term interest rate and the slope of the yield curve. The model is summarised in Appendix B. Anderson and Sleath (1999) assess parametric models, including the Svensson model, against spline-based methods such as those described by Waggoner (1997), and we summarise their results later in this chapter.

5.3.1   Parametric Techniques

Curve-fitting techniques generally fit into two classes, as described, for example, in Chapter 15 of James and Webber (2000), *parametric* methods and *spline-based* methods. Parametric techniques are so-called because they model the forward rate using a parametric function. An early parametric technique was that described by Nelson and Siegel (1987), which models the forward rate curve. Given the relationship between spot and forward rates, such an approach is identical to modelling a spot rate curve by taking a geometric average of the forward rates curve. A fairly flexible function for the forward rate is described in the Nelson-Siegel approach, known as a Laguerre function (plus a constant) and is given by

$$f(T) = \beta_0 + \beta_1 e^{-T/\tau_1} + \frac{\beta_2}{\tau_1} T e^{-T/\tau_1} \qquad (5.7)$$

where T is the variable being calculated and $\beta_0, \beta_1, \beta_2$ and τ_1 are the parameters required to be estimated. Remembering that the spot rate is an average of the forward rates, that is

$$rs = \frac{\displaystyle\int_0^T f(u)\,du}{T} \qquad (5.8)$$

then Equation (5.7) implies that the spot rate is given by

$$rs(T) = \beta_0 + (\beta_1 + \beta_2)\frac{\tau_1}{T}\left(1 - e^{-T/\tau_1}\right) - \beta_2 e^{-T/\tau_1}. \qquad (5.9)$$

To illustrate implementation, we adapt with permission the Anderson and Sleath (1999) evaluation of the Nelson-Siegel method; we set parameter values of:

$$\beta_0 = 5.0 \quad \beta_1 = -1 \quad \tau_1 = 1$$

and denote the remaining parameter as a, which reduces Equation (5.9) to

$$rs(T) = 5 + (-1 + a)\frac{1 - e^{-T}}{T} - ae^{-T}. \qquad (5.10)$$

Setting β_0 as 5.0 means that the spot rate has been set to a common value of 5.0%. As an exercise, we evaluate the possible results with the same parameters used by Anderson and Sleath in their analysis with the exception of the initial spot rate, and change the values for the term to maturity to 10, 20, 30 and 1000 years and the value of a to $-5, -3, -1, 0, 1, 3$ and 5. Our results are given in Table 5.1. As the value for T increases to very high values, the convergence of spot rates to the initial value proceeds only slowly. However, our results illustrate the process.

An evaluation fitting the Nelson-Siegel curve to actual gilt yields from June 1997 is described in the next section.

Another parametric method is described by Svensson (1994, 1995). This adds an extra coefficient to the Nelson-Siegel model and has been described as an extended Nelson-Siegel model. The extra parameter introduces greater

TABLE 5.1 Spot Rate Values Using Nelson-Siegel Model and User-Specified Parameters

Maturity	a Values						
(T) Years	−5	−3	−1	0	1	3	5
10	4.4003	4.6002	4.8001	4.9	5.0000	5.1999	5.3998
20	4.7000	4.8000	4.9000	4.9500	5.0000	5.1000	5.2000
30	4.8000	4.8667	4.9333	4.9667	5.0000	5.0667	5.1333
1000	4.9940	4.996	4.9980	4.9990	5.0000	5.0200	5.0040

flexibility, so that the resulting curve can model forward curves that have more than one 'hump'. It is given by Equation (5.11):

$$f(T) = \beta_0 + \beta_1 e^{-T/\tau_1} + \beta_2 \frac{T}{\tau_1} e^{-T/\tau_1} + \beta_3 \frac{T}{\tau_1} e^{-T/\tau_2}. \tag{5.11}$$

In the Svensson model, there are six coefficients $\beta_0, \beta_1, \beta_2, \beta_3, \tau_1$ and τ_2 that must be estimated. The model was adopted by central monetary authorities such as the Swedish Riksbank and the Bank of England (who subsequently adopted a modified version of this model, which we describe shortly, following the publication of the Waggoner paper by the Federal Reserve Bank of England). In their 1999 paper, Anderson and Sleath evaluate the two parametric techniques we have described, in an effort to improve their flexibility, based on the spline methods presented by Fisher et al. (1995) and Waggoner (1997).

5.3.2   Parameterised Yield Curves

The technique for curve fitting presented by Nelson and Siegel and variants on it described by Svensson (1994), Wiseman (1994) and Bjork and Christensen (1997) have a small number of parameters, and generally one obtains a relatively close approximation to the yield curve with them. As we saw above, the Nelson and Siegel curve contains four parameters while the Svensson curve has six parameters. The curve presented by Wiseman contains $2 \times (n+1)$ parameters, given by $\{\beta_j, k_j\}_{j=0,...,n}$. The curve is $f_2(\tau)$:

$$f_2(\tau) = \sum_{j=0}^{n} \beta_j e^{-k_j \tau}. \tag{5.12}$$

The original Nelson and Siegel curve does not produce close approximations for all types of yield curves, because the small number of parameters limits

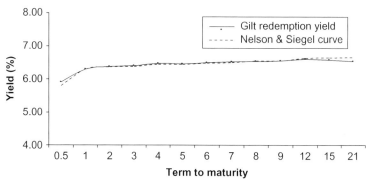

FIGURE 5.1   A Nelson and Siegel fitted yield curve and gilt redemption yield curve.

flexibility. It can be used to model the spot rate or the forward rate curve, but does not produce accurate results if used to model the discount curve. An example of a fitted Nelson and Siegel curve is shown in Figure 5.1 for United Kingdom gilt yields from June 1997. The table of actual gilt yields is shown as well (Table 5.2).

The fitted curve is a close approximation to the redemption yield curve, and is also very smooth. However, the fit is inaccurate at the very short end, indicating an underpriced 6-month bond, and also does not approximate the long end of the curve. For this reason, B-spline methods are more commonly used.

TABLE 5.2 Gilt redemption Yields

Term to Maturity	Gilt Redemption Yield %	Term to Maturity	Gilt Redemption Yield %
0.5	5.90	7	6.52
1	6.29	8	6.54
2	6.37	9	6.55
3	6.40	12	6.60
4	6.47	15	6.58
5	6.45	21	6.54
6	6.50		

Source: Butler Gilts

5.4   THE CUBIC SPLINE METHOD FOR ESTIMATING AND FITTING THE YIELD CURVE

In mathematical applications a *spline* is *piecewise polynomial*, this being a function that is composed of a number of individual polynomial segments that are joined at user-specified points known as *knot points*. The function is twice differentiable at each knot point, which produces a smooth curve at each connecting knot point. The commonest approach uses regression methods to fit the spline function, and an excellent and accessible account of this technique is given in Suits et al. (1978); the article is summarised in Choudhry (2001). In this section, we summarise with permission the spline approach described by Waggoner in his ground-breaking article published by the Federal Reserve Bank of Atlanta in 1997.

Spline methods are commonly used to derive spot and forward rate curves and the discount function from the observed yields of bonds in the market. A popular method is that proposed by McCulloch (1975), which uses regression cubic splines to derive the discount function. Waggoner (1996) has written that this method however, while accurate and stable, produces forward rate curves that oscillate. In fact, this property is exhibited by virtually all curve-fitting techniques, but the objective for the analyst is to produce curves with the smallest amount of oscillation. A technique posited by Fisher et al. (1995) used a cubic spline that incorporated a 'roughness penalty' when extracting the forward rate curve. This approach produces a decreased level of oscillation, but also reduces the fit of the curve to the actual observed yields. A later technique modified this method by using a 'variable roughness penalty' (Waggoner, 1997) and this approach is described here.

5.4.1   Using a Cubic Spline: The Waggoner Model

A cubic spline approach can be used as the functional form for the discount function or the forward rate curve. We define a function g on the interval $[t_1, t_N]$ as a cubic spline with node points $t_1 < t_2 < \ldots < t_n$ if it is a cubic polynomial on each of the subintervals $[t_{j-1}, t_j]$ for $1 < j < n$ and if it can be continuously differentiated over the interval $[t_1, t_N]$. The node points are $\tau_1 < \tau_2 < \ldots < \tau_N$ which are the cash flow and maturity dates of the set of bonds (assuming the bonds are semiannual coupon instruments). Following Waggoner (1997), we set $\tau_0 = 0$ so that the curve is derived from the point 0 to the point of the longest dated bond in the sample. It is possible to use all the node points in the interval to produce the yield curve; however, the more points there are in a cubic spline, the greater the tendency for the derived forward curve to oscillate, more so at longer maturities. We wish to minimise the level of oscillation, because for monetary policy purposes the curve is used to provide information on expected future interest rates. A fluctuating yield curve would imply oscillations in expected future prices, and this can produce illogical results, particularly at the long end of the curve. For example, a curve may imply that while the current yield of a 6-month T-bill is £97.50, the price

1w	1m	3m	6m	9m	1y	2y	3y	4y	5y	6y	7y	8y	9y	10y

3m	6m	1y	2y	3y	4y	5y	7y	10y	15y	20y	25y	30y

FIGURE 5.2   Suggested node points.

of a 6-month bill in 1-year's time will be £98, while the price of such a bill in 2-years' time will be £95. This is not an unreasonable expectation. However, the same implications for 6-month bill prices in 25-, 26- and 27-years' time is less reasonable. Therefore, the fitted curve should smooth out the forward rates at longer maturities, which calls for a reduced level of oscillation. The McCulloch technique uses regression splines to reduce forward rate fluctuation, while the Fisher et al. and the Waggoner approach use a smoothed spline and a modified smoothed spline.

In a regression spline, a smaller number of node points are used in order to reduce the level of oscillation. This affects the flexibility of the cubic spline over the interval that is being considered; there is a trade-off between accuracy and the level of oscillation. By reducing node points at the longer end but keeping more at the short end, oscillation is reduced, but the curve retains accuracy at the short end. In practice, it is common for node points to be set in one of the ways shown in Figure 5.2, but obviously there are any number of ways that node points may be set.

Once we have chosen the node points we set the yield curve ψ as the cubic spline that minimises the function (5.13):

$$\sum_{i=1}^{N} \left(P_i - \hat{P}_i(\psi) \right)^2. \tag{5.13}$$

The technique proposed by McCulloch (1975) used a regression cubic spline to approximate the discount function, and he suggested that the number of node points that are used be roughly equal to the square root of the number of bonds in the sample, with equal spacing so that an equal number of bonds mature between adjacent nodes. A number of writers have suggested that this approach produces accurate results in practice.[5] The discount function is constrained to set $v(0) = 1$. Given these parameters the discount function chosen is the one that minimises the function (5.14). As this is a discount function and not a yield curve, Equation (5.14) can be solved using the least squares method.

$$\sum_{i=1}^{N} \left(P_i - \hat{P}_i^{\nu}(\nu) \right)^2. \tag{5.14}$$

For a smoothed spline, the level of oscillation is controlled by setting a 'roughness penalty' in the function, and not by reducing the number of node points. The yield curve ψ is chosen that minimises the objective function (5.15):

---

5. For example, see Bliss (1997).

$$\sum_{i=1}^{N} \left(P_i - \hat{P}_i^*(\psi)\right)^2 + \lambda \int_0^{t_N} (\psi''(t))^2 \, dt \qquad (5.15)$$

for all the cubic splines over the node points $\tau_0 < \tau_1 < \tau_2 < \ldots < \tau_N$. In minimising this function there is a trade-off between the goodness of fit, which is given by the first term, and the degree of smoothness, which is measured by the second term. This trade-off is known as the 'roughness penalty' and is given by λ, which is a positive constant. If λ is set to 0 the function reverts to a regression spline, and as it increases g approaches a linear function. The flexibility of the spline is a function of both the spacing between the node points and the magnitude of λ, although as λ increases the impact of the node spacing decreases. For large values of λ, the flexibility of the spline is essentially similar across all terms. This is not necessarily ideal because as we saw from Figure 5.1 we require the spline to be more flexible at the short end, and less so at the long end. Therefore, Waggoner (1997) has proposed a modified smoothed spline. For a modified smoothed spline, the objective function (5.16) is minimised over the whole term covering the node points $\tau_0 < \tau_1 < \tau_2 < \ldots < \tau_N$.

$$\sum_{i=1}^{N} \left(P_i - \hat{P}_i^*(\psi)\right)^2 + \int_0^{\tau_N} \lambda(t)(\psi''(t))^2 \, dt. \qquad (5.16)$$

The approach used by Fisher et al. (1995) is a smoothed cubic spline that approximates the forward curve. The number of nodes to use is recommended as approximately one-third of the number of bonds used in the sample, spaced apart so that there is an equal number of bonds maturing between adjacent nodes. This is different to the theoretical approach, which is to have node points at every interval where there is a bond cash flow; however, in practice using the smaller number of nodes as proposed by Fisher et al. produces essentially an identical forward rate curve, but with fewer calculations required. The resulting forward rate curve is the cubic spline that minimises the function (5.17):

$$\sum_{i=1}^{N} \left(P_i - \hat{P}_i^f(f)\right)^2 + \lambda \int_0^{\tau_N} (f''(s))^2 \, ds. \qquad (5.17)$$

The value of λ is obtained by a method known as generalised cross validation (GCV). It is the value that minimises the expression in Equation (5.18):

$$\gamma(\lambda) = \frac{rss(\lambda)}{(N - \theta ep(\lambda))^2} \qquad (5.18)$$

where N is the number of bonds in the sample and $rss\,(\lambda)$ is the residual sum of squares, given by

$$rss(\lambda) = \sum_{i=1}^{N} \left(P_i - \hat{P}_i^f(f_\lambda)\right)^2$$

where f_λ is the forward rate curve that minimises the expression; $ep(\lambda)$ is the effective number of parameters and θ is the cost or tuning parameter.

The higher the value for θ, the more rigid is the resulting spline. Fisher et al. and Waggoner both set θ equal to 2. Expression (5.17), for a fixed term λ can be solved using a nonlinear least squares method. The GCV method can be implemented by using a method known as a *line search*.

Following Fisher et al., Waggoner (1997) proposes using a cubic spline to approximate the forward rate function, with the number of nodes again being approximately one-third of the number of bonds in the sample, and spaced so that there is an equal number of bonds maturing between adjacent nodes. The Waggoner approach is termed the 'variable roughness penalty method' (VRP). The cubic spline forward rate curve is selected that will minimise the function (5.19):

$$\sum_{i=1}^{N} \left(P_i - \hat{P}_i(f) \right)^2 + \int_0^{\tau_N} \lambda(s)(f''(s))^2 \mathrm{d}s. \tag{5.19}$$

The roughness penalty λ is set as follows:

$$\lambda(t) = \begin{cases} 0.1 & 0 \leq t \leq 1 \\ 100 & 1 \leq t \leq 10 \\ 100,000 & 10 \leq t \end{cases}$$

where t is measured in years. The VRP method is nonlinear and can be solved using the nonlinear least squares method.

5.4.2   The Anderson-Sleath Model

Anderson and Sleath presented a model in the Bank of England *Quarterly Bulletin* in November 1999. The main objective of this work was to evaluate the relative efficacy of parametric versus spline-based methods. In fact, different applications call for different methods; the main advantage of spline methods is that individual functions in between knot points may move in fairly independent fashion, which makes the resulting curve more flexible than that possible using parametric techniques. In Section 5.5.1 we reproduce their results with permission, which shows that a shock introduced at one end of the curve produces unsatisfactory results in the parametric curve.

The Anderson-Sleath model, which is the method adopted by the Bank of England, is a modification of the Waggoner approach in a number of significant ways. The $\lambda(t)$ function of Waggoner was adapted thus:

$$\log \lambda(m) = L - (L - S)\mathrm{e}^{-m/\mu} \tag{5.20}$$

where the parameters to be estimated are L, S and μ. In addition, the difference in bond market and theoretical prices is weighted with the inverse of the modified duration of the bond. This accounts for observed pricing errors for bonds that are more volatile than others.

The model, therefore, minimises the expression in Equation (5.21):

$$X = \sum_{i=1}^{N} \left(\frac{P_i - \pi_i(c)}{MD_i} \right)^2 + \int_0^M \lambda_t(m) (f''(m))^2 \, dm \qquad (5.21)$$

where P and MD are the price and modified duration of bond; i, c is the parameter vector of the polynomial spline being estimated and M is the time to maturity of the longest dated bond.

The outstanding feature of the Anderson-Sleath approach is their adaptation of both spline and parametric techniques.

5.4.3   Applications

Each of the methods described in this section can be used to fit the zero-coupon curve with validity. In practice, results produced by each method imply that certain techniques are more suitable than others under specific conditions. Generally, the incorporation of a 'roughness' penalty that varies across maturities produces more accurate pricing of short-dated bonds, and this is the case in the Fisher et al. and Waggoner methods. The McCulloch technique is reasonably accurate and, as it is a linear method, is more straightforward to implement than the other techniques. It produces a similar curve to the VRP method in terms of goodness of fit and smoothness. Therefore, in most cases, it is reasonable to use this method. The advantage of the VRP method is that it allows the user to select the degree of smoothing.

In deciding which method to use, practitioners will need to consider the effectiveness of each approach with regard to flexibility, simplicity and consistency. The requirements of central monetary authorities differ in some respects to investment and commercial banks, as we noted at the start of the chapter. Generally, however, curves should fit as wide a range of term structures as possible, and be tractable, or straightforward to compute. They should also be consistent with a yield curve model. For example, the approach presented by Bjork and Christensen (1997) is compatible with the Hull-White or extended Vasicek yield curve model. In the same paper, it is stated that the Nelson and Siegel technique is not consistent with any common term structure model. James and Webber (2000) state that the simplicity of the Nelson and Siegel approach, which is an advantage of the technique, is also its main drawback. In the same review, it is concluded that B-spline methods are the most flexible and consistent, along with that described by Bjork and Christensen.

5.5   THE ANDERSON-SLEATH EVALUATION

5.5.1   Fitting the Spot Curve

In this section we summarise, with permission, results obtained in highly innovative research by Anderson and Sleath (1999), comparing the different methods. The accuracy of any of the techniques is usually tested by using a goodness-of-fit measure, for example, if we fit the curve using n bonds we wish to minimise the measure given by Equation (5.22):

$$X_P = \sum_{i=1}^{N} \left(\frac{P_i - \prod_i(\rho)}{MD_i} \right)^2 \tag{5.22}$$

where P_i is the market price of the i-th bond; MD_i is the modified duration of the i-th bond and $\prod_i(\rho)$ is the fitted price of the i-th bond.

A popular technique is the spline-based method of curve fitting. Unlike other methods (such as the parametric Svensson method) which specify a single short rate to describe the instantaneous forward rate curve, spline-based methods fit a curve to observed data that is composed of a number of sections, but with constraints to ensure that the curve is smooth and continuous. As this is one of the aims we stated at the beginning, this is an advantage of the spline-based method, as it allows individual sections of the curve to move independently of each other. This is demonstrated in Figures 5.3 and 5.4, which show a hypothetical yield curve that has been fitted, from an assumed set of bond prices, using the cubic spline method and a parametric method such as Svensson. The change of the long bond yield has a significant effect on the Svensson curve, notably at the short end of the curve. The spline curve, however, undergoes only a slight change in response to the change in yield, and only at the long end.

The effect of a change in yield on the Svensson curve is amplified because the technique specifies a constraint that results in yields converging to a constant level. This assumption is based on the belief that forward rates reflect market expectations of the future level of short rates, and following this the 30-year

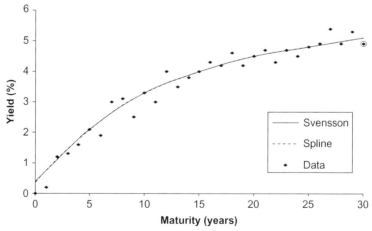

FIGURE 5.3 Yield curves fitted using cubic spline method and Svensson parametric method, hypothetical bond yields. *(Reproduced with permission from the Bank of England Quarterly Bulletin, November 1999.)*

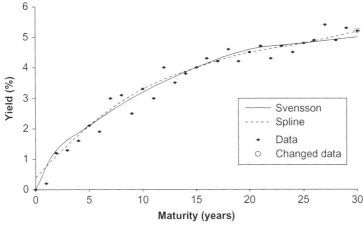

FIGURE 5.4   Effect on fitted yield curves of change in long-dated bond yield. *(Reproduced with permission from the Bank of England Quarterly Bulletin, November 1999.)*

forward rate will be expected to be not significantly different from the 25- or 20-year forward rate. This causes the forward rate after about 10 years to converge to a constant level.

We can compare fitted yield curves to an actual spot rate curve wherever there is an active government (risk-free) zero-coupon market in operation. In the United Kingdom, a zero-coupon bond market was introduced in December 1997. In theory any derived spot rate curve can be compared to the actual spot rate curve, this comparison serving to provide an instant check of the accuracy of the yield curve model. In practice, however, discrepancies between the observed and fitted curves may not have that much significance, because of the way that strip yields behave in practice. In the United Kingdom market, there is a certain level of illiquidity associated with strip yields at certain points of the term structure; the United Kingdom market also exhibits a common trait of strip markets everywhere that the longest dated issue traded dear to the yield curve. Another factor is that coupon strips trade cheaper to principal strips; which yield should be used in the comparison?[6] In Figure 5.5 we compare the theoretical spot curve fitted using the Svensson method to the observed coupon strip curve in July 1998, at a time when the United Kingdom gilt yield curve was inverted.

The fitted curve exhibits the constant long yield that we observed in the hypothetical yield curve in Figure 5.1, while the strip curve trades expensive at the long end, which as we noted is a common observation. Nevertheless, for the purposes of accurate fitting, the parametric method exhibits a significant difference to the

6. This is the observation that, due to demand and liquidity reasons, zero-coupon bonds sourced from the principal cash flow of a coupon bond trade at a lower yield than equivalent-maturity zero-coupon bonds sourced from the coupon cash flow of a conventional bond.

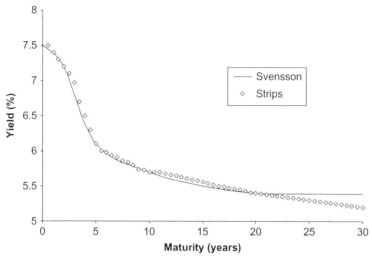

FIGURE 5.5 Comparison of fitted spot yield curve to observed spot yield curve. *(Reproduced with permission from the Bank of England Quarterly Bulletin, November 1999.)*

observed curve. A cubic spline-based fitted curve such as that proposed by Waggoner (1997) produces a more realistic curve, as shown in Figure 5.6.

This reflects the properties of the spline curve, including the fact that forward rates are described by a series of segments that are in effect connected together. This has the effect of localising the influence of individual yield movements to only the relevant part of the yield curve; it also allows the curve to match more closely the observed yield curve. The goodness of the spline-based method is measured using Equation (5.23):

$$X_s = X_P + \int_0^M \lambda_t(m)(f''(m))^2 \, dm \qquad (5.23)$$

where $f''(m)$ is the second derivative of the fitted forward curve and M is the maturity of the longest dated bond. The term $\lambda_t(m)$ is the 'roughness penalty'. Figure 5.6 shows that the spline-based method generates a more realistic curve, that better mirrors the strip yield curve seen in Figure 5.5.

5.5.2 Repo and Estimating the Short End of the Yield Curve

For the purposes of conducting monetary policy and for central government requirements, little use is made of the short end of the yield curve. This is for two reasons; one is that monetary and government policy is primarily concerned with medium-term views, for which a short-term curve has no practical input, the second is that there is often a shortage of data that can be used to fit the short-term curve accurately. In the same way that the long-term term structure

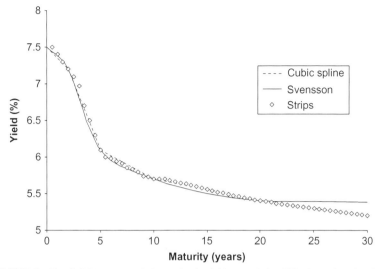

FIGURE 5.6   Fitted yield curves and observed strip yield curve, July 1998. *(Reproduced with permission from the Bank of England Quarterly Bulletin, November 1999.)*

must be fitted using risk-free instruments, the short-term curve can only be estimated using treasury bills. The T-bill can be restricted to only a small number of participants in some markets; moreover, the yield available on T-bills reflects its near cash, risk-free status, and so may not be the ideal instrument to use when seeking to extract market views on forward rates. So for liquidity purposes, the existence of an alternative instrument to T-bills would be useful. In most respects, the government repurchase market or repo market is a satisfactory substitute for T-bills, although there is an element of counterparty risk associated with repo that does not apply to T-bills, they can be considered to be essentially risk-free instruments, more so if margin has been taken by the party lending cash. We can, therefore, consider general collateral repo to be essentially a liquid, short-term and risk-free instrument.[7]

The fitted spot curve can differ considerably if yields on short-term repo are included. The effect is shown in Figure 5.7, which is reproduced from Anderson and Sleath (1999). Note that this is a short-term spot curve only; the maturity extends out to only 2 years. Two curves have been estimated; the cubic spline-based yield curve using the repo rate and without the repo rate. The curve that uses repo data generates a curve that is much closer to the money market yield curve than the one that does not. The only impact is at the very short end. After about 1 year, both approaches generate very similar curves.

---

7. See Choudhry (2002) for more information on the repo markets and the United Kingdom gilt repo market.

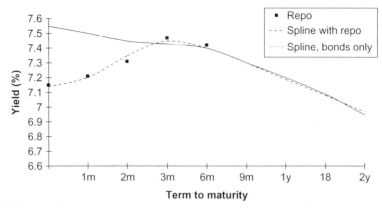

FIGURE 5.7   Fitting short-term yield curves using government repo rates. *(Reproduced with permission from the Bank of England Quarterly Bulletin, November 1999.)*

For an account of the impact of 'special' repo rates on term structure modelling see Barone and Risa (1994) and Duffie (1993), which are available from the respective institution Web sites.

5.6   MULTICURRENCY YIELD CURVE

The Credit Support Annexe (CSA) side agreement to the standard ISDA derivatives agreement often allows counterparties to a derivative to post collateral in the form of cash in a different denomination to the currency of the trade. As a result, banks now construct multicurrency yield curves to assist them with the funding decision when paying or receiving collateral.

The concept of the single-currency curve is straightforward and is covered in detail elsewhere in this chapter. Here we consider the concept of the multicurrency curve. As this is most relevant to collateralised interest-rate swaps (IRS), we place the discussion in this context.

5.6.1   IRS Rates and Discounting Levels

Generally, the market consensus has been to use Libor levels to discount swaps.[8] In a conventional positive sloping yield curve environment, forward Libor rates will be increasing along the term structure. In this environment a vanilla IRS, paying floating and receiving fixed, will have net positive cash flows at the start of its life (when the floating rate payment, typically 3- or 6-month Libor, is lower than the fixed rate), and net negative flows towards the end of its life (when the floating Libor fix is higher than the fixed rate).

---

8. We refer to the BBA Libor fixings for 0-12 months and the fixed rate on interbank swaps for 2-20 years as 'Libor rates'.

If discounting rates rise, then this will affect cash flows at the end of the swap's life by more than it affects flows at the start of the swap.

In other words, if market interest rates rise, the mark-to-market (mtm) value of a receive-fixed swap will be increasing as discounting rates rise. In turn, this means that the break-even rate of the swap moves lower; hence a market making swap bank will require a lower fixed rate if it is to price the swap correctly as discounting rates rise.

On the other hand, consider a receive-fixed IRS where the fixed payment is on an annual basis, while the floating leg pays quarterly 3-month Libor. If discounting rates rise, then this will affect the fixed leg payments by more than the floating leg payments, because fixed payments are received on a lower frequency and at a later time, so there is more time for the impact of discounting to take effect. In this case, the value of the receive-fixed swap is decreasing as discounting rates rise. Here, the break-even rate of the swap moves higher as rates rise.

The break-even rate to use when pricing an IRS is a function of the current discounting level. This is separate to the current interbank swap rate. The question then is what discount level to use when constructing the forward Libor curve from current swap rates. This is where the funding impact of swaps traded under a CSA agreement becomes pertinent. The party that is negative mtm on a collateralised swap will, under London Clearing House and SwapClear rules, will pass collateral in the local currency, which attracts the overnight-index swap (OIS) interest rate.

This, therefore, dictates that a dealer bank should use the local currency OIS curve as inputs to construct a curve of projected Libor rates from current interbank swap rates. Swaps traded in euro currency would be priced off the EONIA curve, sterling swaps off the SONIA curve, and so on.

5.6.2 Multicurrency Yield Curves

Where a swap is being priced in the local currency, it uses the projected 3-month Libor rate and OIS curve for valuation. A different issue arises when a bank posts collateral to cover a negative mtm swap in a currency other than that of the swap. This means a dealer bank needs to consider using a discount curve to value a swap across different currencies. The best way to look at this is to view it from the angle of a cross-currency swap, and the spread for such products. These swaps, which exchange currencies at inception and then return the same amount, pay floating-fixed (or floating-floating) interest in two different currencies. The principle for discounting them is identical to that of vanilla IRS.

We illustrate with an example. Consider a floating-floating cross-currency swap between EUR and GBP. The latter currency has higher forward rates. If the discount rate falls in both currencies, the EUR leg value will decrease by more than the GBP side. This is because a higher value of the EUR cash flows than the GBP cash flows is paid at maturity on the reexchange of principal.

To allow for this, the price of the GBP leg needs to be higher, to cover against this impact.

The question here is what discount level to use when pricing the cross-currency swap. In general, the market uses the OIS rate. Therefore, this rate should be used when building the multicurrency curve.

The starting point is that we set discount curves in all the main currencies, which are the relevant OIS curve. We can extract the discount factors for each currency from these curves, which we call Df_{CCY} for a general discount factor and Df_{OIS} for the relevant discount factor for the OIS in that currency. If we assume that FX rates are not correlated to interest rates (a big assumption, but necessary in this analysis), this implies that forward FX rates – which are a deposit product, as forward FX rates are simply spot FX rate adjusted for the deposit interest rate in each currency – are not a function of the discounting level in each currency. This further implies that the ratio of forward discount factors is constant.

This enables us to set the following relationship for any two currencies and any two rates:

$$\frac{Df_{CCY1}^{REFB}(t)}{Df_{CCY2}^{REFB}(t)} = \frac{DF_{CCY1}^{REFA}(t)}{DF_{CCY2}^{REFA}(t)}$$

We can then use this relationship to obtain the discount factor for any currency pair. Taking the base currency of euro, we set the currency to euro and the reference level to EONIA, as follows:

$$\frac{Df_{CCY}^{REF}(t)}{Df_{EUR}^{REF}(t)} = \frac{Df_{CCY}^{EONIA}(t)}{DF_{EUR}^{EONIA}(t)}$$

Setting one reference level to EONIA, we use these EONIA levels to obtain the reference level between any two currencies CCY1, CCY2, shown below:

$$\frac{Df_{CCY2}^{REF}(t)}{Df_{CCY1}^{REF}(t)} = \left(\frac{Df_{CCY2}^{REF}(t)}{Df_{EUR}^{REF}(t)} \bigg/ \frac{Df_{CCY1}^{REF}(t)}{Df_{EUR}^{REF}(t)}\right) = \left(\frac{Df_{CCY2}^{EONIA}(t)}{Df_{EUR}^{EONIA}(t)} \bigg/ \frac{Df_{CCY1}^{EONIA}(t)}{Df_{EUR}^{EONIA}(t)}\right)$$

$$= \frac{Df_{CCY2}^{EONIA}(t)}{Df_{CCY1}^{EONIA}(t)}$$

Using this relationship, we build the yield curve by obtaining the relevant reference rate for regular intervals on the term structure, and then obtaining the discount factors for each point along the term structure. This set of discount factors is then used to extract the yield curve.

Where the CSA in place allows a choice of two or more currencies out of EUR, GBP or USD for cash collateral, we will need to account for more than one reference level. This is done by constructing curves for each separate reference level as before, and then building a new curve by looking at each daily forward rate from the three curves, and taking the highest point for each point

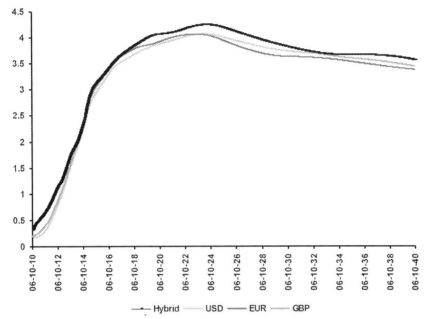

FIGURE 5.8   Hybrid discount yield curve.

along the curve as the data point for the curve. This process has 'equalised' the curves of the three different currencies. (Note that this process does not take into account the optionality value inherent in the fact that the poster of collateral has a choice as to which currency it posts.) A stylised illustration of such a 'hybrid' curve is shown in Figure 5.8.

The graph at Figure 5.8 shows the cross-currency basis-adjusted discount curves for IRS traded under four CSA scenarios: USD cash only, EUR cash only, GBP cash only and a choice of either of the three. A hybrid curve is not like a conventional yield curve constructed using Nelson-Siegel or cubic spline, because it is not a smooth curve. As the underlying forward curve changes from one currency to another, there is a kink at the changeover point. Hence as we show at Figure 5.8, at each point in time the orange hybrid curve overlaps with exactly one of the three single-currency curves and only three curves can be seen at any given time. Under conventional analysis, the bank that is negative mtm will post the currency of highest yield, or conversely of lowest funding cost.

The assumption of forward FX rates being uncorrelated to funding rates is perhaps the biggest issue for discussion. Certainly one would be right to state that FX spot rates do have positive correlation with changes in interest rates. The impact is greater where one of the currencies is a core currency such as USD, EUR, GBP and possibly CHF, which are held as reserve deposits by other country central banks. However, we make the assumption with respect to forward FX rates to enable us to construct a multicurrency curve. The issue of which currency we wish to receive as collateral is a separate discussion.

APPENDIX A   THE MCCULLOCH CUBIC SPLINE MODEL

This was first described by McCulloch (1975) and is referred to in Deacon and Derry (1994). We assume the maturity term structure is partitioned into q knot points with $q_1,\ldots,q_q$ where $q_1=0$ and q_q is the maturity of the longest dated bond. The remaining knot points are spaced such that there is, as far as possible, an equal number of bonds between each pair of knot points. With $j<q$, we employ the following functions:

- for $m<q_{j-1}$

$$f_j(m)=0 \qquad (5.24)$$

- for $q_{j-1}\le m\le q_j$

$$f_j(m)=\frac{(m-q_{j-1})^3}{6(q_j-q_{j-1})} \qquad (5.25)$$

- for $q_i\le m\le q_{j+1}$

$$f_j(m)=\frac{c^2}{6}+\frac{cf}{2}+\frac{f^2}{2}-\frac{f^3}{6(q_{j+1}-q_j)} \qquad (5.26)$$

- where

$$c=q_j-q_{j-1}$$
$$f=m-q_j$$

- for $q_{j+1}\le m$

$$f_j(m)=(q_{j+1}-q_{j-1})\left(\frac{2q_{j+1}-q_j-q_{j-1}}{6}+\frac{m-q_{j+1}}{2}\right) \qquad (5.27)$$

- for $j=q$

the function $f_q(m)=m$ for all values of m.

APPENDIX B   PARAMETRIC AND CUBIC SPLINE YIELD CURVE MODELS

In the Nelson and Siegel (1987) method, we may model the implied forward rate yield curve along the entire term structure using the following function:

$$rf(m, \ \beta) = \beta_0 + \beta_1 \exp\left(\frac{-m}{t_1}\right) + \beta_2 \left(\frac{m}{t_1}\right) \exp\left(\frac{-m}{t_1}\right) \tag{5.28}$$

where $\beta = (\beta_0, \beta_1, \beta_2 \ t_1)'$ is the vector of parameters describing the yield curve and m is the maturity at which the forward rate is calculated. There are three components, the constant term, a decay term and a term reflecting the 'humped' nature of the curve. The shape of the curve will gradually lead into an asymptote at the long end, the value of which is given by β_0, with a value of $\beta_0 + \beta_1$ at the short end.

Svensson (1994) presents a modification of this, by means of an adjustment to allow for the humped characteristic of most yield curves. This is fitted by adding an extension, as shown by Equation (5.29):

$$rf(m, \ \beta) = \beta_0 + \beta_1 \exp\left(\frac{-m}{t_1}\right) + \beta_2 \left(\frac{m}{t_1}\right) \exp\left(\frac{-m}{t_1}\right) + \beta_3 \left(\frac{m}{t_2}\right) \exp\left(\frac{-m}{t_2}\right).$$
$$\tag{5.29}$$

So we note that the Svensson curve is modelled using six parameters, the additional inputs being β_3 and t_2.

A different approach is adopted by smoothing cubic spline models. A generic spline is a segmented polynomial, or a curve that is constructed from individual polynomial segments that are joined together at user-specified 'knot points'. That is, the x-axis is divided into selected segments (the knot points). The segments can be at equal intervals or otherwise. At the knot points, the curve and its first derivative are continuous at all points along the curve. Generally the market uses cubic functions, resulting in a cubic spline. A cubic spline is given by Equation (5.30):

$$S(x) = ax^3 + \beta x^2 + \gamma x + \delta + \sum_{i=1}^{N-1} \eta_i |x - k_i|^3 \tag{5.30}$$

for a range of constants a, β, γ, δ, η and where k_i, $i = [0, N]$ is the set of knot points. The expression in Equation (5.30) is the most common one used for a cubic spline; however, in practice it is unwieldy for the purposes of calculation. Therefore, splines are usually constructed as a linear combination of cubic basis splines or B-splines. This is a general transformation which removes the numerical problems associated with Equation (5.30). A B-spline of order n can be written in the form:

$$B_{i,n}(x) = \frac{x - k_i}{k_{i+n-1} - k_i} B_{i,n-1}(x) + \frac{k_{i+n} - x}{k_{i+n} - k_{i+1}} B_{i+1,n-1}(x) \qquad (5.31)$$

where $B_{i,1}(x) = 1$ if $k_i \leq x < k_{i+1}$, and $B_{i,1}(x) = 0$ otherwise. This approach was described in Lancaster and Šalkauskas (1986). When a large number of knot points are used a cubic spline can be used for interpolation; however, as noted by Anderson and Sleath (1999) this approach is not used for monetary policy purposes, because it does not produce a smooth curve.

SELECTED BIBLIOGRAPHY AND REFERENCES

Anderson, N., Sleath, J., 1999. New estimates of the UK real and nominal yield curves. Bank of England Quarterly Bulletin, November, 39, 384–392.

Anderson, N., Breedon, F., Deacon, M., Derry, A., Murphy, M., 1996. Estimating and Interpreting the Yield Curve. Wiley, Chichester.

Bank of England, 1999. Quarterly Bulletin.

Barone, E., Risa, S., 1994. Valuation of Floaters and Options on Floaters Under Special Repo Rates. Instituto Mobiliare Italiano, Rome.

Bjork, T., Christensen, B., 1997. Interest Rate Dynamics and Consistent Forward Rate Curves. University of Aarhus, Aarhus, Denmark, Working Paper.

Bliss, R., 1997. Testing term structure estimation methods. Adv. Fut. Opt. Res. 9, 197–231.

Brenner, R., Jarrow, R., 1993. A simple formula for options on discount bonds. Adv. Fut. Opt. Res. 6, 45–51.

Choudhry, M., 2001. Bond Market Securities. FT Prentice Hall, London.

Choudhry, M., 2002. The Repo Handbook. Butterworth-Heinemann, Oxford.

Cox, J., Ingersoll, J., Ross, S., 1985. A theory of the term structure of interest rates. Econometrica 53, 385–407.

Dahlquist, M., Svensson, L., 1996. Estimating the term structure of interest rates for monetary policy analysis. Scand. J. Econ. 98, 163–183.

Deacon, M., Derry, A., 1994. Estimating the Term Structure of Interest Rates. Bank of England, London, Working Paper, No. 24.

Dothan, U., 1978. On the term structure of interest rates. J. Financ. Econ. 6, 59–69.

Duffie, D., 1993. Special Repo Rates. Stanford University, Graduate School of Business, Stanford, CA.

Edmister, R.O., Madan, D.P., 1993. Informational content in interest rate term structures. Rev. Econ. Stat. 75 (4), 695–699.

Fisher, M., Nychka, D., Zervos, D., 1995. Fitting the Term Structure of Interest Rates with Smoothing Splines. Federal Reserve Board, Finance and Economic Discussion Series 95–1.

Harrison, J., Pliska, S., 1981. Martingales and stochastic integrals in the theory of continuous trading. Stochastic Process. Appl. 11, 215–260.

Heath, D., Jarrow, R., Morton, A., 1992. A new methodology for contingent claims valuation. Econometrica 60, 76–106.

James, J., Webber, N., 2000. Interest Rate Modelling. Wiley, Chichester.

Kim, J., 1993. A Discrete-Time Approximation of a ONE-FACTOR MARKOV MODEL of the Term Structure of Interest Rates. Graduate School of Industrial Administration, Carnegie-Mellon University, Pittsburgh, PA.

Lancaster, P., Šalkauskas, K., 1986. Curve and Surface Fitting: An Introduction. Academic Press, London, UK.

Mastronikola, K., 1991. Yield Curves for Gilt-Edged Stocks: A New Model. Bank of England, London, Discussion Paper (Technical Series), No. 49.

McCulloch, J., 1971. Measuring the term structure of interest rates. J. Bus. 44, 19–31.

McCulloch, J., 1975. The tax adjusted yield curve. J. Financ. 30, 811–829.

Nelson, C., Siegel, A., 1987. Parsimonious modelling of yield curves. J. Bus. 60, 473.

Schaefer, S., 1981. Measuring a tax-specific term structure of interest rates in the market for British government securities. Econ. J. 91, 415–438.

Shea, G., 1985. Interest-rate term structure estimation with exponential splines: a note. J. Financ. 40 (1), 319–325.

Suits, D., Mason, A., Chan, L., 1978. Spline functions fitted by standard regression methods. Rev. Econ. Stat. 60, 132–139.

Svensson, L., 1994. Estimating and Interpreting Forward Interest Rates: Sweden 1992–94. International Monetary Fund, Working Paper 114.

Svensson, L., 1995. Estimating forward interest rates with the extended Nelson & Siegel method. Sveriges Riksbank Quart. Rev. 3, 13.

Vasicek, O., 1977. An equilibrium characterization of the term structure. J. Financ. Econ. 5, 177–188.

Vasicek, O., Fong, H.G., 1982. Term structure modelling using exponential splines. J. Financ. 37 (2), 339–356.

Waggoner, D., 1996. The Robustness of Yield and Forward Rate Extraction Methods. Federal Reserve Bank of Atlanta, Atlanta, GA, Unpublished Working Paper.

Waggoner, D., 1997. Spline Methods for Extracting Interest Rate Curves from Coupon Bond Prices. Federal Reserve Bank of Atlanta, Atlanta, GA, Working Paper, No. 97–10.

Wiseman, J., 1994. The Exponential Yield Curve Model. European Fixed Income Research, Technical Specification, JP Morgan.

Zheng, C., 1994. An arbitrage-Free SAINTS Model of Interest Rates. First National Bank of Chicago, Chicago, Working Paper.

Chapter 6

Advanced Analytics for Index-Linked Bonds

Chapter Contents

Bonds that have part or all of their cash flows linked to an inflation index form an important segment of several government bond markets. In the United Kingdom, the first index-linked bonds were issued in 1981 and at the end of 2012 they accounted for approximately 25% of outstanding nominal value in the gilt market. Index-linked bonds were also introduced in the United States Treasury market but are more established in Australia, Canada, the Netherlands, New Zealand and Sweden. There is no uniformity in market structure and as such there are significant differences between the index-linked markets in these countries. There is also a wide variation in the depth and liquidity of these markets.

Index-linked or inflation-indexed bonds present additional issues in their analysis, due to the nature of their cash flows. Measuring the return on index-linked bonds is less straightforward than with conventional bonds, and in certain cases there are peculiar market structures that must be taken into account as well. For example, in the United States market for index-linked treasuries (known as 'TIPS' from Treasury Inflation-Indexed Securities) there is no significant lag between the inflation link and the cash flow payment date. In the United Kingdom, there is an 8-month lag between the inflation adjustment of the cash flow and the cash flow payment date itself, while in New Zealand there is a 3-month lag. The existence of a lag means that inflation protection is not available in the lag period, and that the return in this period is exposed to inflation risk; it also must be taken into account when analysing the bond.

From market observation we know that index-linked bonds can experience considerable volatility in prices, similar to conventional bonds, and therefore, there is an element of volatility in the real yield return of these bonds. Traditional economic theory states that the level of real interest rates is constant; however, in practice they do vary over time. In addition, there are liquidity and supply and demand factors that affect the market prices of index-linked bonds. In this chapter, we present analytical techniques that can be applied to index-linked bonds, the duration and volatility of index-linked bonds and the concept of the real interest rate term structure. Moreover, we show the valuation of inflation-linked bonds with different cash flow structures and embedded options.

6.1 INDEX-LINKED BONDS AND REAL YIELDS

The real return generated by an index-linked bond, or its real yield, is usually defined as yield on risk-free index-linked bonds, or in other words the long-term interest rate on risk-free funds minus the effect of inflation. There may also be other factors involved, such as the impact of taxation. Therefore, the return on an index-linked bond should in theory move in line with the real cost of capital. This will be influenced by the long-term growth in the level of real gross domestic product in the economy. This is because in an economy experiencing rapid growth, real interest rates are pushed upwards as the demand for capital increases, and investors, therefore, expect higher real yields. Returns are also influenced by the demand for the bonds themselves.

The effect of general economic conditions and the change in these over time results in real yields on index-linked bonds fluctuating over time, in the same way nominal yields fluctuate for conventional bonds. This means that the price behaviour of indexed bonds can also be fairly volatile.

The yields on indexed bonds can be used to imply market expectations about the level of inflation. For analysts and policy makers to use indexed bond yields in this way, it is important that a liquid secondary market exists in the bonds themselves. For example, the market in Australian index-linked bonds is relatively illiquid, so attempting to extract an information content from their yields may not be valid. Generally, though, the real yields on indexed bonds reflect investors' demand for an inflation premium, or rather a premium for the uncertainty regarding future inflation levels. This is because holders of indexed bonds are not exposed to inflation-eroded returns; therefore, if future inflation was expected to be 0, or known with certainty (whatever its level) there would be no requirement for an inflation premium, because there would be no uncertainty. In the same way, the (nominal) yields on conventional bonds reflect market expectations on inflation levels. Therefore, higher volatility of the expected inflation rate will lead to a higher inflation risk premium on conventional bonds, and a lower real yield on indexed bonds relative to nominal yields. It is the uncertainty regarding future inflation levels that creates a demand for an inflation risk yield premium, rather than past experience of inflation levels. However, investor sentiment may well demand a higher inflation premium in a country with a poor record in combating inflation.

Therefore, the inflation expectation could be assumed comparing the yield of a conventional bond to the yield of an inflation-linked bond with similar maturity.[1] This average inflation expectation is known as 'break-even inflation rate' and is given by Fisher's equation (6.1):

$$BE = \frac{(1+r)}{(1+r_y)} - 1 \qquad (6.1)$$

where BE is the break-even inflation rate; r is the yield on the conventional bond and r_y is the yield on the inflation-linked bond. The yield breakdown is shown in Figure 6.1.

Therefore, the break-even analysis allows to determine the *spread* that equals the price of a conventional bond to the one of an inflation-linked bond. This approach assumes a risk-neutral pricing by which an investor treats conventional and inflation-linked bonds the same. Under break-even hypothesis, both bonds have the same nominal yield. Note if the inflation breakeven is greater than expected inflation, for an investor is favorable to buy a conventional bond. Conversely, the inflation-linked bond is more attractive. If inflation breakeven and expectations are equal, the investor bond's choice will be then indifferent. Figure 6.2 shows the trend of UKGGBE10 and UKGGBE20 Index

1. See Section 6.3.2.

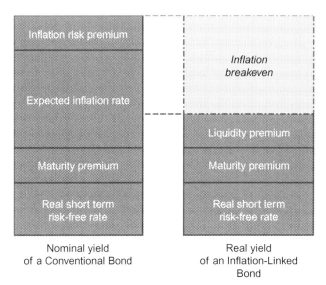

Nominal yield
of a Conventional Bond

Real yield
of an Inflation-Linked
Bond

FIGURE 6.1 Inflation Breakeven. *(Source Reproduced from J.P. Morgan 2013.)*

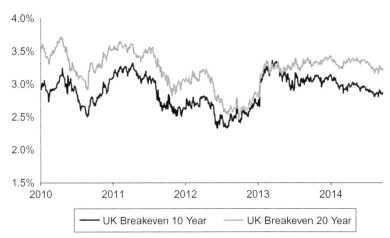

FIGURE 6.2 Ten years Inflation Breakeven, UKGGBE10 Index and UKGGBE20 Index. *(Data source: Bloomberg.)*

(2010-2014) that represent the break-even rates between nominal and real United Kingdom Treasury bonds with maturity of 10 and 20 years.

Also the simple difference between the yield of conventional and inflation-linked bonds or *yield spread* is an indicator for expected inflation. For example, on 18 September 2014 the 10-year UK 0 1/8% inflation-linked 2024 had a money yield of 2.125% and a real yield of –0.410%, assuming an inflation of 2.571%. Differently, the 10-year benchmark, the UK 2¼% 2023 had a gross

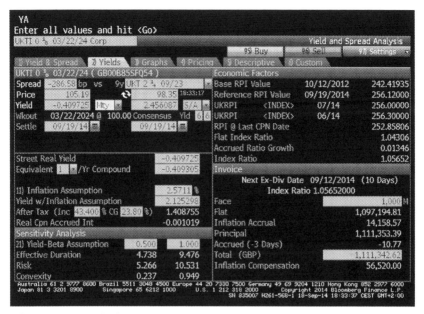

FIGURE 6.3 Example of index-linked yield analysis, UK 0 1/8% Treasury 2024 (assumed annual inflation rate 2.57%, base inflation index 242.4, reference RPI value 256.1), showing real yield and money yield, 18 September 2014. (*©Bloomberg L.P. Reproduced and used with permission.*)

redemption yield of 2.456%. Figure 6.3 shows the Bloomberg YA page for the UK 0 1/8% inflation-linked 2024.

Therefore, the yield spread is around 2% reflecting the expected inflation during the life of the bond. A higher inflation expectation will mean a greater spread between inflation-linked and conventional bonds.

This obviously approximates the expected inflation in which the yield spread cannot be attributed to the inflation only.

Traditionally, information on inflation expectations has been obtained by survey methods or theoretical methods. These have not proved reliable however, and were followed only because of the absence of an inflation-indexed futures market.[2] Certain methods for assessing market inflation expectations are not analytically valid; for example, the suggestion that the spread between short- and long-term bond yields cannot be taken to be a measure of inflation expectation, because there are other factors that drive this yield spread, and not just inflation risk premium.

Equally, the spread between the very short-term (overnight or 1 week) interest rate and the 2-year bond yield cannot be viewed as purely driven by inflation expectations. Using such approaches to glean information on inflation

---

2. The New York Coffee, Sugar and Cocoa Exchange traded a futures contract on the United States consumer prices index (CPI) in the 1980s.

expectations is logically unsound. One approach that is valid, as far as it goes, would be to analyse the spread between historical real and nominal yields, although this is not a forward-looking method. It would, however, indicate the market's inflation premium over a period of time. The best approach though is to use the indexed bond market; given a liquid market in conventional and index-linked bonds it is possible to derive estimates of inflation expectations from the yields of both sets of bonds. This is reviewed later in the chapter.

6.2   DURATION AND INDEX-LINKED BONDS

In earlier chapters, we reviewed the basic features of index-linked bonds and their main uses. We also discussed the techniques used to measure the yield on these bonds. The largest investors in indexed bonds are long-dated institutions such as pension fund managers, who use them to match long-dated liabilities that are also index linked; for example, a pension contract that has payments linked to the inflation index. It is common though for investors to hold a mixture of indexed and conventional bonds in their overall portfolio.

The duration of a bond is used as a measure of its sensitivity to changes in interest rate. The traditional measure, if applied to indexed bonds, will result in high values due to the low coupon on these bonds and the low real yield. In fact, the longest duration bonds in most markets are long-dated indexed bonds. The measure, if used in this way however, is not directly comparable to the duration measure for a conventional bond. Remember that the duration of a conventional bond measures its sensitivity to changes in (nominal) yields, or put another way to changes in the combined effect of inflation expectations and real yields. The duration measure of an indexed bond on the other hand, would be a measure of its sensitivity to changes in real yields only, that is, to changes in real interest-rate expectations. Conventionally, the price of an inflation-linked bond is less volatile than a conventional bond because the real yields of the former are less volatile than nominal yield of the second. Therefore, it is not valid to compare traditional duration measures between conventional and indexed bonds, because one would not be comparing like for like. If this analysis is made, the main assumption is that the implied inflation rate is 0 or constant for the overall observed time horizon. The current approach could be adjusted introducing the concept of *beta* or *inflation beta*. In corporate finance and portfolio theory, beta measures the sensitivity between an asset to the market portfolio or an index. In inflation-linked bonds, this analysis is known as 'inflation beta-adjusted duration'. The advantage of this adjustment is that it mitigates the protection for inflation included in this asset class. In practice, the beta is calculated as the sensitivity between real and nominal yields, given the same maturity or also between real yields and inflation rates. The choice of the time period influences the value of beta, in which a shorter time period determines higher volatility of beta and vice versa.

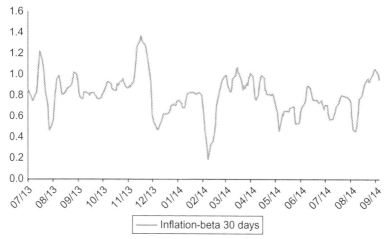

FIGURE 6.4 Inflation-beta calculated over 30 days. *(Data source: Bloomberg.)*

Figure 6.4 shows the inflation beta calculated as the correlation between nominal and real yield of the United Kingdom gilts, based to 30 days. How can be seen the inflation beta is unstable over time.

Moreover, the disadvantage of this analysis is that beta is calculated from historical data and not looking forward. Mathematically, the duration for an inflation-linked instrument is corrected as follows Equation (6.2)[3]:

$$D_{adj} = \beta_{ILB} \times D \tag{6.2}$$

where D_{adj} is the adjusted duration; β_{ILB} is the inflation beta and D is the unadjusted duration.

For instance, considering again the example of UK 0 1/8% inflation-linked 2024 shown in Figure 6.3. If we assume the analysis without the beta adjustment, the duration is equal to 9.48. Assuming a beta of 0.5, the adjusted duration becomes equal to 4.74.

The particular duration feature for inflation-linked bonds has important implications for the portfolio level. If a portfolio is composed of both conventional and indexed bonds, how does one measure its combined duration? The traditional approach of combining the duration values of individual bonds would have no meaning in this context, because the duration measure for each type of bond is measuring something different. For example, consider a situation where there are two portfolios with the same duration measure. If one portfolio was composed of a greater amount by weighting of index-linked bonds, it would have a different response to changes in market yields, especially so if investors' economic expectations shifted significantly, compared to the

---

3. The inflation adjustment can be made on both, Macaulay and Modified duration.

portfolio with a lower weighting in indexed bonds. Therefore, a duration-based approach to market risk would no longer be adequate as a means of controlling portfolio market risk.

Therefore, the key focus of fund managers that run combined portfolios of conventional and indexed bonds is to manage the duration of the conventional and indexed bonds on a separate basis, and to be aware of the relative weighting of the portfolio in terms of the two bond types. A common approach is to report two separate duration values for the portfolio, which would measure two separate types of risk exposure. One measure would be the *portfolio real yield duration*, which is the value of the combined durations of both the conventional and indexed bonds. This measure is an indication of how the portfolio value will be affected by a change in market real yields, which would impact both indexed and conventional bond yields. The other measure would be the *portfolio inflation duration*, which is a duration measure for the conventional bonds only. This duration measure indicates the sensitivity of the portfolio to a change in market inflation expectations, which have an impact on nominal yields, but not real yields. Portfolio managers also follow a similar approach with regard to interest-rate volatility scenarios. Therefore if carrying out a parallel yield curve shift simulation, which in terms of a combined portfolio would actually correspond to a real-yield simulation, the portfolio manager would also need to undertake a simulation that mirrored the effect of a change in inflation expectations, which would have an impact on nominal yields only.

The traditional duration approach can be used with care in other areas. For instance, the Bank of England monetary policy committee is tasked with keeping inflation at a level of 2.5%. If, therefore, the 10-year benchmark gilt is trading at a yield of 6.00% while the 10-year index-linked gilt is trading at a real yield of 3.00%, this implies that the market expectation of average inflation rates during the next 10 years is 3.00%. This would suggest that the benchmark gilt is undervalued relative to the indexed gilt. To effect a trade that matched the market maker's view, one would short the 10-year index-linked gilt and buy the conventional gilt. If the view turned out to be correct and market inflation expectations declined, the trade would generate a profit. If on the other hand real interest-rate expectations changed, thus altering real yields, there would be no effect. The other use of the traditional duration approach is with regard to hedging. Indexed bonds are sometimes difficult to hedge because of the lack of suitable hedging instruments. The most common hedging instrument is another indexed bond, and the market maker would use a duration weighting approach to calculate the nominal value of the hedging bond.

In the traditional approach the duration value is calculated using nominal cash flows, discounted at the nominal yield. A more common approach is to assume a constant average rate of inflation, and adjust cash flows using this inflation rate. The real yield is then used to discount the assumed future cash flows. There are a number of other techniques that can be used to calculate a duration value, all requiring the forecasting of the level of future cash flows and discounting using the nominal yield. These include:

- As above, assuming a constant average inflation rate, which is then used to calculate the value of the bond's coupon and redemption payments. The duration of the cash flow is then calculated by observing the effect of a parallel shift in the zero-coupon yield curve. By assuming a constant inflation rate and constant increase in the cash flow stream, a further assumption is made that the parallel shift in the yield curve is as a result of changes in real yields, not because of changes in inflation expectations. Therefore, this duration measure becomes in effect a real yield duration;
- A repeat of the above procedure, with the additional step, after the shift in the yield curve, of recalculating the bond cash flows based on a new inflation forecast. This produces a duration measure that is a function of the level of nominal yields. This measure is in effect an inflation duration, or the sensitivity to changes in market inflation expectations, which is a different measure to the real yield duration;
- An assumption that the inflation scenario will change by an amount based on the historical relationship between nominal yields and the market expectation of inflation. This is in effect a calculation of nominal yield duration, and would be a measure of sensitivity to changes in nominal yields.

Possibly the most important duration measure is the real yield duration, which is more significant in markets where there is a lag between the indexation and cash flow dates, due to the inflation risk exposure that is in place during the lag period. This is the case in both the United Kingdom and Australia, although as we noted the lag is not significant in the United States market. It is worth noting that index-linked bonds do not have stable nominal duration values, that is, they do not exhibit a perfectly predictable response to changes in nominal yields. If they did, there would be no advantage in holding them, as their behaviour could be replicated by conventional bonds. For this reason, index-linked bonds cannot be hedged perfectly with conventional bonds, although this does happen in practice on occasions when no other hedging instrument is available.

One final point regarding duration is that it is possible to calculate a *tax-adjusted duration* for an index-linked bond in markets where there is a different tax treatment to indexed bonds compared to conventional bonds. In the United States market, the returns on indexed and conventional bonds are taxed in essentially the same manner, so that in similar fashion to Treasury strips, the inflation adjustment to the indexed bond's principal is taxable as it occurs, and not only on the maturity date. Therefore, in the US-indexed bonds do not offer protection against any impact of after-tax effects of high inflation. That is, Tips real yields reflect a premium for only pretax inflation risk. In the United Kingdom market however, index-linked gilts receive preferential tax treatment, so their yields also reflect a premium for after-tax inflation risk. In practice, this means that the majority of indexed gilt investors are those with high marginal tax rates.[4] This factor also introduces another element in analysis; if the demand for indexed or conventional bonds were to be a function of expected after-tax returns, this would imply that pretax real yields should rise as expected inflation rates rise, in order to maintain a constant after-tax real yield. This has not been observed explicitly in practice, but is a further factor of uncertainty about the behaviour of real yields on index-linked bonds.[5]

6.3 ESTIMATING THE REAL TERM STRUCTURE OF INTEREST RATES

In Chapter 11 of the author's book *The Bond and Money Markets*, we show some approaches used to measure inflation expectations, with reference to the United Kingdom index-linked gilts. To recap, these measures include:

- The 'simple' approach, where the average expected inflation rate is calculated using the Fisher identity, so that the inflation estimate is regarded as the straight difference between the real yield on an index-linked bond, at an assumed average rate of inflation, and the yield on a conventional bond of similar maturity;
- The 'break-even' inflation expectation, where average inflation expectations are estimated by comparing the return on a conventional bond against that on an indexed bond of similar maturity, but including an application of the compound form of the Fisher identity. This has the effect of decomposing the nominal rate of return on the bond into components of real yield and inflation;
- A variation of the break-even approach, but matching stocks by duration rather than by maturity.

The drawbacks of each of these approaches are apparent. A rather more valid and sound approach is to construct a term structure of the real interest rates, which would indicate, in exactly the same way that the conventional forward rate curve does for nominal rates, the market's expectations on future inflation rates. In countries where there are liquid markets in both conventional and inflation-indexed bonds, we can observe a nominal and a real yield curve. It then becomes possible to estimate both a conventional and a real term structure; using these allows us to create pairs of hypothetical conventional and indexed bonds that have identical maturity dates, for any point on the term structure.[6] We could then apply the break-even approach to any pair of bonds

---

4. For example, see Brown and Schaefer (1996).
5. For further detail on this phenomenon, see Roll (1996).
6. We are restricted, however, to the longest dated maturity of either of the two types of bonds.

to obtain a continuous curve for both the average and the forward inflation expectations. To maximise use of the available information, we can use all the conventional and indexed bonds that have reasonable liquidity in the secondary market.

In this section, we review one method that can be used to estimate and fit a real term structure.

6.3.1   The Term Structure of Implied Forward Inflation Rates

In previous chapters, we reviewed the different approaches to yield curve modelling used to derive a nominal term structure of interest rates. We saw that the choice of yield curve model can have a significant effect on the resulting term structure; in the same way, the choice of model will impact the resulting real rate term structure as well. One approach has been described by McCulloch (1975), while in the United Kingdom market the Bank of England uses a modified version of the approach posited by Waggoner (1997) which we discussed in the previous chapter. McCulloch's approach involves estimating a discount function by imposing a constraint on the price of bonds in the sample to equal the sum of the discounted values of the bonds' cash flows. The Waggoner approach uses a cubic spline-based method, like McCulloch, with a roughness penalty that imposes a trade-off between the smoothness of the curve and its level of forward rate oscillation. The difference between the two approaches is that with McCulloch it is the discount function that is specified by the spline function, whereas in the Waggoner model it is the zero-coupon curve. Both approaches are valid, in fact due to the relationship between the discount function, zero-coupon rate and forward rate, both methods will derive similar curves under most conditions.

Using the prices of index-linked bonds, it is possible to estimate a term structure of real interest rates. The estimation of such a curve provides a real interest counterpart to the nominal term structure that was discussed in the previous chapters. More important it enables us to derive a real forward rate curve. This enables the real yield curve to be used as a source of information on the market's view of expected future inflation. In the United Kingdom market, there are two factors that present problems for the estimation of the real term structure; the first is the 8-month lag between the indexation uplift and the cash flow date, and the second is the fact that there are fewer index-linked bonds in issue, compared to the number of conventional bonds. The indexation lag means that in the absence of a measure of expected inflation, real bond yields are dependent to some extent on the assumed rate of future inflation. The second factor presents practical problems in curve estimation; in December 1999 there were only 11 index-linked gilts in existence, and this is not sufficient for most models. Neither of these factors presents an insurmountable problem however, and it is still possible to estimate a real term structure.

6.3.2   Estimating the Real Term Structure[7]

There are a number of techniques that can be applied in estimating the real term structure. One method was described by Schaefer (1981). The method we describe here is a modified version of the cubic spline technique described by Schaefer. This is a relatively straightforward approach. The adjustment involves simplifying the model, ignoring tax effects and fitting the yield-to-maturity structure. A reduced number of nodes defining the cubic spline is specified compared with the conventional term structure, because of the fewer number of index-linked bonds available, and usually only three node points are used. Our approach, therefore, estimates three parameters, defining a spline consisting of two cubic functions, using 11 data points. The approach is defined below.

In the first instance, we require the real redemption yield for each of the indexed bonds. This is the yield that is calculated by assuming a constant average rate of inflation, applying this to the cash flows for each bond, and computing the redemption yield in the normal manner. The yield is, therefore, the market-observed yield, using the price quoted for each bond. These yields are used to define an initial estimate of the real yield curve, as they form the initial values of the parameters that represent the real yield at each node point. The second step is to use a nonlinear technique to estimate the values of the parameters that will minimise the sum of the squared residuals between the observed and fitted real yields. The fitted yield curve is viewed as the real par yield curve; from this curve we calculate the term structure of real interest rates and the implied forward rate curve, using the technique described in Chapter 5. In estimating the real term structure in this way, we need to be aware of any tax effects. In the United Kingdom market, there is a potentially favourable tax effect, which may not apply in say, the United States Tips market. Generally for UK-indexed gilts, high marginal taxpayers are the biggest holders of index-linked bonds because of the ratio of capital gain to income, and their preference is to hold shorter dated indexed bonds. On the other hand pension funds, which are exempt from income tax, prefer to hold longer dated indexed gilts. The approach we have summarised here ignores any tax effects, but to be completely accurate any tax impact must be accounted for in the real term structure.

6.3.3   Fitting the Discount Function

The term structure method described by McCulloch (1971) involved fitting a discount function, rather than a spot curve, using the market prices of a sample

---

7. This section follows the approach (with permission) from Deacon and Derry (1994), a highly accessible account. This is their Bank of England working paper, 'Deriving Estimates of Inflation Expectations from the Prices of UK Government Bonds'.

of bonds. This approach can be used with only minor modifications to produce a real term structure. Given the bond price Equation (6.3):

$$P_i = C_i \int_0^{T_i} df(\mu)d\mu + M_i df(T_i) \qquad (6.3)$$

where P_i, C_i, T_i and M_i are the price, coupon, maturity and principal payment of the i-th bond, we set the set of discrete discount factors as the discount function df, defined as a linear combination of a set of k linearly independent underlying basis functions, given by Equation (6.4):

$$df(T) = 1 + \sum_{j=1}^{k} a_j f_j(T) \qquad (6.4)$$

where $f_j(T)$ is the j-th basis function and a_j is the corresponding coefficient, with $j = 1, 2, \ldots, k$. It can be shown (see Deacon and Deny (1994)) that for index-linked bonds equation (6.4) can be adapted by a scaling factor Δ_i that is known for each bond, once an assumption has been made about the future average inflation rate, to fit a discount function for indexed bonds. We estimate the coefficients a_j from:

$$y_i = \sum_{j=1}^{k} a_j x_{ij}$$

where

$$y_i = P_i - \Delta_i C_i T_i - \Delta_i M_i$$
$$x_{ij} = \Delta_i C_i \int_0^{T_i} f_j \mu \, d\mu + \Delta_i M_i f_j(T_i)$$
$$u = (1 + \pi^e)^{-1/2}$$

$$\Delta_i = \begin{cases} [u^{t\,dj}]_i \cdot \dfrac{\text{RPID}_j}{\text{RPIB}_i} & \text{if } \text{RPID}_j \text{ is known} \\ [u^{t\,dl - L/6}]_i \cdot \dfrac{\text{RPIL}}{\text{RPIB}_i} & \text{otherwise} \end{cases}$$

where P_i, C_i, T_i, M_i are as before, but this time representing the index-linked bond. The scaling factor Δ_i is that for the i-th bond, and depends on the ratio of the retail price index (RPI) at the time compared to the RPI level in place at the time the bond was issued, known as the *base* RPI.[8] If in fact the RPI that is used to index any particular cash flow is not known, it must be estimated using the latest available RPI figure, in conjunction with an assumption about the path of future inflation, using π^e.

8. Due to the lag in the United Kingdom gilt market, for index-linked gilts the base RPI is actually the level recorded for the 8 months before the issue date.

6.3.4 Deriving the Term Structure of Inflation Expectations

Using any of the methods described in Chapter 5 or the discount function approach summarised above, we can construct curves for both the nominal and the real implied forward rates. These two curves can then be used to infer market expectations of future inflation rates. The term structure of forward inflation rates is obtained from both these curves by applying the Fisher identity:

$$1 + \frac{f}{2} = (1 + i)^{1/2} \left(1 + \frac{r}{2}\right) \tag{6.5}$$

where f is the implied nominal forward rate; r is the implied real forward rate and i is the implied forward inflation rate. As with the term structure of real spot rates, the real implied forward rate curve is dependent on an assumed rate of inflation. To make this assumption consistent with the inflation term structure that is calculated, we can use an iterative procedure for the assumed inflation rate. Essentially this means that the real yield curve is reestimated until the assumed inflation term structure and the estimated inflation term structure are consistent. Real yields are usually calculated using either a 3% or a 5% flat inflation rate. This enables us to estimate the real yield curve, from which the real forward rate curve is derived. Using (6.5) we can then obtain an initial estimate of the inflation term structure. This forward inflation curve is then converted into an average inflation curve, using Equation (6.6):

$$i_i = \prod_{j}^{k} (1 + if_i)^{-1/k} - 1 \tag{6.6}$$

where if_i is the forward inflation rate at maturity i and i_i is the average inflation rate at maturity i.

From this average inflation curve, we can select specific inflation rates for each index-linked bond in our sample. The real yields on each indexed bond are then recalculated using these new inflation assumptions. From these yields the real forward curve is calculated, enabling us to produce a new estimate of the inflation term structure. This process is repeated until there is consistency between the inflation term structure used to estimate the real yields and that produced by Equation (6.5).

Using the modified Waggoner method described in Chapter 5, the nominal spot yield curve for the gilt market in July 1999 is shown in Figure 6.5. The real term structure is also shown, which enables us to draw the implied forward inflation expectation curve, which is simply the difference between the first two curves.

6.3.5 Application

Real yield curves are of some use to investors, for a number of reasons. These include applications that arise in insurance investment management and corporate finance, such as the following:

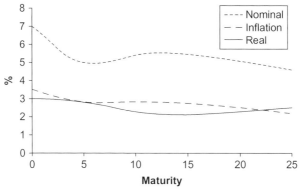

FIGURE 6.5 United Kingdom market nominal and real term structure of interest rates, July 1999. *(Yield source: BoE)*

- They can be used to value inflation-linked liabilities, such as index-linked annuity contracts;
- They can be used to value inflation-linked revenue streams, such as taxes that are raised in line with inflation, or for returns generated in corporate finance projects; this makes it possible to assess the real returns of project finance or government revenue;
- They can be used to estimate the present value of a company's future staff costs, which are broadly linked to inflation.

Traditionally, valuation methods for such purposes would use nominal discount rates and an inflation forecast, which would be constant. Although the real term structure also includes an assumption element, using estimated market real yields is equivalent to using a nominal rate together with an implied market inflation forecast, which need not be constant. This is a more valid approach; a project financier in the United Kingdom in July 1999 can obtain more meaningful estimates on the effects of inflation using the rates implied in Figure 6.2, rather than an arbitrary, constant inflation rate. The inflation term structure can be used in other ways as well; for example, an investor in mortgage-backed bonds, who uses a prepayment model to assess the prepayment risk associated with the bonds, will make certain assumptions about the level of prepayment of the mortgage pool backing the bond. This prepayment rate is a function of a number of factors, including the level of interest rates, house prices and the general health of the economy. Rather than use an arbitrary assumed prepayment rate, the rate can be derived from market inflation forecasts.

In essence, the real yield curve can and should be used for all the purposes for which the nominal yield curve is used. Provided that there are enough liquid index-linked bonds in the market, the real term structure can be estimated using standard models, and the result is more valid as a measure of market inflation expectations than any of the other methods that have been used in the past.

6.4 THE VALUATION OF INFLATION-LINKED BONDS

To obtain the price of an inflation-linked bond, it is necessary to determine the value of coupon payments and principal repayment. Inflation-linked bonds can be structured with a different cash flow indexation. As noted above, duration, tax treatment and reinvestment risk, are the main factors that affect the instrument design. For instance, index-annuity bonds that give to the investor a fixed annuity payment and a variable element to compensate the inflation have the shortest duration and the highest reinvestment risk of all inflation-linked bonds. Conversely, inflation-linked zero-coupon bonds have the highest duration of all inflation-linked bonds and do not have reinvestment risk. In addition, also the tax treatment affects the cash flow structure. In some bond markets, the inflation adjustment on the principal is treated as current income for tax purpose, while in other markets it is not.

6.4.1 Forecasting the Inflation-Index Level

The first step for estimating future streams is to know the expected inflation. To do this, the procedure needs the future trend of index in which the inflation expectation is built. The inflation expectation determined by countries is based on a different basket of products and services. For instance, inflation-linked bonds issued in the United Kingdom or *UK index-linked gilts*, are linked to the Retail Price Index (RPI); inflation-linked bonds issued in the United States or *TIPS* are linked to the Consumer Price Index (CPI). Table 6.1 summarizes the key global inflation indices used by the major issuers of inflation-linked bonds.

Therefore, in order to obtain the future index level we consider the actual index level as at bond issue and we assume a constant inflation rate. The expected 1 year index level is given by Equation (6.7):

$$I_1 = I_0 \times (1 + \tau) \tag{6.7}$$

where I_1 is the expected index level for 1 year; I_0 is the actual index level and τ is the annual inflation rate.

6.4.2 Valuing the Inflation-Linked Bonds

The price of an inflation-linked bond is determined as the present value of future coupon payments and principal at maturity. Like a conventional bond, the valuation depends on the cash flow structure. We can have three main cash flow structures of index-linked bonds.

6.4.2.1 Inflation-Linked Bonds with Zero-Coupon Indexation

Zero-coupon bonds linked to the inflation do not pay coupons. Therefore, the unique adjustment is made to the principal. These types of bonds offer no

TABLE 6.1 Key Global Inflation Indices

Key global inflation indices

Country	Issue	Inflation Index
United States	Treasury Inflation-Protected Securities (TIPS)	US Consumer Price Index (NSA)
United Kingdom	Inflation-Linked Gilt	Retail Price Index
Japan	JGBI	Japan CPI
Germany	Bund Index and BO Index	EU HICP exTobacco
France	OATI and OATei	France CPI ex-tobacco (OATI), EU HICP (OATei)
Canada	Real Return Bond	Canada All-items CPI
Australia	Capital Indexed Bonds	ACPI
Sweden	Index-Linked Treasury Bonds	Swedish CPI
Italy	BTP€i	EU HICP exTobacco

Reproduced from Standard Life Investments, 2013.

reinvestment risk due to the absence of coupon payments and have the longest duration than other inflation-linked bonds. The value is given by Equation (6.8):

$$P_{IL} = \frac{M_{IL}}{(1+r)^N} \tag{6.8}$$

where P_{IL} is the fair price of an inflation-linked bond; M_{IL} is the indexed principal repayment and r is the money or nominal yield.

The inflation adjustment on the redemption value can be derived as follows Equation (6.9):

$$M_{IL} = M \times \frac{I_M}{I_i} \tag{6.9}$$

where M is the redemption value; I_M is the expected index level as at maturity date and I_i is the actual index level as at issue date.

Table 6.2 illustrates the cash flow structure of an inflation-linked bond with zero-coupon indexation.

6.4.2.2   Inflation-Linked Bonds with Coupon Indexation

The pricing of this type of bond is similar to a straight bond, that is, the value is found as the present value of expected coupons and principal. The main

TABLE 6.2 The Cash Flow Structure with Zero-Coupon Bond Indexation

	0	1	2	3	4	5
Coupon payment		0	0	0	0	0
Expected inflation		2.1%	1.8%	2.0%	2.0%	1.9%
Compounded expected inflation		1.02	1.04	1.06	1.08	1.10
Inflation adjusted Coupon payment		0	0	0	0	0
Indexed Principal repayment						110.18

difference is that coupon payments are linked to the inflation. The value of bond is given by Equation (6.10):

$$P_{IL} = \sum_{t=1}^{t=N} \frac{C_{ILt}}{(1+r)^t} + \frac{M}{(1+r)^N} \qquad (6.10)$$

where P_{IL} is the fair price of an inflation-linked bond; C_{ILt} is the inflation-adjusted coupon payment; M is the redemption value and r is the money or nominal yield.

As noted above for inflation-linked bonds with zero-coupon indexation, the coupon can be adjusted in a similar way:

$$C_{IL} = C \times \frac{I_t}{I_i} \qquad (6.11)$$

where C_{IL} is the inflation-adjusted coupon payment; C is the coupon payment; I_t is the expected index level as at next coupon date and I_i is the actual index level as at issue date.

Table 6.3 illustrates the cash flow structure of an inflation-linked bond with coupon indexation.

6.4.2.3 Inflation-Linked Bonds with Coupon and Principal Indexation

Another structure for inflation-linked bonds is when both, coupons and principal, are linked to the inflation.[9] The value is given by (6.12):

$$P_{IL} = \sum_{t=1}^{t=N} \frac{C_{ILt}}{(1+r)^t} + \frac{M_{IL}}{(1+r)^N} \qquad (6.12)$$

---

9. See in Appendix A the example of bond pricing.

TABLE 6.3 The Cash Flow Structure with Coupon Indexation

	0	1	2	3	4	5
Coupon payment		2	2	2	2	2
Expected inflation		2.1%	1.8%	2.0%	2.0%	1.9%
Compounded expected inflation		1.02	1.04	1.06	1.08	1.10
Inflation adjusted Coupon payment		2.04	2.08	2.12	2.16	2.20
Principal repayment						100

or

$$P_{IL} = \frac{C_1 \times (I_1/I_0)}{(1+r)} + \frac{C_2 \times (I_2/I_0)}{(1+r)^2} + \cdots + \frac{M \times (I_N/I_0)}{(1+r)^N}$$
$$= \frac{C_{IL1}}{(1+r)} + \frac{C_{IL2}}{(1+r)^2} + \cdots + \frac{M_{IL}}{(1+r)^N} \qquad (6.13)$$

where P_{IL} is the fair price of an inflation-linked bond; C_{IL} is the inflation-adjusted coupon payment; M_{IL} is the indexed principal repayment and r is the money or nominal yield.

Table 6.4 illustrates the cash flow structure of an inflation-linked bond with coupon and principal indexation.

TABLE 6.4 The Cash Flow Structure with Coupon and Principal Indexation

	0	1	2	3	4	5
Coupon payment		2	2	2	2	2
Expected inflation		2.1%	1.8%	2.0%	2.0%	1.9%
Compounded expected inflation		1.02	1.04	1.06	1.08	1.10
Inflation adjusted Coupon payment		2.04	2.08	2.12	2.16	2.20
Indexed Principal repayment						110.18

EXAMPLE 6.1 Inflation premium

Consider the example in which a hypothetical conventional bond and inflation-linked bond pay an annual coupon of 2%, with a discount rate of 3%. The second one pays coupons and principal linked to the inflation. To understand the effect of the inflation, Figure 6.6 shows the loss of value of a conventional bond compared to an inflation-linked bond. The evidence is that maintaining a flat discount rate, a change of the inflation rate affects only to an inflation-linked bond, increasing its value, while the value of a conventional bond remains unchanged. In reality, over the bond's life, the value of the first one remains unchanged while the value of second one depreciates as the inflation increases.

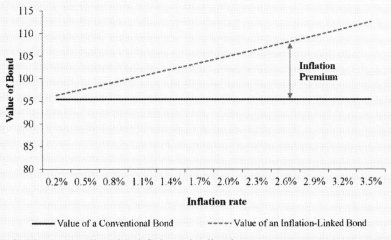

FIGURE 6.6 The effect of the inflation on bond's value.

If the price of an inflation-linked bond is 104.95 and the price of a conventional bond is 95.42, the difference of value represents the inflation premium, or 9.53.

6.4.3 Other Features of Inflation-Linked Securities

6.4.3.1 Bond valuation with real cash flows and yields

We currently illustrate the pricing of inflation-linked bonds adopting real cash flows. As noted earlier, according to Fisher's theory, the real yield is given by the following equation:

$$r_y = \frac{(1+r)}{(1+\tau)} - 1 \tag{6.14}$$

where r_y is the real yield; r is the money or nominal yield and τ is the annual inflation rate.

In hypothesis by which both coupons and redemption value are linked to the inflation, we can rearrange the Equations (6.12) and (6.13) as follows:

$$P_{\text{IL}} = \sum_{t=1}^{t=N} \frac{C}{(1+r_y)^t} + \frac{M}{(1+r_y)^N} = \frac{C_1}{(1+r_y)} + \frac{C_2}{(1+r_y)^2} + \cdots + \frac{M}{(1+r_y)^N} \quad (6.15)$$

Therefore, in Equations (6.12) and (6.13) we use both nominal cash flows and discount rates. Conversely, in Equation (6.15) the real yield is the appropriate discount rate for discounting real cash flows. This relationship is true only in the perfect indexation scenario without indexation lag.

6.4.3.2   The Deflation Floor

In a deflationary environment a conventional bond performs very well, while an inflation-linked bond gives negative returns. Some of inflation-linked bonds include deflation protection.[10] In practice, in the event of deflation, the bondholder will receive at maturity the par value although the redemption value is less than 100. Therefore, the bondholder will obtain at least the par value. Note that the deflation floor applies to the redemption value only leaving coupon payments exposed to the deflation risk.

This feature can be assimilated as an embedded put option by which the investor will receive the par value, in the case of deflation, or the redemption value linked to the inflation. The payoff is given by Equation (6.16):

$$\text{Redemption value} = M_{\text{IL}} + \max\left(0, M - M_{\text{IL}}\right) \quad (6.16)$$

or by Equation (6.17):

$$\text{Redemption value} = \max\left(M, M_{\text{IL}}\right) \quad (6.17)$$

Therefore, we propose an example in which we price an inflation-linked bond by using a binomial tree. Conventionally, this type of pricing model is not implemented in the reality, but it allows to understand the impact of the embedded option on bond's value.

Considering the example in which a 5-year bond pays an annual coupon of 1%, with a discount rate of 2%. The bond price is given by the following steps:

- Determining the binomial inflation rate tree;
- Determining the value of coupon payments and principal repayment;
- Determining the value of a European put option;
- Determining the value of an inflation-linked bond.

The first step determines the binomial inflation rate tree according to the inflation expectations. The binomial tree is used for pricing a hypothetical annual

---

10. For example, inflation-linked bonds issue in the United States, Italy, France, Sweden and Germany. Note that inflation-linked bonds issue in the United Kingdom does not include deflation protection.

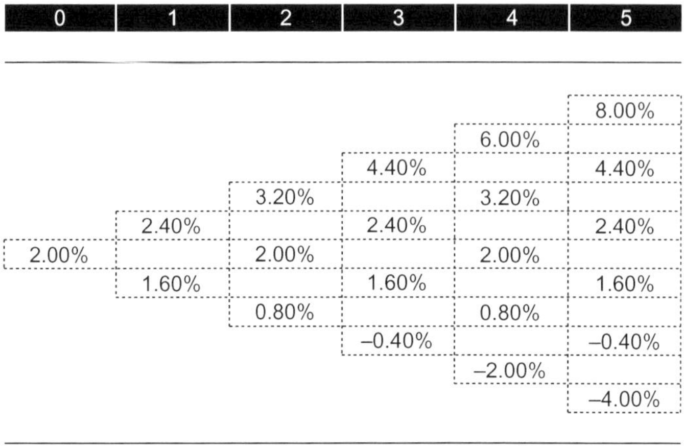

0	1	2	3	4	5
					8.00%
				6.00%	
			4.40%		4.40%
		3.20%		3.20%	
	2.40%		2.40%		2.40%
2.00%		2.00%		2.00%	
	1.60%		1.60%		1.60%
		0.80%		0.80%	
			−0.40%		−0.40%
				−2.00%	
					−4.00%

FIGURE 6.7 Binomial inflation rate tree.

inflation-linked bond. In order to predict the evolution of the inflation rate we assume a volatility of 0.4%, calculated as 30 days annualized standard deviation of the break-even inflation rate. Figure 6.7 shows the binomial inflation rate tree.

However, this is not the market inflation rate. Therefore, the binomial inflation rate tree is fitted with the market inflation rate curve because the inflation rate derived by the model differs from the one observed in the market or implied inflation rate. Thus, using the *drift* factor, the binomial inflation rate tree is adjusted with the numerical iteration process setting the *pricing error* (difference between model inflation rate curve and market inflation rate curve) equal to 0. Note that in an environment with higher expected inflation the pricing error will be greater and vice versa. Note also that in an environment with lower expected inflation the probability of deflation scenario rises, increasing the value of the embedded option. Figure 6.8 shows the binomial tree with the market inflation rate.

After having determined the binomial inflation rate tree, we calculate the value of coupon payments and principal repayment. Each coupon is linked to the inflation rate in the binomial inflation rate tree and the value is obtained as the present value of coupon payments.

In the same way, the value of the principal repayment is given at maturity as the par value linked to the inflation rate (Figure 6.9). Consequently, the principal is discounted at time 0. For instance, at higher node t_5, the pricing is given by (6.18):

$$P_{IL} = \frac{(108.70 \times 0.5) + (105.10 \times 0.5)}{(1+0.02)} = 104.80 \qquad (6.18)$$

Note that when the binomial inflation rate tree is negative, therefore, with a deflation rate, the value of both coupons and principal decreases. For

0	1	2	3	4	5
					8.70%
				6.56%	
			4.82%		5.10%
		3.48%		3.76%	
	2.54%		2.82%		3.10%
2.00%		2.28%		2.56%	
	1.74%		2.02%		2.30%
		1.08%		1.36%	
			0.02%		0.30%
				−1.44%	
					−3.30%

FIGURE 6.8 Binomial inflation rate tree with market expectations.

0	1	2	3	4	5
					1.09
				2.11	
			3.09		1.05
		4.04		2.06	
	4.96		3.03		1.03
4.83		3.98		2.03	
	4.89		3.00		1.02
		3.92		2.01	
			2.94		1.00
				1.95	
					0.97

0	1	2	3	4	5
					108.70
				104.81	
			101.40		105.10
		98.43		102.06	
	95.69		99.39		103.10
93.02		96.78		100.69	
	94.07		98.04		102.30
		95.13		99.32	
			96.02		100.30
				96.57	
					96.70

FIGURE 6.9 Binomial tree of coupon payments and principal repayment.

instance, in the last year and node, the value of the principal is lower than 100 (96.70).

Therefore, without considering the deflation floor, the value of an inflation-linked bond is equal to $4.83 + 93.02 = 97.85$.

The benefit of the deflation floor is assimilated to a European put option in which the payoff is given by Equation (6.19):

$$P_T^{\text{put option}} = \max\left(0, M - M_{\text{IL}}\right) \qquad (6.19)$$

in which M is the strike price of the option or par value, in this case 100, and M_{IL} is the value of the principal at maturity T that follows the binomial inflation rate tree.

In other words, the option is valuable when the principal is lower than 100. When the inflation rate drops and the economy is in a hypothetical deflation scenario, the option is in the money. This increases the value of an inflation-linked bond. Note that the probability of a deflation scenario depends on the market sentiment and implied inflation rate between conventional and

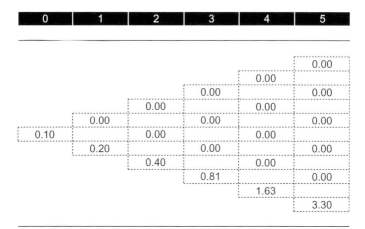

| 0 | 1 | 2 | 3 | 4 | 5 |

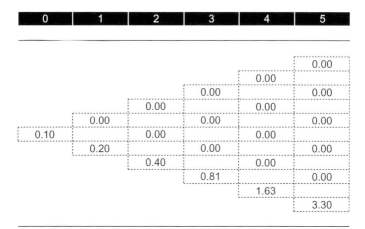

FIGURE 6.10   Binomial Tree of a European Put Option.

inflation-linked bonds.[11] For instance, at last node, the value of a European put option is given by Equation (6.20):

$$P_5^{\text{put option}} = \max\left(0, 100 - 96.70\right) = 3.30 \qquad (6.20)$$

Then, the value of the option is discounted in each node with a discount rate assumed equal to 1% as follows:

$$P_t^{\text{put option}} = \frac{0.5 \times P_u + 0.5 \times P_d}{(1+r)} \qquad (6.21)$$

where it is the value of the option for a further period; P_u is the value of the option in the up state and P_d is the value of the option in the down state. Figure 6.10 shows the binomial tree of a put option.

Finally, the value of an inflation-linked bond is determined as the sum of the value of coupon payments, principal and put option at time 0. The value is given by Equation (6.22):

$$P_{\text{IL}} = C_{\text{IL}} + M_{\text{IL}} + P = 4.83 + 93.02 + 0.10 = 97.94 \qquad (6.22)$$

6.4.3.3   Accrued Interest

In order to obtain the full or invoice price, we need to take into account the accrued interest. The accrued interest should be adjusted with the inflation for each period. The adjusted accrued interest is given by Equation (6.23):

$$\text{AI}_{\text{adj}} = C \times \frac{t}{T} \times I_R \qquad (6.23)$$

---

11. See Section 6.3.

where AI_{adj} is the adjusted accrued interest; C is the coupon payment; t is the number of days accrued; T is the number of days in the coupon period and I_R is the index ratio.

Therefore, adding the accrued interest to the clean or flat price including the inflation adjustment we obtain the full or invoice price. The invoice price is given by Equation (6.24):

$$P_i = (P_f \times I_R) + AI_{adj} \qquad (6.24)$$

where P_i is the full or invoice price; P_f is the flat or clean price and I_R is the index ratio.

6.4.3.4 Indexation Lag

As described above, inflation-linked bonds allow to save investors from changes in the general level of prices. However, the indexation is not perfect creating a lag between the index prices and the adjustment to the bond cash flows. According to Deacon and Derry (2004) at the end of a bond's life there is no inflation protection, matched with an equal period before the issue in which the inflation compensation is paid. Figure 6.11 shows an example of indexation lag according to Deacon and Derry (2004).

There are several ways in which the indexation lag could be reduced:

- First of all, choosing the index with the most frequent updating;
- Secondly, increasing the frequency of coupon payments;
- Finally, adopting the method proposed by Barro (1994), which the inflation for the previous coupon is assumed as a proxy of the actual inflation.

For the last point, we consider the following example. We assume to have an indexation lag of 1 year. Without indexation lag, at first payment date, the coupon should be adjusted with the inflation rate τ_1 between the issue date and first coupon date. The adjustment is given by Equation (6.25):

$$C_{IL} = C \times (1 + \tau_1) \qquad (6.25)$$

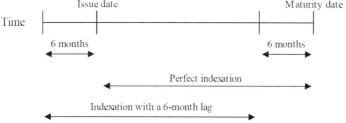

FIGURE 6.11   Indexation lag. *(Reproduced from Deacon and Derry (2004).)*

where C_{IL} is the inflation-adjusted coupon payment; C is the coupon payment and τ_I is the inflation between issue date and first coupon payment.

Conversely, under Barro's method the inflation used for the first coupon is 1 year before the issue date. The Barro's adjustment is given by Equation (6.26):

$$C_{IL} = C \times (1 + \tau_0) \tag{6.26}$$

where τ_0 is the inflation between 1 year before issue date and issue date.

After the first coupon payment, Barro attributes a double weight on the periodical inflation rate before the coupon payment. For instance, in the case of perfect indexation, the second coupon payment should be adjusted in the following way:

$$C_{IL} = C \times (1 + \tau_1) \times (1 + \tau_2) \tag{6.27}$$

while under Barro's approach we give a double weight to the inflation τ_I between the issue date and first coupon date as follows:

$$C_{IL} = C \times (1 + \tau_1) \times (1 + \tau_1) \tag{6.28}$$

6.5 WEB SITE MODELS

The Web site associated with this book contains an Excel spreadsheet demonstrating the valuation of inflation-linked bonds, as described in this chapter. The reader may use the spreadsheet to value such bonds using his or her own parameter inputs.

Details of how to access the Web site are contained in the preface.

APPENDIX A INFLATION-LINKED BOND PRICING

Considering the example shown in Table A1 of a hypothetical bond with coupons and principal linked to the inflation. We assume a 5-year inflation-linked bond with a 2% annual coupon payment. The expected cash flows, coupons and principal, are discounted with a discount rate of 3%. The valuation is performed by the following steps.

Determining the Expected Inflation Rate

The inflation rate is determined by the inflation index expectations. For instance, at first coupon date, the inflation rate is 2.1% and is given by:

$$\tau_1 = \frac{I_1}{I_0} - 1 = \frac{102.3}{100.2} - 1 = 2.1\%$$

TABLE A1 The Valuation of An Inflation-Linked Bond

	0	1	2	3	4	5
Inflation Index	100.2	102.3	104.1	106.2	108.3	110.4
Coupon payment		2	2	2	2	2
Expected inflation		2.1%	1.8%	2.0%	2.0%	1.9%
Compounded expected inflation		1.02	1.04	1.06	1.08	1.10
Inflation adjusted Coupon payment		2.04	2.08	2.12	2.16	2.20
Indexed Principal repayment						110.18
Cash Flow		2.04	2.08	2.12	2.16	112.38
Discounted Cash flow		1.98	1.96	1.94	1.92	96.94
Price of an Inflation-Linked Bond	104.74					

Determining the Coupon Payment

The coupon payments are determined as percentage on the par value and they are adjusted to the expected inflation rate. For instance, at first payment date, the coupon is calculated as follows:

$$C_1 = C \times (1 + \tau_1) = 2 \times (1 + 0.021) = 2.04$$

The present value of the coupon at first payment date is equal to 1.98.

The second coupon payment is calculated as the compounded inflation rate at time t_2 as follows:

$$C_2 = C \times (1 + \tau_1) \times (1 + \tau_2) = 2 \times (1 + 0.021) \times (1 + 0.018) = 2.08$$

or

$$C_2 = 2 \times \frac{104.1}{100.2} = 2.08$$

The present value of the second coupon payment is 1.96.

Determining the Principal Repayment

As made for coupon payments, also the redemption value is adjusted for inflation. The nominal redemption value is equal to 110.18 and is given by:

$$M_{IL} = M \times \frac{I_5}{I_0} = 100 \times \frac{110.4}{100.2} = 110.18$$

Determining the Value of an Inflation-Linked Bond

Finally, the value of an inflation-linked bond is calculated as the sum of the present value of coupons and principal, assuming a nominal discount rate of 3%. The bond value obtained is 104.74.

BIBLIOGRAPHY

Arak, M., Kreicher, L., 1985. The real rate of interest: inferences from the new UK indexed gilts. Int. Econ. Rev. 26 (2), 399–408.

Barro, R.J., 1994. A suggestion for revising the inflation adjustment of payments on indexed bonds.

Bootle, R., 1991. Index-Linked Gilts, second ed. Woodhead-Faulkner.

Brown, R., Schaefer, S., 1996. Ten years of the real term structure: 1984–1994. J. Fixed Income 5 (4), 6–22.

Brynjolfsson, J., Fabozzi, F. (Eds.), 1999. Handbook of Inflation-Indexed Bonds. FSF Associates, New Hope, PA.

Choudhry, M., Moskovic, D., Wong, M., 2014. Fixed Income Markets: Management, Trading and Hedging, second ed. John Wiley & Sons, Singapore.

Deacon, M., Derry, A., 1994. Deriving estimates of inflation expectations from the prices of UK government bonds. Working Paper No. 23, Bank of England.

Deacon, M., Derry, A., 1998. Inflation-Indexed Securities. Prentice Hall, London.

Deacon, M., Derry, A., 2004. Inflation-Indexed Securities: Bonds, Swaps and Other Derivates, 2nd ed. John Wiley & Sons, Chichester.

Diedrich, S., 2011. Inflation-linked bonds: not always the best answer to inflation. PAAMCO Research Paper.

Fleckenstein, M., 2012. The inflation-indexed bond puzzle. Working Paper, UCLA.

Huber, S., 2014. Inflation-linked bonds – Preserving real purchasing power and diversifying risk. Credit Suisse.

Jarrow, R., Yildirim, Y., 2003. Pricing treasury inflation protected securities and related derivates using an HJM model. J. Financ. Quant. Anal. 38 (2), 337–358.

Krämer, W., 2013. An introduction to inflation-linked bonds. Lazard Asset Management.

McCulloch, J., 1971. Measuring the term structure of interest rates. J. Bus. XLIV, 19–31.

McCulloch, J., 1975. The tax-adjusted yield curve. J. Financ. 30 (3), 811–830.

Roll, R., 1996. US Treasury inflation-indexed bonds: the design of a new security. J. Fixed Income 6 (3), 321–335.

Schaefer, S., 1981. Measuring a tax-specific term structure of interest rates in the market for British government securities. Econ. J. 91, 415–438.

Standard Life Investments, 'Guide to inflation-linked bonds', June 2013.

Sundaresan, S., 2009. Fixed Income Markets and Their Derivates, third ed. Elsevier, Burlington.

Waggoner, D., 1997. Spline methods for extracting interest rate curves from coupon bond prices. Working Paper, No. 97–10, Federal Reserve Bank of Atlanta.

Wrase, J.M., 1997. Inflation-indexed bonds: how do they work? Federal Reserve Bank of Philadelphia.

Chapter 7

Analysing the Long-Bond Yield

Chapter Contents

A common observation in government bond markets is that the longest dated bond trades expensive to the yield curve. It also exhibits other singular features that have been the subject of research, for example, by Phoa (1998), which we review in this chapter. The main feature of long-bond yields is that they reflect a convexity effect. Analysts have attempted to explain the convexity effects of long-bond yields in a number of ways. These are discussed first. We then consider the volatility and convexity bias that is observed in long-bond yields.

7.1 THEORIES OF LONG-DATED BOND YIELDS

In both the United States and the United Kingdom government markets, extremely long-dated bonds have been actively traded. These include 'century' bonds in the United States and undated or irredeemable bonds in the United Kingdom, including gilt issues such as the 'consols' or War Loan. At what yields should very long-dated bonds trade? Under the conventional hypothesis investors might believe that if the yield on the 30-year government bond is 6.00%, the yield on a hypothetical 100-year government bond will be higher, say 6.25%, the higher rate signifying the term premium payable on the longer bond. In fact, this is extremely unlikely, and it has been shown that, for such a term structure to be observed, we would require forward interest rates to be very high. Expected rates will not, therefore, be as high as the forward rates. We explore the issues in this section.

Theories of very long-dated interest rates have been proposed that on observation would appear to hold; these include:

- That very long-dated yields are not an unbiased average of expected future interest rates, but rather can be estimated using a weighting of various interest-rate scenarios; at sufficiently long maturities, the highest interest-rate scenarios do not impact the long-dated yield (Dybvig and Marshall, 1996);
- Extremely long-dated zero coupon and forward rates can never decline, even when expected long-term future interest rates fall; therefore, this limits the extent to which very long-dated bond yields are affected by a change in the current interest-rate environment (Dybvig et al., 1996).

The very long-dated zero-coupon yield is taken to be the infinite maturity zero-coupon yield, that is, the limiting yield of a risk-free zero-coupon bond whose maturity approaches infinity. Although it might appear so, the infinite maturity yield is not identical to the yield on an irredeemable bond, which pays coupons during its life and so has a shorter dated yield. It is also not identical to the long-term interest rate, which is defined as the expected long-term rate of return on bonds or the expected rate of return on a bond with infinite duration. The long rate is a measure of the expected future rate of *return*, rather than a present bond *yield*. The two interest-rate hypotheses above are general and apply to both conventional and index-linked bonds. They use the principle of no-arbitrage pricing, in terms of a trading strategy, in their derivation, which we do not present here. They do, however, have a practical significance in terms of the valuation of long-dated bonds.

7.1.1 Long-Dated Yields

In an environment of interest-rate uncertainty, from previous chapters we know the price today of a zero-coupon bond of maturity T to be a function of the expectation of future short rates, which at time t are not known; this is given in Equation (7.1):

$$P(t,T) = \exp\left(-\int_t^T r(s)\,ds\right). \tag{7.1}$$

Expression (7.1) states that the price of a zero-coupon bond is equal to the discount factor from time t to its maturity date or the average of the discount factors under all interest-rate scenarios, weighted by their probabilities. It can be shown that the T-maturity forward rate at time t is given by

$$f(t,T) = \frac{E_t\left[r_T\exp\left(-\int_t^T r(s)\,ds\right)\right]}{E_t\left[\exp\left(-\int_t^T r(s)\,ds\right)\right]} \tag{7.2}$$

which expresses the T-term forward rate in terms of the dynamics of the T-maturity short rate r_T under all possible interest-rate scenarios, that is, along all possible random interest-rate paths. The weightings are in terms of the probabilities of each interest-rate path occurring and the discount factors from the period t to T that occur in each scenario. So, for instance, consider an environment where there are only two possible interest-rate scenarios, each with a probability of $p(1)$ and $p(2)$. Phoa (1998) states that the T-maturity forward rate is given by the weighted average, shown in Equation (7.3), where Df is the discount factor:

$$f(t,T) = \frac{p(1)\mathrm{Df}_1(t,T) \cdot r_{T,(1)} + p(2)\mathrm{Df}_2(t,T) \cdot r_{T,(2)}}{p(1)\mathrm{Df}_1(t,T) + p(2)\mathrm{Df}_2(t,T)}. \tag{7.3}$$

The effect of weighting using discount factors is to make the lower level interest-rate scenario more significant because the discount factors are higher under these scenarios. This means that a lower interest-rate scenario has more influence on the forward rate than a higher rate scenario, and this influence steadily increases as the forward rate term grows in maturity, since the difference between the discount factors increases. This is an important result.

7.1.2   Long-Dated Forward Rates

We can illustrate this with a hypothetical example. Consider a binomial interest-rate environment under which there are the following interest-rate scenarios:

- The short rate is at a constant level of 8.00%, with a probability of 70%;
- The short rate is at a constant level of 4.00%, with a probability of 30%.

The expected future short rate at any point in the future will be 8%, given the probabilities; however, the forward rate will be lower than 8% because it is calculated by weighting each interest-rate scenario by the relevant discount factors. This is illustrated in Figure 7.1.

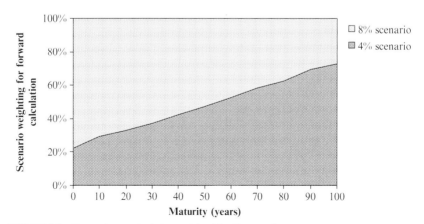

FIGURE 7.1   Forward rate calculation weighted by discount factors.

The weight attached to the lower 4% interest-rate scenario increases with increasing term-to-maturity, while the weight on the higher rate will diminish. Therefore, the 30-year forward rate will be below 8%, while the 100-year forward rate will be around half the short rate for the most probable scenario. Put another way, over a long period, only the lowest interest-rate scenario is relevant, which is the theorem posited by Dybvig and Marshall. This tendency for the forward rate curve to fall with very long maturities is as a result of a *convexity bias* in the behaviour of the yield curve, which we consider later. This effect influences zero-coupon yields, which also exhibit a tendency to gravitate towards the lowest interest-rate scenario. Consider now another hypothetical example, where the current short rate is 6% and that there are now three (and only three) possible interest-rate scenarios, which are:

- that the short rate increases from 6% to a long-term rate of 10%;
- that the short rate increases from 6% to a long-term rate of 8%;
- that the short rate decreases from 6% to a long-term rate of 4%.

The probabilities of each of these occurrences are 10%, 80% and 10%, respectively; that is, the most likely scenario is a rise in the short rate from 6% to 8%. For each scenario, we assume that the short rate approaches the expected long-term level in exponential fashion. The expected interest-rate scenario, therefore, is a rise from 6% to 8%. From Figure 7.2, we see that the forward rate curve behaves differently to expected future short-rate levels. The forward rates peak at around 12-14 years and then steadily decline as the term to maturity increases. The zero-coupon yield curve, which can be derived from the forward yield curve, has a different shape and starts to decline from the 20-year term period.

Figure 7.2 suggests that the unbiased expectations hypothesis, which states that forward rates are equal to the expected level of future short-term rates, is incorrect, and so it is not valid to calculate par and zero-coupon yield curves using the expected short-rate curve. Instead, the forward rate curve

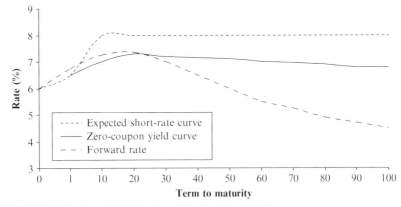

FIGURE 7.2 The theoretical behaviour of the long-bond yield.

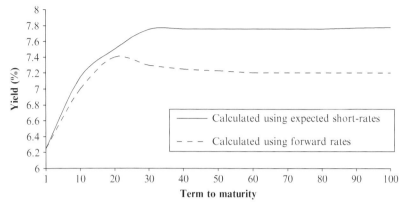

FIGURE 7.3   Zero-coupon yield curves calculated using expected short- and forward rates.

should be used. Figure 7.3 illustrates the extent of the error that might be made using the expected short-rate curve to calculate the zero-coupon yield curve, which is magnified over longer terms to maturity.

From Figure 7.3, we see that to price a very long-dated bond off the yield of the 30-year government bond would lead to errors. The unbiased expectations hypothesis suggests that 100-year bond yields are essentially identical to 30-year yields; however, this is in fact incorrect. The theoretical 100-year yield in fact will be approximately 20-25 basis points lower. This reflects the convexity bias in longer dated yields. In our illustration, we used a hypothetical scenario where only three possible interest-rate states were permitted. Dybvig and Marshall showed that in a more realistic environment, with forward rates calculated using a Monte Carlo simulation, similar observations would result. Therefore, the observations have a practical relevance.

This is an important result for the pricing of longer dated bonds. Certain corporate bonds including those issued by Walt Disney, Coca-Cola and British Gas, to name three instances in the past years, have been very long-dated bonds, from 50 to 99 years' maturity. The analysis above suggests that such bonds priced at a spread over the 30-year government bond are theoretically undervalued. While investor sentiment would appear to demand a yield premium for buying such long-dated bonds, the theoretical credit-risk spread for a 100-year corporate bond is essentially the same as that for a 30-year corporate bond. For instance, if a 30-year corporate bond has a default probability of 1% each year, while a 100-year corporate bond has a default probability of 1% for the first 30 years and a subsequent default probability of 3% for the remainder of its life, the longer dated bond appears at first sight to hold considerably more credit risk. However, it can be shown that the yield premium an investor should demand for holding the longer dated bond will not be much more than 15-20 basis points. This is because the impact of future loss scenarios is weighted by the discount factor that applies from today to the loss date; the influence of each discount factor steadily diminishes over an increasing term to maturity.

7.2 PRICING A LONG BOND

In a conventional positive yield curve environment, it is common for the 30-year government bond to yield say 10-20 basis points above the t10-year bond. This might indicate to investors that a 100-year bond should yield approximately 20-25 basis points more than the 30-year bond. Is this accurate? As we noted in the previous section, such an assumption would not be theoretically valid. Marshall and Dybvig have shown that such a yield spread would indicate an undervaluation of the very long-dated bond and that should such yields be available an investor, unless he or she has extreme views on future interest rates, should hold the 100-year bond.

This is intuitively apparent. In the first instance, long-dated forward rates have very little influence on the prices of bonds, and therefore for there to be a yield spread of, say, 20 basis points between 30 and 40 years, forward rates would have to be very high. This reflects the relationship between spot and forward rates, the former being an average of the latter to the longest maturity. Similarly, expected future short rates are assumed to be composed of the market's expectation of these rates and a premium for interest-rate risk. For there to be a high enough expectation such that there is a yield premium of 20 basis points between 30 and 100 years, it would require very high expectations about the future level of short rates or a very high risk premium. We now consider this in greater detail.

7.2.1 The Impact of Forward Rates on the Long-Bond Yield

From elementary financial arithmetic, we know that an investment of £1 at a continuously compounded interest rate of r will have a value at time t given by e^{-rt} so that the value of a coupon C at this time is given by Ce^{-rt}.

This enables us to set the value of a bond with a coupon of C maturing at time T and redemption value of M as Equation (7.4):

$$\int_0^T MCe^{-rt}ds + Me^{-rT} \tag{7.4}$$

which can also be given as

$$\frac{MC}{r}\left(1 - e^{-rT}\right) + Me^{-rT}. \tag{7.5}$$

We assume that the zero-coupon rate r-term structure is flat until the time s and that forward rates are flat at f. The value of £1 to be received at time $t > s$ is given by:

$$e^{-rs-f(t-s)} \tag{7.6}$$

while the price of a bond maturing at T is given by (7.7):

$$P = \int_0^t MCe^{-rt}\,ds + \int_t^T MCe^{-rs-f(t-s)}\,ds + Me^{-rs-(T-t)f}. \tag{7.7}$$

Equation (7.7) can be integrated to give:

$$\frac{MC}{r}(1 - e^{-rt}) + \frac{MC}{f}e^{-f(T-t)} + Me^{-rt-f(T-t)}. \tag{7.8}$$

This can be illustrated with an example. Consider a situation where the zero-coupon rates term structure is flat at 6% for 30 years and that forward rates are flat at f for terms from 30 to 100 years. This results in the price of a 30-year bond with a coupon of 6% and a redemption value of £100 having a price of par, shown below:

$$P = 100 = \frac{6}{0.06}(1 - e^{-0.06 \times 30}) + 100e^{-0.06 \times 30}.$$

Now let us imagine that the yield on a 100-year government bond with a coupon of 6.00% is 6.20%. This fits investor expectations that the very long-dated bond should have a yield premium of approximately 20 basis points. This would set the price of the 100-year bond as:

$$P = 100$$
$$= \frac{6.20}{0.06}(1 - e^{-0.06 \times 30}) + e^{-0.06 \times 30}\left(\frac{6.20}{f}\right)(1 - e^{70f}) + e^{-0.06 \times 30}100e^{-f \times 70}$$

where the price of the bond is par. The forward rate given by the expression above must be greater than 6.20% and is higher because long-dated forward rates have very little influence on the price of a coupon bond. The size of the coefficient $e^{-0.06 \times 30}$, in this instance, indicates the extent of the impact of the forward rate on the price of the bond. In fact, in a term structure environment that is flat or only very slightly positive out to 30 years, the zero-coupon term structure beyond this term is flat.

Let us look now at the T-period forward rate again as a function of the range of spot rates from the time t today to point T in more detail than in Section 7.1. If $P(t, T)$ is the price today of a zero-coupon bond that has a redemption value of £1 at time T, then this price is given in terms of the instantaneous structure of forward rates by Equation (7.9):

$$P(t, T) = \exp\left(-\int_t^T f(t, s)\,ds\right) \tag{7.9}$$

where the forward rate $f(t, T)$ is given by:

$$f(t, T) = -\frac{\partial \ln P(t, T)}{\partial T}. \tag{7.10}$$

However, the price of the zero-coupon bond is also given in terms of the spot rate as the expression in (7.1), where E_t is the expectation under the risk-free probability function. Therefore, forward rates are related to the expected level of the instantaneous spot rates, and if we differentiate the expression in (7.10), we obtain a result that states that the forward rate is a weighted average of the range of spot rates in the period t to T. This is given in Equation (7.11), which we encountered earlier as Equation (7.2):

$$f(t, T) = \frac{\exp\left(-\int_t^T r(s)\,ds\right)}{E_t\left[\exp\left(-\int_t^T r(s)\,ds\right)\right]}. \tag{7.11}$$

In the spot-rate scenario where the expected future rate is high, the interest rate $r(T)$ will exert very little influence, while it exerts more weight at lower levels. Therefore, the forward rate will be lower than the expected spot rate, and this is described below, where

$$E_t\left[r(T)\Big|\int_t^T r(s)\,ds\right]$$

is an increasing function in $\int_t^T r(s)\,ds$.

Therefore, we may write for long-term forward rates $f(t, T) \le E_t\,[r(T)]$, where interest rates are assumed to not be deterministic. This result has an important effect on the pricing of very long-dated bonds. Since forward rates lie below the level of expected short-term rates, for a very long-dated bond to trade at a yield of 6.20% means that the average level of future short rates over the life of the bond would have to be higher than 6.20%. If this is not the case, a yield premium of 20-25 basis points between the long bond and a very long-dated bond would indicate an unrealistically low price for the latter instrument. And crucially, for there to be a spread of this magnitude for up to, say, 50 years beyond the benchmark long bond, we would observe unrealistically high forward rates and an exploding forward rate curve.

7.3 FURTHER VIEWS ON THE LONG-DATED BOND YIELD

In the previous section, we described a theorem from Dybvig, Ingersoll and Ross stating that extremely long-dated bond yields cannot decline. This carries implications about the level of interest-rate risk attached to the very long-dated yield. We present a summary of their results here.

Assume that along all random interest-rate paths ω, the short rate gravitates towards a long-term equilibrium level of r_ω^∞, which is dependent on the path ω. A long-term level r can result if the set of interest-rate paths ω for which $r_\omega^\infty \le r$ has a positive probability. Consider then the lowest possible value r^∞ of the long-term equilibrium level r_ω^∞. The result from the previous section, that very long-dated forward rates do not reflect the unbiased expectations hypothesis but rather a disproportionate weighting of the lowest yields, implies that long-dated rates are determined by r^∞. That is, as the maturity approaches infinity, both the forward and the zero-coupon rate are essentially equal to the lowest possible long-term interest rate r^∞. Over time, a particular long-term interest-rate level r^∞_ω that was previously possible may become impossible so that r^∞ may rise over time. However, a previously unattainable level r^∞_ω will remain impossible, and if it is possible today, it will have been possible before. Therefore, r^∞ cannot fall over time, which indicates that very long-dated forward and zero-coupon rates cannot fall. This means that long-dated yields are essentially given by the lowest interest-rate scenario and will remain sticky at this level. It also means that there is a limit to the extent to which long-dated yields will be affected by changes in the expectations of future interest rates. The yield on a 100-year bond is essentially determined by the lowest yield scenario, and a fall in expected future short-term rates will have very little impact indeed.

We can illustrate this with the same example as before. Consider now that there is a 50-basis point decline in the short rate and that the probabilities of the three interest-rate scenarios are now:

- that there is a zero probability that the short rate increases from 5.50% to a long-term rate of 10%;
- that there is an 80% probability that the short rate increases from 5.50% to a long-term rate of 8%;
- that there is a 20% probability that the short rate decreases from 5.50% to a long-term rate of 4%.

The change in the short rate will result in a 50-basis point decline in all the expected future interest rates. However, this will not result in a uniform fall in all bond yields. The impact on the zero-coupon curve and the forward rate curve is shown in Figure 7.4.

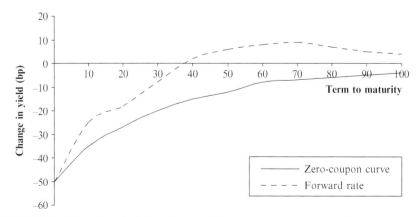

FIGURE 7.4   The effect of a decline in expected short rates on zero coupon and forward curves.

From Figure 7.4, we observe that at the very short end, yields fall by 50 basis points. However, the 100-year spot rate falls by only approximately four basis points, while the 100-year forward rate actually rises. This is because under the probabilities used in our scenario the 6% scenario has a higher weight at these forward dates.

What are the practical implications of these results? We may conclude that if there is a rally in the government bond market, very long-dated bond yields should be virtually unaffected. More important though, the results indicate that any term structure model that allows very long-dated yields to fall is inconsistent with the Dybvig-Ingersoll-Ross theorem, and is therefore invalid because it would permit arbitrage. Such a model would also price 100-year bonds incorrectly (although it may well price 30-year bonds correctly). The theorem is still consistent with the concept of mean reversion, and a term structure model that assumes that long-term yields will revert to a constant long-term level will fit in with the theorem. Dybvig et al. state that the long-term level must be the 'lowest possible level' of the average level of interest rates, but calculating this level is problematic. The issues involved in accurately pricing a very long-dated bond, and the fact that term structure modelling out to this maturity is not yet consistently applied, may explain why, despite there being no theoretical basis for it, the yields on 50-, 90- and 100-year corporate bonds sometimes lie some way above the 30-year risk-free yield.

7.4 ANALYSING THE CONVEXITY BIAS IN LONG-BOND YIELDS

In theory, the results implied by a discussion of convexity imply that if there are two fixed income portfolios that have identical durations and yields, the portfolio with the higher convexity will outperform the other under conditions of a parallel yield curve shift. In fact, in practice, this will not be the case, as such portfolios will have lower yields, which reflects the price paid for convexity in the market.[1] We can observe this yield/convexity trade-off in the government bond yield curve: in a positive sloping yield curve environment, the yield on the longest dated (usually 30-year) bond is almost always lower than the 15- or 20-year bond yield. This is explained by the fact that the longer dated bond has higher convexity and that the value of this convexity is the difference in the yields. This *convexity bias* is evident in other markets, and in Chapters 41 and 43 of Choudhry (2001) we review the convexity bias that exists between the swap yield curve and the yield curve implied by long-dated interest-rate future contracts. For example, in one study[2], the 10-year interest-rate swap rate was found to be significantly lower than the rate implied by the equivalent strip of 10-year Eurodollar future contracts. This reflects the fact that the swap

---

1. For example, see Lacey and Nawalkha (1993).
2. See Burghardt and Hoskins (1995).

instrument has convexity, while the future position does not. Therefore, it is theoretically possible to benefit from a position where the trading book is short the swap (receiving fixed) and short the future strip, as the combined effect is to be long convexity.

7.4.1   Estimating the Convexity Bias

Phoa (1998) presents an approximation of the convexity bias as follows. Consider a conventional fixed coupon bond, which has a yield at a future time t of r and a price at this time of $P(r)$. The convexity bias is estimated using

$$E[r] - r_{\text{fwd}} \approx (C/D)\sigma^2 t \qquad (7.12)$$

where $E[r] - r_{\text{fwd}}$ is the difference between the forward yield and the expected future yield (which is the convexity adjustment to the bond yield), C is the convexity divided by two, D is the duration of the forward bond position and σ is the basis point volatility of bond yields.

The volatility value used can be estimated in two ways. We can estimate volatility separately and then use this to calculate what the approximate convexity adjustment should be, or we may observe the convexity bias directly and derive a volatility value from this. This would require an examination of market swap rates and bond yields, and use these to estimate the volatility implied by these rates.

REFERENCES

Burghardt, G., Hoskins, B., 1995. A question of bias. Risk 8 (3).

Choudhry, M., 2001. The Bond and Money Markets. Butterworth-Heinemann.

Dhillon, U., Lasser, D., 1998. Term premium estimates from zero-coupon bonds: new evidence on the expectations hypothesis. J. Fixed Income 8, 52–58.

Dybvig, P., Marshall, W., 1996. Pricing long bonds: pitfalls and opportunities. Financ. Anal. J. 52, 32–39.

Dybvig, P., Ingersoll, T., Ross, S., 1996. Long forward and zero-coupon rates can never fall. J. Bus. 69 (1), 1–25.

Lacey, N., Nawalkha, S., 1993. Convexity, risk, and returns. J. Fixed Income 3 (3), 129–145.

Phoa, W., 1998. Advanced Fixed Income Analytics. FJF Associates, New York (chapter 4).

Chapter 8

The Default Risk of Corporate Bonds

Chapter Contents

In the companion volume to first edition of this book, part of the Fixed Income Markets Library, we looked at the range of corporate bond instruments that are held by investors. Institutions are interested in holding non-government bonds because of the higher yield that these bonds offer, relative to government bonds. The existence of a credit default risk on such bonds means that bondholders must ensure that the return is satisfactory and compensates them for the risk of the bond portfolio. This can be done by measuring the risk premium obtainable from the corporate bond, the total return that is expected from holding the bond, and assessing whether this is sufficient to compensate for all the risks associated with the bond, excluding the interest-rate risk. These risks must be identified and quantified, and the higher the risk, the higher the risk premium should be. A common measure for the risk premium is the *option-adjusted spread* (OAS). It is basically

155

the spread of the corporate bond over the equivalent-maturity risk-free bond. A bond's OAS measures the constant spread that must be added to the current short-term interest rate to make the theoretical price of the corporate bond, as calculated by the pricing model, identical to the observed market price. This means that it is a quantification of the excess return of the bond over the short rate. There is no one measure of OAS however, and it means different things depending on what type of bond it is applied to. This means that if it is used to measure the yield premium on a corporate bond that reflects a particular bond's credit risk, any specific limitations of the measure must be accounted for. There are other measures that may be considered however, in terms of the default risk of a bond, and these are considered in this chapter. We also present theoretical default spread models.

8.1 CORPORATE BOND DEFAULT SPREAD RISK

8.1.1 Spread Risk

The general rule of corporate bonds is that they are priced at a spread to the government yield curve. In absolute terms, the yield spread is the difference between the yield to maturity of a corporate bond and the benchmark, generally a yield to maturity of a government bond with the same maturity. Corporate bonds include a yield spread on a risk-free rate in order to compensate two main factors, liquidity premium and credit spread. The yield of a corporate bond can be assumed as the sum of parts of the elements as shown in Figure 8.1, in which the yield spread relative to a default-free bond is given by the sum of default premium (credit spread) and liquidity premium.

The yield of a benchmark government bond depends on expected inflation rate, currency rate, economic growth, monetary and fiscal policy. Conversely, the spread of a corporate bond is influenced by the credit risk of the issuer, taxation and market liquidity. Moreover, the yield spread depends on other factors such as:

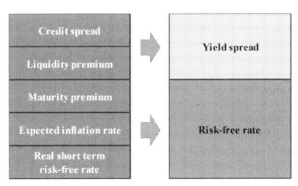

FIGURE 8.1 The yield of a corporate bond.

- *Economic environment*: Where weak economic conditions and low expected growth increase the credit spread. Therefore, credit spread tends to increase during the economic recession and decrease during economic boom;
- *Financial market trend*: In which credit spread tends to be narrow in strong financial markets and vice versa;
- *Supply and demand*: Where higher supply brings wider spreads, whereas higher demand decreases spreads;
- *Maturity*: Generally default spreads are larger for longer date bonds and narrow for short-term bonds.

8.1.1.1   Benchmark Spread

There are several ways to measure the yield spread of a corporate bond:

- *G-spread*: It is the yield spread over the government bond curve. This spread takes into account the credit risk, liquidity risk and other risks that affect corporate bonds;
- *I-spread*: It is the yield spread of a corporate bond relative to an interpolated swap rate. According to this approach, the yield of a corporate bond is built in the following way:

$$Y = I + S + T \qquad (8.1)$$

  Where Y is the yield of a corporate bond; I is the I-spread over the swap; S is the swap spread and T is the yield of a treasury bond;
- *Asset-swap spread*: It is determined by combining an interest-rate swap and cash bond. Generally, bonds pay fixed coupons; therefore, it will be combined with an interest-rate swap in which the bondholder pays fixed coupons and receives floating coupons. The spread of the floating coupon over an interbank rate is the asset-swap spread.[1]
- *Z-spread*: The Z-spread or *zero volatility spread* calculates the yield spread of a corporate bond by taking a zero-coupon bond curve as benchmark. Conversely to other yield spreads, the Z-spread is constant. In fact, it is found as an iterative procedure, which is the yield spread required to get the equivalence between market price and the present value of all its cash flows. The Z-spread is given by Equation (8.2):

$$P = \sum_{t=1}^{T} \frac{C_t}{[1 + (T + S + Z)]^t} + \frac{M}{[1 + (T + S + Z)]^T} \qquad (8.2)$$

where P is the price of a corporate bond; C_t is the coupon payment; M is the redemption value and Z is the Z-spread.

---

1. For example, Libor or Euribor.

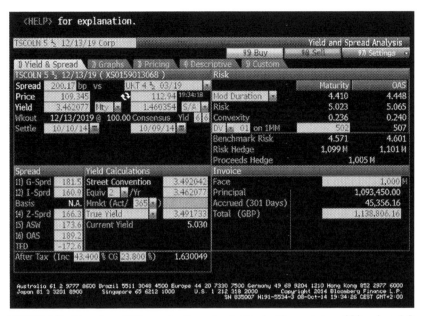

FIGURE 8.2   Bloomberg YAS page for Tesco bond. *(Used with permission of Bloomberg L.P. Copyright© 2014. All rights reserved.)*

- *Option-adjusted spread*: The *OAS* is used for bonds with embedded options. This spread is calculated as the difference between the Z-spread and option value expressed in basis points.

Figure 8.2 shows the Bloomberg YAS page for Tesco bond 5½% 2019, as at October 9, 2014. The bond has a price of 109.345 and yield to maturity of 3.46%. On the date, the yield spread over a government bond benchmark UK 4½% Treasury 2019 is 200 basis points. The *G*-spread over an interpolated government bond is 181.5 basis points. Conventionally, the difference between these two spreads is narrow. We see also that the asset-swap spread is 173.6 basis points and Z-spread is 166.3 basis points.

8.1.1.2   Spread Duration

The price of a corporate bond is a yield spread for conventional bonds or on an OAS basis for callable or other option-embedded bonds. If an OAS calculation is undertaken in a consistent framework, price changes that result in credit events will result in changes in the OAS. Therefore, we can speak in terms of a sensitivity measure for the change in value of a bond or portfolio in terms of changes to a bond's OAS measure. One of these measures is the *spread duration*. The spread duration of a bond is the sensitivity of its OAS to a change in yield of one basis point. For a conventional bond, the spread duration is essentially its modified duration because a change in the OAS would have an identical effect on the price of such a bond as a similar magnitude change in the yield on the equivalent government bond. For the same reason, the spread duration of a callable bond is essentially identical to its modified duration. However, the spread duration for an asset-backed security such as a mortgage-backed bond is not equal to its modified duration. This is because a change in the OAS will not have the same effect necessarily as a similar change in government bond yields.

The effect of a change in OAS for mortgage-backed bonds can be explained thus. For instance a rise in yields will lead to a rise in the level of mortgage rates, which will have the effect of decreasing prepayment rates. This will change the expected cash flow profile of the bond. However, a change in the OAS of the bond will only have an effect on the bond's expected cash flows if it also leads to a rise in the prevailing mortgage interest rate.

The spread duration of a bond can be applied to calculate the break-even spread change. Remember that investors who are looking to outperform government bonds will set up portfolios to include corporate bonds, whose yields are higher than those of government bonds. However, it is important for them to determine the extent to which yield spreads can widen before the additional income from the higher yield corporate bonds is offset by the negative price effect of these bonds with regard to the price of government bonds. This measure will indicate the extent of the risk profile of their portfolios. One approach is to calculate break-even spreads for a holding period of up to 1 year using Equation (8.3):

$$\text{Break-even spread} = \frac{\text{Income excess}}{\text{Spread duration}} = \frac{\text{Holding period} \times \text{spread}}{\text{Spread duration}}. \quad (8.3)$$

EXAMPLE 8.1 Spread Duration

An investor's corporate bond portfolio has an identical duration to a benchmark portfolio of government bonds, and an OAS of 50 basis points. Assume that the portfolio has a spread duration of 5. During a 12-month holding period, the excess income of the portfolio compared to government bonds is 0.25%. How much can the OAS widen before the corporate bond portfolio begins to underperform the government portfolio?

Break-even spread shift $= 0.25/5 = 5$ basis points.

Therefore, if spreads widen by five basis points or more over the 12-month period, or if the OAS of the portfolio widens beyond 55 basis points, the portfolio will underperform the government portfolio.

Note that this is an approximation that is valid for short-term holdings only.

8.1.2   Spread Risk and Government Bond Yields

The risk premium available on a corporate bond reflects the total risk exposure of the bond, over and above the interest-rate risk which is expected to be identical in theory to the interest-rate risk on an otherwise risk-free bond. This means that the discussion of spread risk above implies that it is independent of interest-rate risk. In practice, this is not so. Observation shows that the yield spread of corporate bonds is positively correlated to the outright government bond yield: when yields increase, the yield spread often decreases, while when yields fall the yield spread usually increases. Empirically though this effect can only be measured for specific issuers, and not for a class of identical credit-quality bonds. This is because the group of same-rated bond issuers is constantly fluctuating, and measuring the change in yield spread for a group of say, single-A-rated borrowers will reflect changes to the group of issuers as some are re-rated, and others enter or leave the group. In most OAS calculations, the relationship between outright yield levels and corporate yield spreads is not taken into account, resulting in an OAS spread of a corporate bond being equal to its nominal spread over the government yield curve.

To assess the impact of changing yield spreads therefore, it is necessary to carry out a simulation on the effect of different yield curve assumptions. For instance, we may wish to analyse 1-year holding period returns on a portfolio of investment-grade corporate bonds, under an assumption of widening yield spreads. This might be an analysis of the effect on portfolio returns if the yield spread for triple-B-rated bonds widened by 20 basis points, in conjunction with a varying government bond yield. This requires an assessment of a different number of scenarios, in order to capture this interest-rate uncertainty.

8.2   DEFAULT RISK AND DEFAULT SPREADS

8.2.1   The Theoretical Default Spread

We have stated that the yield premium required on a corporate bond accounts for the default risk exposure of such a bond. The level of yield spread is determined by the expected default loss of the bond and it is assumed that investors can assess the level of the default risk. This makes it possible to calculate the level of the theoretical default spread.

We set p_t as the probability that a bond will default in year t, and is the probability of default up to year t, while r_y is the expected recovery rate on the bond should it default. The default probability is assumed to fluctuate over time, while the recovery rate remains constant. Therefore, the probability that the bond will not have defaulted up to the beginning of year t is given by:

$$s_t = \prod_{\tau=1}^{t-1} (1 - p_\tau) \tag{8.4}$$

while the probability that the bond will default in year t is given by:

$$p(t) = p_t s_t \qquad (8.5)$$

If the bond has a maturity of T, there are $T+1$ scenarios, represented by default in years 1 to T or survival until maturity. The final scenario has a probability of

$$Q = s_{T+1} = 1 - \sum_{\tau=1}^{T} p(\tau). \qquad (8.6)$$

Therefore, using the assumed recovery rate, we may calculate the cash flows of the bond under each of the possible scenarios. For any given yield r, we can then calculate the present value of the bond's cash flows for each of these scenarios. These are denoted by PV_1, PV_2, ..., PV_T and PV_{T+1}. Let $p(r)$ be the probability-weighted average for all the possible scenarios, shown by Equation (8.5):

$$p(r) = \left(\sum_{t=1}^{T} p_r \cdot PV_t \right) + Q \cdot PV_{T+1}. \qquad (8.7)$$

This means that $p(r)$ is the expected value of the present value of the bond's cash flows, that is, the expected yield gained by buying the bond at the price $p(r)$ and holding it to maturity is r. If our required yield is r, for example this is the yield on the equivalent-maturity government bond, then we are able to determine the coupon rate C for which $p(r)$ is equal to 100. The default-risk spread that is required for a corporate bond means that C will be greater than r. Therefore, the theoretical default spread is $C - r$ basis points. If there is a zero probability of default, then the default spread is 0 and $C = r$.

Generally, the theoretical default spread is almost exactly proportional to the default probability, assuming a constant default probability. Generally, however, the default probability is not constant over time, nor do we expect it to be. In Figure 8.3, we show the theoretical default spread for triple-B-rated bonds of various maturities, where the default probability rises from 0.2% to 1% over time. The longer dated bonds, therefore, have a higher annual default risk and so their theoretical default spread is higher. Note that after around 20 years the expected default probability is constant at 1%, so the required yield premium is also fairly constant.

For lower- and non-rated bonds, the observed effect is the opposite to that of an investment-grade corporate. Over time the probability of default decreases; therefore, the theoretical default spread decreases over time. This means that the spread on a long-dated bond will be lower than that of a short-dated bond because if the issuer has not defaulted on the long-dated bond in the first few years of its existence, it will then be viewed as a lower risk credit, although the investor may well continue to earn the same yield spread.

Default probabilities are not known with certainty, and credit rating agencies suggest that higher risk bonds have more uncertain default probabilities. The agencies publish default rates for each rating category (which are used in credit

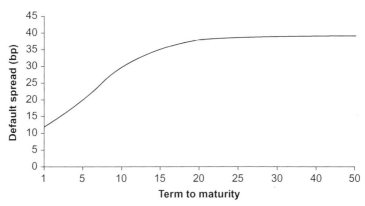

FIGURE 8.3   Theoretical default spread on BBB-rated corporate bond.

value-at-risk calculations), but the default probability values assume wider spreads for lower rated bonds. For example, a long-dated triple-B bond may have a default probability of between 0.5% and 2%, whereas a medium-dated single-B-rated bond may have default probabilities of between 5% and 15%. This uncertainty will influence the calculation of the theoretical default yield spread. To estimate this, one approach involves the use of a probability distribution of the default probability, and applying the analysis using a range of possible default probabilities, rather than a single default probability. This results in a range of theoretical yield spreads. The result of this approach, somewhat surprisingly, is that the greater the range of uncertainty about the future default probability, the lower the theoretical default spread. This result has a significant impact on the yield spreads of high-risk or 'junk' bonds. The reason behind this is that an assumption of lower default probabilities results in the generation of scenarios with higher cash flows, and the scenarios generated by these lower default probability assumptions carry a correspondingly higher weight. The default-adjusted yield being earned under a given default assumption is essentially the coupon rate minus the loss rate, where the loss rate is the product of the annual default probability and the recovery rate. Therefore, the assumption of a low default probability corresponds to a lower default-adjusted yield, and has a higher weight in determining the theoretical default spread than does a high-default probability assumption. A greater level of uncertainty about the level of the default probability means that more extreme high- and low-default probability assumptions are being used, and as the low assumptions carry greater weight in the calculation, the theoretical default spread emerges as lower.

8.2.2   The Default Spread in Relation to the Outright Government Bond Yield

In the previous section, we noted that in practice there is a positive correlation between the extent of the default yield spread and outright yield levels. We may wish to analyse the effect of a correlation that results in a higher level of default

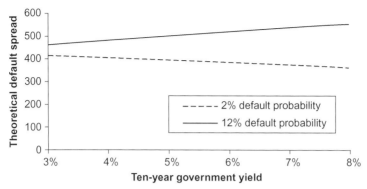

FIGURE 8.4 Correlation of theoretical yield spread with outright government bond yield, 10-year corporate bonds.

in a lower yield environment, or a recessionary environment when interest rates are lower. In fact, the outcome will depend on whether the default probability rate that is used is assumed to rise or fall over time. If the default probability rises over time, as it does for an investment-grade bond, then the theoretical yield spread has a negative correlation with the outright yield level, whereas for a lower rated bond or junk bond, where the default probability falls the further we move into the future, the theoretical yield spread is positively correlated with the outright yield level. This is illustrated in Figure 8.4.

Portfolio managers must also take account of a further relationship between default risk and interest-rate risk. That is, if two corporate bonds have the same duration but one bond has a higher default probability, it essentially has a 'shorter' duration because there is a greater chance that it will experience premature cash flows, in the event of default.

This means that an investor who holds bonds that carry an element of default risk should in theory take this default risk into consideration when calculating the duration of his or her portfolio. In practical terms this only has an effect with unrated or junk bonds, which have default probabilities much greater than 1%. Figure 8.5 shows how the theoretical duration of a bond decreases as its assumed default probability increases.

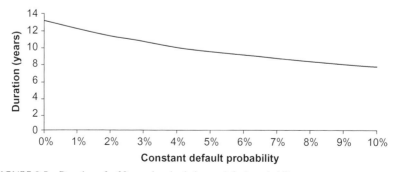

FIGURE 8.5 Duration of a 30-year bond relative to default probability.

8.3   MODELING THE CREDIT RISK

8.3.1   Structural Approach

As shown in previous sections, the credit spread on a corporate bond takes into account its expected default loss. Structural approaches are based on the option pricing theory of Black & Scholes and the value of debt depends on the value of the underlying asset. The determination of yield spread is based on the firm value in which the default risk is found as an option to the shareholders. Other models proposed by Black and Cox (1976), Longstaff and Schwartz (1995) and others try to overcome the limitation of the Merton's model, like the default event at maturity only and the inclusion of a default threshold. This class of models is also known as 'first passage models'.

8.3.1.1   Merton's Model

Merton's model is one of the most important models of credit risk. Merton (1974) and Black and Scholes (1973) proposed a model to assess the credit risk recalling the concept of capital structure, according to Modigliani and Miller's theorem (1958, 1963). According to the Black and Scholes's assumptions, at basis of the model the critical ones are two:

- The first one (Merton, 1974) requires assets that trade in continuous time;
- The second one, in which the dynamic of the firm value can be described by a diffusion-type stochastic process, is as follows[2]:

$$dV = (\alpha V - \gamma)dt + \sigma V dz \qquad (8.8)$$

where V is the firm value; α is the expected rate of return for the firm per unit time; γ is the dollar payouts in terms of dividend and interest payments, respectively, to shareholder and liabilities holders; σ is the standard deviation of returns per unit time and dz is the standard Gauss-Wiener process.

At the heart of the Merton's assumptions, equity holders have an embedded put option by which if at maturity the firm value is greater than promised obligation or *face value*, the lender gets back the bond's amount and shareholder maintains the ownership of the company; otherwise, if the firm value is lower than the promised payment, the bondholders receive an amount less than bond's face value and the firm defaults. Therefore, in the case of high-put option value, shareholders will have an advantage to walk away from the loan payment, leaving the asset value to the bondholders.

In practice, Sundaresan (2009) shows that when the firm value is low, shareholders can put the firm to bond investor according to the following equation:

$$\text{Risky loan} = \text{Risk free loan} - \text{Put option} \qquad (8.9)$$

2. See Chapter 2.

or

$$\text{Put option} = \text{Risk free loan} - \text{Risky loan} \qquad (8.10)$$

where the value of a put option is the spread between a risk-free loan and risky loan.

Therefore, the valuation of corporate bonds needs to consider the put option value in which the payoff at maturity is given by Equation (8.11):

$$D_T = F - \max(0, F - V_T) \qquad (8.11)$$

where D_T is the value of debt at maturity; F is the promised payment or face value and V_T is the value of firm at maturity.

Putting the strike price equal to the promised payment F, when the firm value is greater than that amount, the value of the option is 0 and the debt holder will receive the face value; conversely, the value of debt at maturity is lower than face value and the option has value. In the second case, the bondholders receive a payment value equal to the firm value and shareholders get nothing.

The equity can be assumed as a call option where the payoff is given by Equation (8.12):

$$E_T = F - \max(0, V_T - F) \qquad (8.12)$$

where E_T is the equity value at maturity.

Differently, the current equity value is given by Equation (8.13):

$$E(t, T) = V_t N(d_1) - Fe^{-r(T-t)}N(d_2) \qquad (8.13)$$

and the value of debt depends on the value of equity and is given by Equation (8.14):

$$D(t, T) = Fe^{-r(T-t)}N(d_2) + V_t N(-d_1) \qquad (8.14)$$

where

$$d_1 = \frac{\ln\left(\frac{V_t}{F}\right) + \left(r + \frac{1}{2}\sigma^2\right)(T-t)}{\sigma\sqrt{T-t}} \qquad (8.15)$$

and

$$d_2 = d_1 - \sigma\sqrt{T-t} \qquad (8.16)$$

where r is the risk-free rate and $N(d)$ is the value from the standardized normal distribution.

This equation can also be defined in terms of yield spread that reflects the yield premium required by a bondholder above the risk-free rate. The credit spread is given by Equation (8.17):

$$s = R_{(t,T)} - r = -\frac{1}{T-t} \ln\left[N(d_2) + \frac{V_t}{Fe^{-r(T-t)}} N(-d_1) \right] \tag{8.17}$$

or

$$s = R_{(t,T)} - r = \frac{-\ln\left[N(d_2) + \dfrac{N(-d_1)}{d} \right]}{T-t} \tag{8.18}$$

where we define $d = \dfrac{Fe^{-r(T-t)}}{V}$ the debt ratio to the firm value; R, the risky rate and τ^*, the time to maturity $T-t$. Therefore, the implied spread depends on the leverage d, volatility σ and time to maturity τ^*. Increasing the value of these parameters, the implied spread becomes wider. However, Merton (1974) shows that the dynamic of credit spread is different according to the maturity and leverage. When the leverage is low, a greater time to maturity increases the implied spread; differently, if the leverage is high with a short time to maturity, the implied spread is wider. This is shown in Figure 8.6.

8.3.1.2 Black and Cox's Model

Black and Cox (1976) proposed a modified version of the Merton's model by considering three main elements:

- First, the *safety covenants* that allow bondholders to force the firm into bankruptcy if the firm falls to a specified level. The level is given by Equation (8.19):

$$V_B = Fe^{-y(T-t)} \tag{8.19}$$

where V_B is the value barrier. Conversely to the Merton's model, the default can happen prior to maturity.
- Second, the Black & Cox's model includes subordinated debt in which the payment of the junior bond is subordinated to the senior debt. At maturity, the payment to the junior debt is made only if the debt obligation of the senior debt holder is satisfied;
- Finally, Merton's model assumes that when the value of firm is lower than the value of debt, equity holders sell assets in order to fulfill their

FIGURE 8.6   The effect of leverage, variance and time to maturity on credit spread. *(Reproduced from Merton (1974).)*

obligations. In this case, the Black & Cox's model supposes a restriction in the sale of assets and the financing of dividends and interest payments is done by issuing new securities.

The inclusion of previous provisions, safety covenants and asset sale restrictions increase the right of creditor and value of debt.

According to Black and Cox (1976), who consider a perpetual debt with continuous interest payment, the value of debt is given by Equation (8.20):

$$D(V) = \frac{C}{r} + \left(V_B - \frac{C}{r}\right)(\rho)^{-\alpha} \tag{8.20}$$

where ρ is the percentage firm value on the firm value with barrier V/V_B; C is the coupon and $\alpha = 2r/\sigma^2$.

According to Sundaresan (2013), the optimal default boundary is reproduced as follows Equation (8.21):

$$V_B = \frac{C}{r + \frac{\sigma^2}{2}} \tag{8.21}$$

The empirical evidence is that by including these assumptions, the Black & Cox's model generates credit spread very similar to the ones observed in the market.

8.3.1.3   Longstaff and Schwartz's Model

Extending the work of Black and Cox, Longstaff and Schwartz (1995) developed a new approach to value both, fixed and floating defaultable bonds. Like Black and Cox (1976), the model proposed overcomes the assumption at basis of the Merton's model in which the defaults occur when the firm exhausts its assets only and adding a value barrier by which the firm defaults. The assumptions at basis of this model are two:

- First, it considers both default risk and interest-rate risk;
- Second, the model overcomes the subordination among several debt categories.

Like Black and Cox's work, the authors find spreads similar to the market spreads. Moreover, they find a correlation between credit spread and interest rate. In fact, they illustrate that firms with similar default risk can have a different credit spread according to the industry. The evidence is that a different correlation between industry and economic environment affects the yield spread on corporate bonds. Then, the duration of a corporate bond changes following its credit risk. For high-yield bonds, the interest-rate sensitivity increases as the time to maturity decreases.

At heart of the model, one of the main assumptions is that if the reorganization occurs the bondholder receives $1 - w$, where w is the percentage write-down. If $w=0$ there is no write-down, when $w=1$ the security holder receives nothing and if $w<0$, the security holder benefits from the firm's restructuring.

For pricing fixed-rate bonds, the value is given by Equation (8.22):

$$P(X, r, T) = D(r, T) - wD(r, T)Q(X, r, T) \tag{8.22}$$

where $P(X, r, T)$ is the price of a fixed-rate bond; X is the ratio between the firm value V and the face value of debt K; $D(r, T)$ is the value of a default-free bond; $wD(r, T)$ is the present value of the write-down and $Q(X, r, T)$ is the probability of default under risk-neutral scenario.

The implication of the model is that the price of a defaultable bond is an increasing function of the value of X and is a decreasing function of w. Increasing the interest rate reduces the probability of default because in an upward interest scenario, the firm value increases at a faster rate of the value of debt.

The findings show that by increasing time to maturity, bonds with high ratings have an increasing/flat credit spread curve, while low rated bonds have a hump-shaped credit curve. Moreover, the credit spread becomes wider as the value of w increases.

8.3.1.4 Leland's Model

Leland (1994) developed structural models of default by including taxes and bankruptcy costs, investigating also on capital structure decision. The model is based on two main assumptions:

- First, the model follows the Modigliani and Miller's theorem in which the firm value is unaffected by the change of capital structure;
- Second, the model assumes a static face value of debt.

The author defines the total value of the firm $v(V)$ as the sum of firm value V, tax benefit from coupon payments $TB(V)$ less the value of bankruptcy costs $BC(V)$. The value is given by Equation (8.23):

$$v(V) = V + TB(V) - BC(V) = V + \left(\frac{\tau C}{r}\right)\left[1 - \left(\frac{V}{V_B}\right)^{-\alpha}\right] - bcV_B\left(\frac{V}{V_B}\right)^{-\alpha} \tag{8.23}$$

where τ is the corporate tax rate and bc are the bankruptcy costs expressed in percentage on firm value. Note that if V rises, the tax benefit $TB(V)$ increases with a concave function of V whereas the value of bankruptcy costs decreases with a convex function of V.

The optimal default boundary is modified from Equation (8.21) including corporate taxation as follows:

$$V_B = \frac{(1-\tau)C}{r + \dfrac{\sigma^2}{2}} \tag{8.24}$$

Leland (1994) studied also the behavior of risky interest rates and yield spreads for unprotected debt. He finds that greater coupons and bankruptcy costs increase the yield spread. Conversely, a greater corporate tax rate decreases the spread because the value of debt will rise.

Leland and Toft (1996) updated Leland's results by investigating the effect of debt maturity on bond value, credit spreads and optimal amount of debt. In particular:

- First, they consider an optimal amount and maturity of debt;
- Second, the bankruptcy is derived as an endogenous condition;
- Third, the model assumes a non-stochastic default-free interest rate.

The findings show that debt with longer maturity better uses the tax benefit while increasing agency costs in which shareholders of highly levered firms can substitute asset with riskier activities. This can be reduced by increasing the amount of short-term debt. The authors highlight that amount and maturity of debt are the two main variables that affect tax advantages, bankruptcy costs and agency costs.

8.3.2   Reduced-Form Approach

In order to solve the probability of default, reduced-form models adopt a different approach. They are mainly based on debt prices rather than equity prices. In fact, they do not take into account the fundamentals of the firm and the default event is determined as an exogenous process without considering the underlying asset movements. In addition, the models are mainly based on $\lambda(t)$, that is the default intensity as a function of time. In particular, these models use the decomposition of the risky rate (risk-free rate and risk premium) in order to determine the default probabilities, recovery rates and debt values. Although structural models have the advantage to follow a reliable measure of credit risk, that is the firm value, reduced-form approach overcomes the limitation in which the balance sheet is not the unique indicator of the default prediction.

8.3.2.1   Fons' Model

Fons (1994) studied the term structure of credit risk based on the historical default probabilities, ratings and recovery rates. In fact, he proposes a bond pricing model in which the value depends on the probability of default and average recovery rate. The model presented is based on the following assumptions:

- Bonds are prices at par;
- The bond is held until maturity, unless prior default;
- Risk-neutral pricing;
- Capital market in the arbitrage-free contest.

The credit spread is defined as the difference between the risky rate of a defaultable bond and the risk-free rate of a default-free bond. In this case, with bonds priced at par, between coupon and risk-free rate, the pricing is performed like a valuation of a straight bond, including the default risk adjustment. The price is given by Equation (8.25):

$$P = \sum_{t=1}^{T} \frac{S_t C + S_{t-1} d_t \mu (C+1)}{(1+i)^t} + \frac{S_T}{(1+i)^T} \qquad (8.25)$$

where S_t is the probability to receive coupon in year t; d_t is the probability of default in year t by considering S_{t-1} the probability of survivor at year $t-1$ and S_T is the probability to receive the principal repayment. The numerator is the default-risk-adjusted cash flow based on expected default rates. S_t is given by Equation (8.26):

$$S_t = \prod_{i=1}^{t} (1 - d_i) \qquad (8.26)$$

This represents the cumulative survival rate. Conversely, D_t is the cumulative default rate, that is the probability that do not receive the coupon in year t. It is given by Equation (8.27):

$$D_t = 1 - S_t \qquad (8.27)$$

Under risk-neutrality assumption, the most appropriate discount rate is the risk-free rate. The model is more sensitive to the change of recovery rates, while less sensitive to the change in interest rates. If we consider a zero-coupon bond rated R with maturity at time T, the price is given by Equation (8.28):

$$P = \sum_{t=1}^{N} S_{(t-1)} d_t \mu B e^{-rt} + S_T B e^{-rT} \qquad (8.28)$$

The spread can be expressed as follows (8.29):

$$s = -\frac{1}{T} \ln \left[\sum_{t=1}^{T} S_{(t-1)} d_t \mu e^{-r(t-T)} + S_T \right] \qquad (8.29)$$

The research compares the model spread to the one observed in the market. In order to determine the term structure of credit spread, Fons uses historical probabilities by Moody's database, adopting a recovery rate of 48.38%. The empirical evidence is that bonds with high investment grade have an upward credit spread curve. Therefore, the spread between defaultable and default-free bonds increases as maturity increases. Conversely, speculative-grade bonds have a negative or flat credit yield curve (Figure 8.7).

8.3.2.2   Jarrow, Lando and Turnbull's Model

Jarrow and Turnbull (1995) developed the first one intensity-based approach for valuing debt involving credit risk. The model is based on three main assumptions:

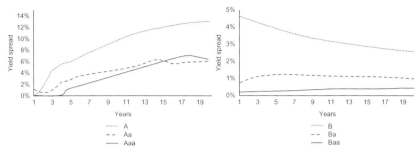

FIGURE 8.7   The term structure of credit spread for investment- and speculative-grade bonds. *(Reproduced from Fons (1994).)*

- *No arbitrage opportunities*: They assume the existence of an unique martingale measure $\bar{Q}$ in which default-free and risky zero-coupon bonds are martingales;
- *The recovery rate δ is constant and exogenously determined*: The recovery rate depends on the seniority of debt to other liabilities, meaning that stochastic structure of credit spread is independent from the recovery rate;
- *The stochastic process for default-free spot rates and default process are independent under martingale measure* $\bar{Q}$: This last assumption implies that the default process is uncorrelated with default-free spot interest rates.

According to this model, the price of a risky bond is given by Equation (8.30):

$$v(t,T) = p(t,T)\left[\delta + (1-\delta)\bar{Q}_t(\tau^* > T)\right] \qquad (8.30)$$

or

$$v(t,T) = p(t,T)\left[1 - (1-\delta)\bar{Q}_t(\tau^* \leq T)\right] \qquad (8.31)$$

where $v(t,T)$ is the price of a defaultable zero-coupon bond at time t, paying a sure dollar at time T, $p(t,T)$ is the price of a default-free zero-coupon bond at time t, paying a sure dollar at time T, τ^* is the random time at which the default occurs and $\bar{Q}_t(\tau^* > T)$ is the likelihood at which under $\bar{Q}_t$ the default occurs after time T. Therefore, the model determines the risky debt by considering the distribution for the time of default $\bar{Q}_t(\tau^* > T)$ only, under martingale probability and the value of a defaultable bond could be explained as the difference between the value of a default-free bond and the present value of the loss if default occurs.

Jarrow et al. (1997) proposed a modified version of the above model, assuming that the bankruptcy process follows a finite Markow process in the firm's credit rating. In particular, the model includes these characteristics:

- Several seniority debt by different recovery rates;
- The model can be included with interest-rate models[3];

---

3. See Chapters 3 and 4.

- It uses historical transition probabilities for different credit rating classes in order to determine the pseudo probabilities.

In practice, assuming the discrete time case, the transition matrix includes the transition probabilities between the possible states. Therefore, in this model, market prices are used to find the credit spread and convert the matrix of transition probabilities to the time-dependent risk-neutral matrices $\bar{Q}_{t,t+1}$. The credit spread is given by Equation (8.32):

$$R(t) - r(t) = 1_{(\tau > T)} \log \frac{1}{1 - (1 - \delta)q_{iK}(t, t + 1)} \tag{8.32}$$

The empirical result gives the survival probabilities and credit spreads. Assuming the risk-neutral hypothesis, the authors calculate the survival probabilities for firms with different credit ratings. The evidence is that survival probabilities for every time to maturity from 1 to 30 years are always greater for firm with better rating and vice versa. Assuming also a recovery rate of 0, the research obtains a similar result as other models explained above in which the spread curve is upward for firms with investment grade ratings and flat/downward for speculative-grade ratings.

8.3.2.3 Duffie and Singleton's Model

Another reduced model is the one proposed by Duffie and Singleton. In this model, the recovery rate of debt is determined prior to default, that is default and recovery rates are assumed exogenous. The price of bond is given by Equation (8.33):

$$v(t, T) = E_t^Q \left[\left(e^{-\int_t^T R_t dt} \right) X \right] \tag{8.33}$$

where E_t^Q is the risk-neutral expectation at time t; R_t is the default-adjusted short rate process and X is the value of contingent claim at maturity T.

According to this model, the adjusted short rate is given by Equation (8.34):

$$R(t) = r(t) + \lambda(t)(1 - \delta) \tag{8.34}$$

where the model takes into account the probability of default and timing of default and the losses at default.

8.3.2.4 Madan and Unal's Model

The model proposed by Madan and Unal (1998) decomposes the risky debt in two main embedded securities:

- *Survival securities*: That makes the payment at maturity in the case of default and nothing otherwise;

- *Default securities*: Paying the recovery rate in the case of default and nothing otherwise.

Therefore, the survival securities face the timing risk of default only and the default securities both, the timing risk of default and the risk of recovery in default.

The model is based on the following assumptions:

- Conversely to the model proposed by Jarrow and Turnbull (1995), Madan and Unal assume that the recovery rate is uncertain;
- The default payouts are independent and identically distributed;
- The risk of default timing depends on the stock price and not interest-rate path;
- The equity value is the main variable for driving the default risk.

According to Madan and Unal, the equity value movement is given by Equation (8.35):

$$dE(t) = \sigma E(t) dW(t) \tag{8.35}$$

where E is the equity value; σ is the volatility and W is the standard Brownian motion.

The price of bond is given by Equation (8.36):

$$v(t, T) = p(t, T)E(\delta) + p(t, T)[1 - E(\delta)]Q(\tau > T) \tag{8.36}$$

8.4   WEB SITE MODELS

The Web site associated with this book contains an Excel spreadsheet demonstrating Merton's model. The reader may use the spreadsheet to value credit risky bonds using this model and also to determine the embedded equity value.

Details of how to access the Web site are contained in the preface.

REFERENCES

Black, F., Cox, J.C., 1976. Valuing corporate securities: some effects of bond indenture provisions. J. Financ. 31 (2), 351–367.

Cohler, G., Feldman, M., Lancaster, B., 1997. Price of risk constant (PORC): going beyond OAS. J. Fixed Income 6(4).

Duffee, G.R., 1996a. Treasury Yields and Corporate Bond Yield Spreads: An Empirical Analysis. Federal Reserve Board, Washington, DC.

Duffee, G.R., 1996b. Estimating the Price of Default Risk. Federal Reserve Board, Washington, DC.

Duffee, G.R., 1998. The relation between treasury yields and corporate bond yield spreads. J. Financ. 53 (6), 2225–2241.

Duffie, D., Singleton, K.J., 1999. Modeling term structure of defaultable bonds. Rev. Financ. Stud. 12 (4), 687–720.

Elton, E.J., Gruber, M.J., Agrawal, D., Mann, C., 2001. Explaining the rate spread on corporate bonds. J. Financ. 56 (1), 247–277.

Fons, J.S., 1994. Using default rates to model the term structure of credit risk. Financ. Anal. J. 50, 25–32.

Hull, M., Nelken, I., White, A., 2004. Merton's model, credit risk, and volatility skews. J. Credit Risk 1 (1), 3–28.

Jarrow, R.A., Turnbull, S.M., 1995. Pricing derivates on financial securities subject to credit risk. J. Financ. 50 (1), 53–85.

Jarrow, R.A., Lando, D., Turnbull, S.M., 1997. A Markov model for the term structure of credit risk spreads. Rev. Financ. Stud. 10 (2), 481–523.

Kopprasch, R., 1994. Option-adjusted spread analysis: going down the wrong path? Financial Analysts Journal, 121–135.

Leland, H.E., 1994. Corporate debt value, bond covenants, and optimal capital structure. J. Financ. 49 (4), 1213–1252.

Leland, H.E., Toft, K.B., 1996. Optimal capital structure, endogenous bankruptcy, and the term structure of credit spreads. J. Financ. 51 (3), 987–1019.

Longstaff, F.A., Schwartz, E.S., 1995. A simple approach to valuing risky fixed and floating rate debt. J. Financ. 50 (3), 789–819.

Madan, D., Unal, H., 1998. Pricing the risks of default. Rev. Deriv. Res. 2 (2/3), 121–160.

Merton, R.C., 1974. On the pricing of corporate debt: the risk structure of interest rates. J. Financ. 29 (2), 449–470.

Saunders, A., Allen, L., 2002. Credit Risk Measurement: New Approaches to Value at Risk and Other Paradigms, second ed. John Wiley & Sons, New York.

Sundaresan, S., 2009. Fixed Income Markets and Their Derivates, third ed. Elsevier.

Sundaresan, S., 2013. A review of Merton's model of the firm's capital structure with its wide applications. Annu. Rev. Financ. Econ. 5, 21–41.

Trück, S., Laub, M., Rachev, S.T., 2004 The terms structure of credit spreads and credit default swaps – an empirical investigation, Working Paper, September.

Trueck, S., Rachev, S.T., 2008. Rating Based Modeling of Credit Risk: Theory and Application of Migration Matrices. Academic Press.

Tudela, M., Young, G., 2003. A Merton-model approach to assessing the default risk of UK public companies, *Bank of England Working Paper*, No. 194, June.

Chapter 9

Convertible Securities: Analysis and Valuation

Chapter Contents

In this chapter we present a discussion on convertible bonds, which have become popular *hybrid* financial instruments. Convertible bonds are financial instruments that give the bondholders the right, without imposing an obligation, to convert the bond into underlying security, usually common stocks, under conditions illustrate in the indenture at the time of issue. The hybrid characteristic defines the traditional valuation approach as the sum of two components: the *option-free bond* and an *embedded option* (call option). The option element makes the valuation not easy, above all in pricing term sheets with specific contract clauses as the inclusion of soft calls, put options and reset features. The chapter shows practical examples of valuation in which financial advisors and investment banks adopts in different contexts.

9.1 WHAT IS GOING ON IN THE CONVERTIBLE MARKET?

Since the financial crisis of 2007-2008, central banks have provided generous liquidity in the market with lower interest rates. This market trend has allowed convertible bonds to become an interesting corporate financing in which specific characteristics as convexity and downside protection, have increased the issuances in 2014. In fact, the market uncertainty, high volatility in stock environment and *credit crunch* under new regulatory capital in banking sector, give benefits for both parties: for *firms*, allowing to finance growth with lower interest rates due to the equity element; for *investors*, due to higher returns and lower risks with other asset classes, including a defensive position to equity exposure. The global convertible bond universe is sizeable at around $500 billion (source: UBS Global Asset Management), in which the United States market remains the largest one, broadly diversified by sector and countries. Figure 9.1 shows that the UBS Global Convertible Index has outperformed the MSCI on an absolute basis, giving a remarkable risk-adjusted return.

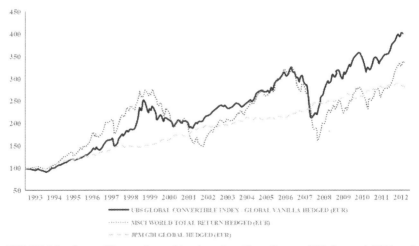

FIGURE 9.1 Convertibles, equity and bond market. *(Data Source: UBS Research 2013 and Bloomberg.)*

9.2   CONVERTIBLE BOND ANALYSIS

As introduced, convertible bonds give the right to exchange the bond to the underlying security. The number of shares received by the investor is determined by the *conversion ratio* as the following formula:

$$\text{Conversion ratio} = \frac{\text{Bond par value}}{\text{Conversion price}} \qquad (9.1)$$

For instance, given the bond par value of 100 and the conversion price of 2.6, the conversion ratio is around 38, that is the investor receives for each bond 38 shares. The *parity* or *intrinsic value* is defined as the ratio between the share price and the *conversion price* (or *conversion ratio*) and is given by Equation (9.2):

$$\text{Parity} = \frac{\text{Share price}}{\text{Conversion price (or Conversion ratio)}} \qquad (9.2)$$

Therefore, the parity allows to understand the instrument structure, in terms of debt and equity. The following chart indicates the parity line in which each value is related to the share price level (Figure 9.2).

As we know convertible bonds give to the investors a yield advantage compared to conventional bonds. This is given by Equation (9.3) (Example 9.1):

$$\text{Yield advantage} = \text{Current yield} - \text{Dividend yield} \qquad (9.3)$$

Convertible bonds give a risk premium above the bond floor, that is the excess of the convertible bond price above the option-free bond price (Figure 9.3).

The risk premium is calculated as follows (Equation 9.4):

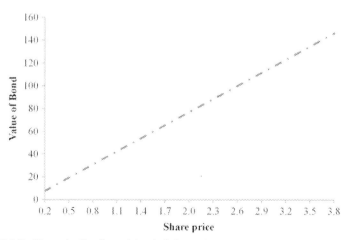

FIGURE 9.2   The parity line for each level of share price.

EXAMPLE 9.1 Yield Advantage

Let us now consider the following example. ABC plc has issued a 5-year convertible bond with a market price of €112.2 and an underlying share with a market price of €0.65. The bond has also a coupon of 5.5%, while the dividend yield of the underlying stock is 2%. If an investor buys just €100 and the bond may be converted into 151.7 shares, the premium over a direct purchase of the ordinary shares expressed in basis points is equal to (112.2 − 98.6) or €13.6 per bond, in which 98.6 is obtained by multiplying the conversion ratio of 151.7 by the current stock price of €0.65. The compensation for this premium is the cash flow differential between the convertible and underlying shares, which is calculated as (€100 × 5.5%) − (98.6 × 2%) or €3.5. The payback period measure is €13.6/3.5 or 3.86 years and the concept is similar to payback period used in corporate finance analysis.

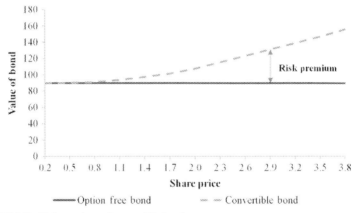

FIGURE 9.3 Risk premium of convertible bonds.

$$\text{Risk Premium} = \frac{\text{Convertible bond price}}{\text{Option free bond price}} - 1 \qquad (9.4)$$

For instance, if the convertible bond price is 107.5 and the bond floor is 89.7, the risk premium is around 20%. This means that an investor is required to pay a risk premium of 20% for the option of the underlying asset.

9.2.1 Issuer's Viewpoint

The main reason for a borrower to issue convertibles is the lower cost of financing than other financial instruments. In fact, the implied equity option feature allows the issuer to pay lower market coupons than a conventional bond. This is because the right of conversion is hold by the bondholder. In a different case, for instance with a callable issue, the coupons will be greater than a convertible because the right to exercise the option is hold by the company. Moreover, conventionally the issuers are able to sell the underlying shares at a greater price than a direct equity offering. This is because in an equity offering, shares are issued at discount of the fair value in order to attract the interest of the investors. For convertibles, the combined package of debt and equity permits to set the price of the underlying shares at fair value. This is incorporated by the conversion premium applied to the reference price. Another benefit for the issuer is the tax advantage. In fact, the interest expenses are deductible from the taxable income while usually dividend payments not.[1]

9.2.2   Bondholder's Viewpoint

The main benefit for an investor is to participate in the appreciation of the underlying asset. In fact, if the price rises, the bondholder can obtain this benefit and convert the bond into shares. There is also a downside benefit. In fact, in the case of falling prices, the investor has the downside protection by receiving the coupon payments from the bond floor. For a fixed income investor, even if the coupons are lower than a conventional bond, however, those are higher than dividend yield from holding the share directly. Equity investors are attracted also by the asymmetrical equity sensitivity of this instrument. In fact while the return of equity is assumed to be symmetrical, convertible bonds are more sensitive from the underlying asset when the implied option is in the money, that is with rising prices than falling prices. This is measured by the risk premium shown in formula (9.4). An increasing risk premium means that the convertible bond price is rising due to the increasing value of the implied option and, therefore, greater share prices.

9.3   CONVERTIBLE BOND VALUATION

As explained in the introduction, the value of a convertible bond is the sum of two main components, the *option-free bond* and a *call option* on underlying security. The value of the option-free bond, or *bond floor*, is determined as the sum of future payments (coupon and principal at maturity). Therefore, the bond component is influenced by three main parameters, that is the maturity, the coupon percentage on par value and the yield to maturity (discount rate). Differently, the value of a call option can be found mainly through two option pricing models, *Black&Scholes* model and *binomial tree* model.

The theory of options was developed in the assumption of *market equilibrium*. The first option pricing model was proposed by Black and Scholes (1973) and then by Merton (1973), in which they did not consider dividend payments. Authors as Schwartz (1975) include dividend payments into valuation model and also consider the possibility of exercising the option before the maturity

---

1. Even if with some limitations, for example under *Earning Stripping Rules* or *Thin Capitalization*.

date (American option). Brennan and Schwartz (1977) consider the appropriate boundary strategy on convertible bond solving the differential equation, mainly focused on optimal strategy in which dividing *optimal conversion strategy* and *optimal call strategy*.

The first one is 'one which maximises the value of the convertible bond at each instant in time'. In practice, the definition starts from the Modigliani and Miller theorem asserting that the firm value is independent of the conversion strategy. Therefore, given the conversion value equal to the conversion ratio times the share price at conversion, the value of the outstanding equity after conversion is given by the pre-conversion firm value divided by the number of shares outstanding shares when the bond is converted.

For investors, it is optimal to convert a bond only if its market price is less than conversion value. Because an uncalled bond cannot sell a low price as the conversion value except prior to a dividend date or in the case of adverse change of conversion terms, the investor will never obtain the optimal conversion strategy. According to Brennan and Schwartz (1977), the value of the bond if called is equal to maximum value of the call price and conversion value. In this case, the bond's value is maximised.

In contrast, the optimal call strategy is 'one which minimises the value of the convertible bonds at each instant in time'. In other words, for a firm, the optimal call strategy is to call the bond when its price if not called is equal to the call price and thus the value of the convertible is minimised.

Cox et al. (1979) developed a binomial tree model in which they determine the option value through a discrete time formula.

9.3.1 Valuation

The proposed methodology determines the theoretical value of convertible bonds as the combination of a straight bond and an embedded call option. The valuation is performed in three steps:

- Determining the value of an option-free bond;
- Determining the value of an embedded option;
- Determining the value of a convertible bond.

9.3.1.1 *Determining the Value of an Option-Free Bond*

The fair value of an option-free bond is the sum of the present values of all its cash flows in terms of coupon payments and principal repayment. The bond value is given by Equation (9.5):

$$P = \sum_{t=1}^{t=N} \frac{C_t}{(1+r)^t} + \frac{M}{(1+r)^N} \tag{9.5}$$

where P is the fair price of a bond; C_t is the annual coupon payment; r is the discount rate and M is the face value of the bond, or principal, or par value.

Consider a hypothetical situation. Assume that an option-free bond paying a semi-annual coupon 5.5% on par value, with a maturity of 5 years and discount rate of 8.04% (EUR 5-year swap rate of 1.04% plus credit spread of 700 basis points). Therefore, the valuation of a conventional bond is performed as follows (Figure 9.4).

Because the discount rate (8.04%) is greater than coupon (5.5%), the bond is valued at *discount*, or 89.71.

The valuation of a conventional bond can be performed also using a binomial tree. On maturity, the bond must be priced at par value plus the semi-annual coupon payment equal to 2.75. Therefore, the value of a conventional bond at maturity t_{10} must be equal to 102.75. The value of the bond in other nodes prior to maturity is calculated using the semi-annual discount rate of 4.02%. For instance, at node t_9 the pricing is given by Equation (9.6):

$$P = \frac{(102.75 \times 0.5) + (102.75 \times 0.5)}{\left(1 + \dfrac{0.0804}{2}\right)} + 2.75 = 101.53 \tag{9.6}$$

The process is continued until time t_0 in which the value of an option-free bond is equal to the one obtained in Figure 9.4, or 89.71. This is shown in Figure 9.5.

Cash flows (Coupon payments + Face value)	2.75	2.75	2.75	2.75	2.75	2.75	2.75	2.75	2.75	102.75
Discount rate	4.02%	4.02%	4.02%	4.02%	4.02%	4.02%	4.02%	4.02%	4.02%	4.02%
Discounted cash flows	**2.64**	**2.54**	**2.44**	**2.35**	**2.26**	**2.17**	**2.09**	**2.01**	**1.93**	**69.28**
Price of an option free bond	**89.71**									

FIGURE 9.4 The valuation of a conventional bond.

0	1	2	3	4	5	6	7	8	9	10
										102.75
									101.53	
								100.36		102.75
							99.23		101.53	
						98.14		100.36		102.75
					97.10		99.23		101.53	
				96.10		98.14		100.36		102.75
			95.13		97.10		99.23		101.53	
		94.21		96.10		98.14		100.36		102.75
	93.32		95.13		97.10		99.23		101.53	
89.71		94.21		96.10		98.14		100.36		102.75
	93.32		95.13		97.10		99.23		101.53	
		94.21		96.10		98.14		100.36		102.75
			95.13		97.10		99.23		101.53	
				96.10		98.14		100.36		102.75
					97.10		99.23		101.53	
						98.14		100.36		102.75
							99.23		101.53	
								100.36		102.75
									101.53	
										102.75

FIGURE 9.5 The valuation of a conventional bond using the binomial tree.

9.3.1.2 Determining the Value of an Embedded Option

The value of an embedded option is found through the binomial tree model. The first step is to forecast the value of the underlying security in which the price S of a security can move, respectively, in the upstate S_u and downstate S_d with a probability of p and $1 - p$. The change in price occurs in discrete time interval Δt and will depend on the level of volatility assumed. An option written on the asset, with maturity T will move in discrete steps as the movements of the share prices. The process can be carried on for any number of time intervals (Figure 9.6).

Therefore, the parameters used in binomial stock price tree are:

$$u = e^{\sigma\sqrt{\Delta t}} \quad d = \frac{1}{u} \quad P_u = \frac{e^{r\Delta t} - d}{u - d} \quad P_d = 1 - p \quad (9.7)$$

where u is the up movement; d is the down movement; r is the risk-free rate; σ is the stock price volatility; P_u is the up probability; P_d is the down probability and t is the time.

Assuming the stock price at time t_0 is 2 and that the option has a time to expiration of 5 years like the bond floor element, the asset will have the following stock path assuming a volatility of 35% as shown in Figure 9.7. In fact, at time t_1, the stock price may be 2.84 in the upstate and 1.41 in the downstate. The spread of the two outcomes will strongly depend on the volatility of the return on S.

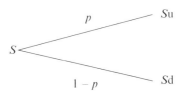

FIGURE 9.6 Binomial stock price outcome.

0	1	2	3	4	5
					11.51
				8.11	
			5.72		5.72
		4.03		4.03	
	2.84		2.84		2.84
2.00		2.00		2.00	
	1.41		1.41		1.41
		0.99		0.99	
			0.70		0.70
				0.49	
					0.35

FIGURE 9.7 Binomial stock price tree.

Therefore, at maturity T, the value of a call option is determined as the relationship between the stock price S_T of the underlying asset and the strike price X as follows (Equation 9.8):

$$C_T = \max(S_T - X, 0) \tag{9.8}$$

For instance, at maturity, the stock price can have a maximum value of 11.51 and a minimum value of 0.35, according to the assumed volatility. Therefore, at higher node, the value of option will be equal to 8.91 as the difference between the stock price of 11.51 and conversion price or strike price of 2.6. In contrast, at lower node, because the stock price of 0.35 is lower than conversion price of 2.6, the option value will be equal to 0. Particular situation is in the middle of the binomial tree in which in the upstate the stock price is 2.84 and downstate is 1.41, meaning that in the first case the option is in the money, while in the second case is out of the money.

However, according to the optimal conversion strategy, the investor maximises the value in each node before maturity date, that is exercising the conversion option C_T or waiting a further period C_t:

$$C_t = e^{-r\Delta t}(P_u \times C_u + P_d \times C_d) \tag{9.9}$$

where C_t is the value of the call option at any node; C_u is the value of the option in the upstate; C_d is the value of the option in the downstate; P_u is the up probability; P_d is the down probability; r is the interest rate and Δt is the time period.

From Figure 9.8, the option value at time t_0 is calculated starting at the final node (time T) by using the formula (9.8) and working backward in each node by applying the formula (9.9). The value of a call option at time t_0 is equal to 0.46.

The value of the *conversion option* is equal to the *conversion ratio* (number of common shares for which each bond may be exchanged) multiplied by the value of a *call option*, that is having a par value of 100 and a conversion price of 2.6, the conversion ratio is 38.5. The value of the conversion option at time t_0 is 17.8 (0.46×38.5). This is the value of the option element.

0	1	2	3	4	5
					8.91
				5.54	
			3.17		3.12
		1.72		1.45	
	0.91		0.67		0.24
0.46		0.31		0.10	
	0.14		0.04		0.00
		0.02		0.00	
			0.00		0.00
				0.00	
					0.00

FIGURE 9.8 Binomial option tree.

9.3.1.3 Determining the Value of a Convertible Bond

The value of a convertible bond is the sum of the option-free bond and the conversion option element, or 107.5.

$$
\begin{aligned}
\text{Value of a Convertible Bond} &= \text{Value of an Option-Free Bond} \\
&\quad + \text{Value of the Conversion Option} \qquad (9.10) \\
&= 89.7 + 17.8 = 107.5
\end{aligned}
$$

9.3.2 Model Parameters Affecting Value of Convertible Bonds

The embedded option component in convertible bonds makes the valuation sensitive from three main parameters: *share price*, *volatility* and *interest rate*. These parameters affect the value of a convertible bond for both situations:

- *At issue*: In which the choice of these inputs will have an impact on the bond pricing, determining also the percentage composition between debt and equity;
- *After issue*: In which the change of these inputs will affect the market price of bond.

9.3.2.1 Share Price

As noted, the share price is a key parameter of the option pricing model. An increase in the underlying share price will result in a rise of the convertible price, and a decrease in the share price will result in a fall of the convertible price. Figure 9.9 illustrates the comparison between the convertible bond price and share price of Intel Corporation.

The chart shown in Figure 9.10 demonstrates that when the stock market is performing badly, the convertible bond trades as a straight bond and the probability of conversion will fall. In this case, the sensitivity of the convertible to

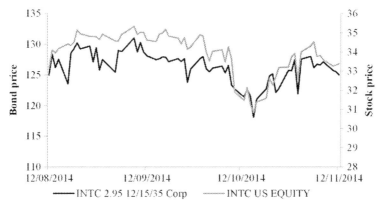

FIGURE 9.9 Comparison between the Intel's convertible bond price and Intel's share price. *(Data source: Bloomberg.)*

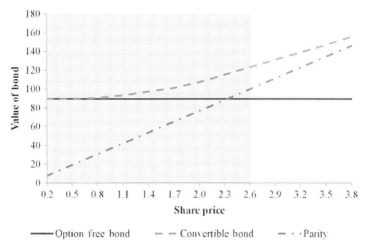

FIGURE 9.10 Convertible price sensitivity.

change in share price is low. Conversely, if the stock market is performing well, then the convertible bond trades as the equity element and the sensitivity between convertible bond and share price rises. The latter case occurs when the parity is overcome, that is when the stock price exceeds the conversion price, or 2.6.

Consider also that the relationship between convertible and share price depends on the degree of the convexity. In fact, if the security has high convexity, its sensitivity is high to the movements of the share price. While in falling share prices, the convertible bond will suffer less.

9.3.2.2 Volatility

The second parameter that affects convertible value is the volatility. In fact, the volatility of the underlying asset is the main element that moves the value of the embedded option, in which pricing models are very sensitive from this parameter. Note that convertible price rises as the volatility increases. The chart shown in Figure 9.11 defines the value of the convertible bond with the volatilities of 25%, 35% and 45%.

Conventionally, investment banks price convertible securities using the *implied volatility* rather *historical volatility*. The implied volatility is different to the historical volatility in which the first one refers to volatility going forward. In other words, banks at issue given all parameters, determine the volatility as a goal seek into the model.

During the book runner phase, banks go in the market with a range of coupons and conversion premium in which each value in the range has a different implied volatility, representing the market sentiment. Thus, the market supply

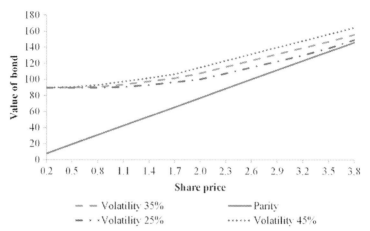

FIGURE 9.11 Convertible price sensitivity – Volatility.

and demand will determine the bond's structure and consequently the implied volatility. In other words, the implied volatility increases with a decreasing coupon value, because if the convertible price is 100, the weight of the bond floor decreases in respect to the equity element and vice versa.

Consider the hypothetical bond explained in Section 9.3.1. The convertible security has a price of 107.5 that includes a historical volatility of 35%. However, the convertible is valued at par (100) using the implied volatility. In practice, given all parameters and given the price of convertible bond (100), the implied volatility is a result of a goal seek value in which the percentage volatility level obtained is 25% (Figure 9.12).

The reason to use implied volatility is that market anticipates mean reversion and uses the implied volatility to gauge the volatility of individual assets relative to the market. Implied volatility represents a market option about the underlying asset and therefore is forward looking. However, the estimate of implied volatility is conditioned by the choice of other inputs; in particular, the credit spread applied in the option-free bond and the conversion premium of the underlying asset (Example 9.2).

Moreover, the volatility input has a different effect depending on if the option is in or out of the money. In fact, the value of the convertible bond is more sensitive to changes in volatility when the option is in the money (price of the underlying asset

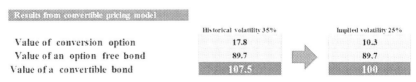

FIGURE 9.12 The value of a convertible bond.

EXAMPLE 9.2 Convertible Bond Pricing with Bloomberg

Consider the example of Beni Stabili SpA. On 11 July 2014 the convertible of Beni Stabili quoted to €112.229. Analysing Figure 9.13 we see that the option-free bond value is €98.5, while the option value is €13.7. In practical terms, the option value can be seen as the difference between market price of convertible and option-free bond (112.2 – 98.5). However, the option value is found through the implied volatility that is equal to 20.6%.

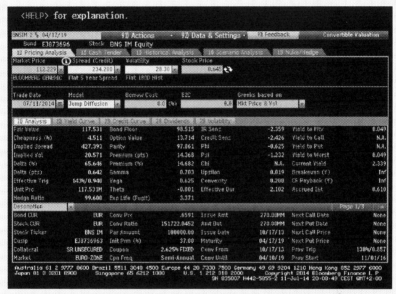

In contrast, the fair value (€117.5) is different from the market price because the first one is calculated using the historical volatility that in this case is 28.3%. Putting the fair value (117.5) into the market price cell, we obtain the same fair value. If the theoretical value is €117.5, then the bond is cheap in the market, with a cheapness of 4.5% calculated as follows (Equation 9.11):

$$Cheapness = \frac{Fair\,Value - Market\,Price}{Fair\,Value} = \frac{117.5 - 112.2}{117.5} = 4.5\% \qquad (9.11)$$

greater than strike price) than the out of the money state. Consider the hypothetical bond shown in Section 9.3.1, if the stock price is 2 and the strike price is 2.6, the option is out of the money. If the volatility increases from 35% to 40%, the value of the convertible bond increases from 107.5 to 111.2 (Figure 9.14).

Results from convertible pricing model	Stock price = 2	
	Volatility 35%	Volatility 40%
Value of conversion option	17.8	21.5
Value of an option free bond	89.7	89.7
Value of a convertible bond	107.5	111.2

FIGURE 9.14 The value of a convertible bond – Volatility sensitivity for out of the money options.

Results from convertible pricing model	Stock price = 2.8	
	Volatility 35%	Volatility 40%
Value of conversion option	38.9	43.1
Value of an option free bond	89.7	89.7
Value of a convertible bond	128.6	132.8

FIGURE 9.15 The value of a convertible bond – Volatility sensitivity for in the money options.

If the stock price is 2.8 and the strike price is 2.6, the option is in the money. If the volatility increases from 35% to 40%, the value of the convertible bond increases from 128.6 to 132.8 (Figure 9.15).

In the first case the change in value of the convertible is 3.7, while in the second case is 4.2.

Finally, the implied volatility can be compared with the historical volatility of the underlying asset. Going to market, if the implied volatility is less than volatility of the underlying share, it means that an investor might speculate and make profit.

9.3.2.3 Interest Rates and Credit Spread

The risk-free rate affects both elements, option-free bond and embedded option. Conversely, the credit spread is applied to the risk-free rate in order to find the price of the option-free bond. If the credit spread is also included into the option pricing model, the option value rises. For instance, consider the scenario in which the risk-free rate is 1.04% and the option value is 0.46. If the risk-free rate is 7.04%, then the option value increases to 0.66. Figure 9.16 shows the effect of a different interest rate level.

For valuing the option-free bond, *market makers* usually adopt a fixed interest rate; for instance, for pricing convertibles issue in Europe, banks use the interest-rate swap as a risk-free rate benchmark with the same time to maturity. In alternative, the bond can be priced using a yield curve of government bonds or Euro curves as a proxy of risk-free rate. However, the yield curve changes overtime and this risk can be hedged using futures or swaps. Figure 9.17 shows the PFC function of Bloomberg.

Consider the case of Tesla Motors Inc., the bond has semi-annual coupon payments. In this case, the present value is determined by using the spot rate for each payment date in which the international yield curve has been implemented.

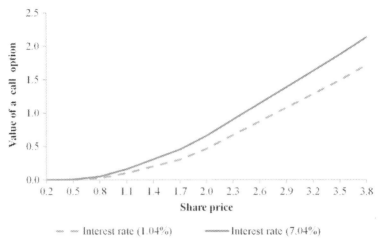

FIGURE 9.16   Value of a call option with a different interest rate.

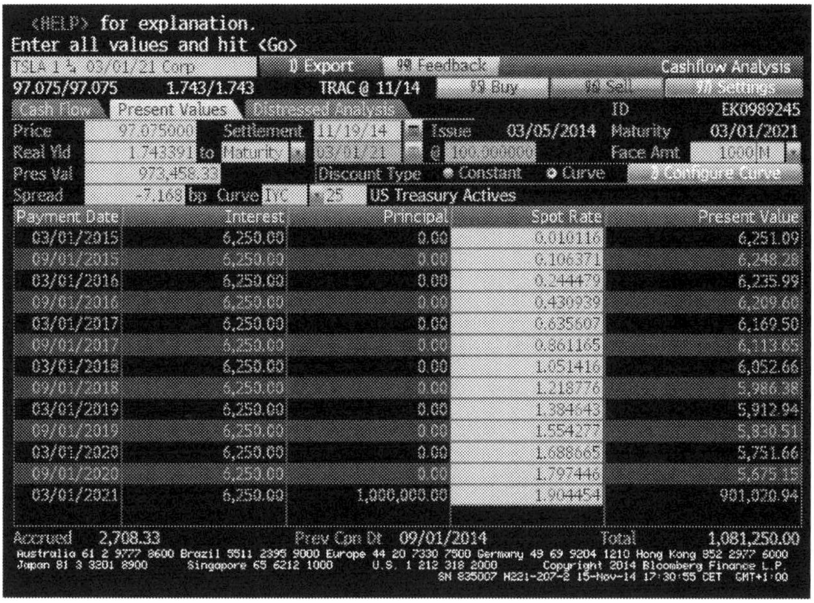

FIGURE 9.17   Cash flow payments of TSLA 1 ¼% 2021, on PFC screen. *(Used with permission of Bloomberg L.P. Copyright© 2014. All rights reserved.)*

Following the risk neutral theory, the credit spread is not included into option valuation because it is independent from the default risk of the underlying asset. The inclusion of credit spread overvalues the option.

As introduced, maintaining fixed all parameters, the implied volatility is found by a goal seek procedure. In the same way, the implied spread depends on model parameters. Since the credit spread affects only the bond floor, the value of the convertible bond is more sensitive from this variable when the embedded option is out of the money than in the money.

9.3.3 Special Market Model Features

9.3.3.1 Justifying the Conversion Premium at Issue

The first important decision for pricing convertible bonds is to decide the conversion premium above the stock price at issue. The conversion premium at issue determines the conversion price, that is the point in which there is parity relationship between the underlying asset and the convertible bond. In fact bonds are often issued with a premium and the conversion price, also known as the *strike price*, is the actual price paid for the shares when conversion occurs.

The conversion price, and indirectly the conversion premium, represents the potential upside of the underlying security. Therefore, the estimate of the conversion premium needs two analyses:

- *Market approach*: Allowing to understand the market sentiment by analysing the conversion premium for other convertible issues. In time of market turmoil and undervalued stocks, the convertible bond allows to incorporate the equity upside potential and ensuring the downside protection through the bond floor component. Therefore, higher is the potential upside of the underlying asset, greater is the conversion premium. The Table in Appendix shows conversion premiums for Italian convertible bond market across different sectors in 2014;
- *Fundamental approach*: Focusing on the value of underlying asset; therefore, the conversion premium and conversion price at issue is also determined using equity valuation methods or simply by looking the target price estimated in equity research reports (Example 9.3).

If the equity value is estimated by using the discounted cash flow method, the cost of capital assumes a particular relevance. Conventionally, the cost of capital is estimated through the capital asset pricing model (CAPM) that was introduced by Sharpe (1964) and subsequently improved by Lintner (1965).[2] One of the most important variables is beta. Beta measures the sensitivity of the asset's or company returns to variation in the market or index returns. Therefore, according to CAPM theory, the risk assumed from an investor depends on the covariance (or correlation) between individual assets and market portfolio. Thus, if these singular assets do not have correlation, they will not add risk; differently, if the correlation is positive they will add risk on market portfolio.

---

2. With free cash flows to firm, we use the Weighted Average Cost of Capital or *WACC*.

EXAMPLE 9.3 Justify the Conversion Premium

Consider a convertible bond issued by our hypothetical borrower ABC plc. In the example, ABC has issued a bond with the following terms (Table 9.1):

TABLE 9.1 Convertible Bond Terms and Conditions

Reference price	€ 3.4
Conversion premium	37.5%
Conversion price	€ 4.7

The equity analysts estimate a target price as shown in Table 9.2.[7]

TABLE 9.2 Target Price Estimation

Eur Per Share	Target Price
Average	4.67
Median	4.80
Min	3.90
Max	5.30

Therefore, target prices allow to understand if the conversion price at issue is fair or not. In this case, the range of expected values between €3.9 and €5.3 per share justifies the conversion price of €4.7 per share. Figure 9.18 clarifies what we explain.

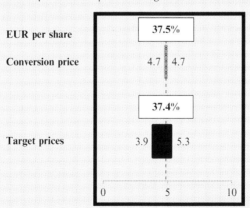

FIGURE 9.18 Conversion price and target price.

---

[7]There are several methods for estimating the equity value, usually equity analysts implement valuations using discounted cash flow model and Market Multiples. See Damodaran (2006).

In other words:

- If beta $= 0$, the investment does not add new risk to market portfolio and the expected return should be equal to risk-free rate $(R_j = R_f)$;
- If beta $= 1$, the investment has the same risk of market portfolio and, therefore, the same expected return $(R_j = R_m)$;
- If beta > 1, the single stock has a covariance (between stock and market portfolio) greater than variance of market portfolio;
- If beta < 1, the single stock has a covariance (between stock and market portfolio) lower than variance of market portfolio.

In rising stock markets, beta ≥ 1 benefits from the index appreciation because the probability of rising stock prices and, therefore, to convert the bond will increase. Therefore, a greater beta determines a greater cost of capital and consequently a lower present value of cash flows. This means that the target price of the underlying asset will be lower, reducing the conversion premium.

Note that the choice of the conversion premium to apply on reference price assumes a great importance in pricing of a convertible bond. A greater conversion premium decreases the value of the embedded option because the underlying asset needs a greater upside to give the right of conversion to the bondholder. For instance, the convertible bond pricing shown in 9.3.1 assumes a conversion premium of 30%, that is a conversion price of 2.6. Figure 9.19 shows that if we decrease this premium, the value of the convertible increases. The limit case is when the convertible is issued with a conversion price equal to the reference price, or conversion premium equals 0. In this case, the value of the convertible is around 123 greater than 107.5 obtained with a premium of 30%.

A premium of 0 is conventionally used in structured notes issued by distressed companies in which the mean reason is to increase the balance sheet

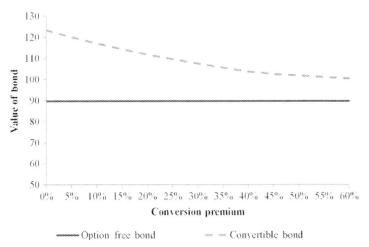

FIGURE 9.19 Convertible price sensitivity – Conversion premium.

strength. In order to rebalance the convertible structure in terms of debt and equity, these convertibles are usually matched with higher coupons than a normal convertible issue.

In contrast, an increasing conversion premium decreases the value of the convertible. For instance, a conversion premium of 60% the convertible bond prices around 100. Therefore, increasing the conversion premium the option element decreases, and the convertible bond prices with values closed to the bond floor.

9.3.3.2   Conversion Premium After Issue

After bond issue, the implied premium fluctuates overtime mainly due to the market movements of the stock price. In fact, the bond floor is enough stable during the convertible bond's life and the change of the convertible prices are due to the moves of the underlying asset.

Because the conversion price is fixed, the implied premium decreases if the stock prices drop and increases if the stock prices go up (see Figures 9.20 and 9.21).[3]

FIGURE 9.20   Convertible bond price and conversion premium of BNSIM 2⅜% 2019, on CNVG screen. *(Used with permission of Bloomberg L.P. Copyright© 2014. All rights reserved.)*

---

3. The indenture can include a *dividend protection* through adjustment to the conversion price.

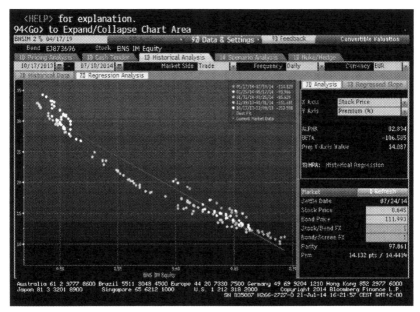

Consider again the example of Beni Stabili SpA. Beni Stabili has issued a convertible bond at an initial premium of 37% and reference price of €0.48. Because the stock price has changed, the implied premium is different to the initial premium. If the current stock price is €0.65 and the market price of bond is €112.2, then the conversion value is given by Equation (9.12):

$$\text{Conversion value} = \text{Share price} \times \text{Conversion ratio} = 0.65 \times 151.72 = €98.6 \tag{9.12}$$

where the conversion value of the bond shows the current value of the shares received in exchange of the bond. Therefore, the implied premium is given by Equation (9.13):

$$\% \text{ conv. price premium} = \frac{\text{Price of bond} - \text{Conversion value}}{\text{Conversion value}} = \frac{112.2 - 98.6}{98.6} = 13.8\% \tag{9.13}$$

9.3.4 Valuing the Option Component with Black and Scholes Model

In 1973, Myron Scholes and Fisher Black developed a model known as B&S model for valuing options. Like the binomial tree, in the B&S model the option value depends mainly on the price of the underlying asset, volatility, interest rate, time to expiration and dividend yield. Because in this chapter, we propose the value of a convertible as the sum of the straight bond and call option, the latter element can be found using the B&S model. However, using B&S, the model treats the financial instrument as a European option by which we assume to exercise the conversion at maturity only.

Therefore, the model is easy to implement and gives similar results as the binomial tree. Because B&S works in continuous compounding while the binomial tree in discrete time, the models give the same results only if the binomial tree has a high number of steps. The more periods in binomial tree are implemented, the nearer is the value that we get in both models. Consider the convertible bond pricing shown in Section 9.3.1. In that analysis we estimate the value of a call option using the binomial tree, obtaining a value per call of 0.46.

Calculating the value of a call option with the same parameters, B&S gives a value of 0.47 greater than the one obtained using the binomial tree of 0.46. However, increasing the number of steps in the binomial tree makes the value similar to the B&S. In fact, increasing the binomial tree steps from 5 to 20 the value of the call is 0.47, with a low error.[4] Moreover, in this case as well a goal seek function can be implemented in which the value error between the B&S model and the binomial tree model is reduced to 0. Increasing the binomial model from 5 to 20 steps, the difference of value between binomial tree and B&S decreases from 0.006 to 0.003. Changing the number of steps, the difference fluctuates between positive and negative values. Therefore, higher is the number of steps, lower is the difference of value between the two models.

Figure 9.22 confirms the sensitivity analysis of the share price implemented by Connolly (1998) in which in some area the binomial tree overvalues the B&S model and in other area not.

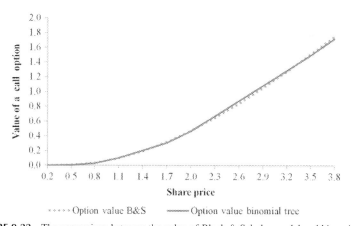

FIGURE 9.22   The comparison between the value of Black & Scholes model and binomial tree.

---

4. Take into account that in special situations, for instance, with the implementation of stock barrier, the binomial tree requires a higher number of steps. Conversely, B&S and binomial results can be very different.

9.4 FURTHER CONVERTIBLE BOND FEATURES

9.4.1 Embedded Options

9.4.1.1 'Hard Call' and 'Soft Call'

Convertible instruments are usually issued with attached call or put options. Such features can be implemented into the valuation model. If a soft call feature has been implemented, it enables the issuer to force the conversion when the share price overcomes a percentage or *trigger level* above the conversion price. However, this option cannot be called in the first years 'hard call'. Differently, after the protection period, the issuer can exercise the option. This second time is referred to 'soft call'. Using the same example shown in Section 9.3.1, we assume that the bond may be redeemed in whole but not in part at their principal amount plus accrued interest on the last 2 years, in which the maturity date is at 20 February 2019. On and after this 'call date', if the share price exceeds 130% of the conversion price the issuer can force the conversion. Figure 9.23 shows the stock price tree in which at years 4 and 5 the stock price is above the threshold.

Therefore, when the stock price reaches the trigger level, the maximum stock price (S^{SC}) is 30% above the conversion price X, or 3.38, and value of the option can be rearranged to[5]:

$$C_t = \max\left[\min\left(S_t, S_t^{SC}\right) - X, 0\right] \tag{9.14}$$

In fact, in that nodes the maximum value of the call option is 0.78 (Figure 9.24).

Multiplying the value of the call option (0.37) by the conversion ratio of 38.462, we obtain the value of conversion option (including soft call) which is equal to 14.3, lower than the one obtained without soft call of 17.8. As in

0	1	2	3	4	5
					11.51
				8.11	
			5.72		5.72
		4.03		4.03	
	2.84		2.84		2.84
2.00		2.00		2.00	
	1.41		1.41		1.41
		0.99		0.99	
			0.70		0.70
				0.49	
					0.35

FIGURE 9.23 Binomial stock price tree.

---

5. (S^{SC}) = stock price with soft call.

0	1	2	3	4	5
					0.78
				0.78	
			3.12		0.78
		1.54		0.78	
	0.76		0.39		0.24
0.37		0.19		0.10	
	0.09		0.04		0.00
		0.02		0.00	
			0.00		0.00
				0.00	
					0.00

FIGURE 9.24 Binomial option tree with trigger level of 30% above the stock price.

Results from convertible pricing model

	Without soft call		With soft call
Value of conversion option	17.8		14.3
Value of an option free bond	89.7		89.7
Value of a convertible bond	107.5		104

FIGURE 9.25 The value of a convertible bond with and without soft call clause.

Figure 9.25, the added call feature reduces the value of the convertible bond from 107.5 to 104.

9.4.1.2   Put Options

The put option gives at the bondholder the right, but not the obligation to redeem the convertible bond to the issuer at the price defined in the indenture. In this case, the value of the convertible bond is greater (the yield is lower) than the one without embedded put option. Usually, the issuer is required to redeem the convertible bond for cash, shares or both elements.

9.4.1.3   Reverse Convertible Bonds

The reverse convertible bonds have increased popularity in Europe and United States. This type of instrument gives to the issuer (not the bondholder) at maturity the right to exchange the bond into shares or to redeem it at par value plus accrued interests. In the first case, the bond is exchanged if the share price is less than conversion price, or if the conversion value is less than par value. Conversely, the issuer can redeem the bond. They typically have a domestic stock as underlying security, but they can also include foreign shares and indexes.

This type of bond is treated as an option-free bond with a European put option attached because the right can only be exercised at maturity. From the investor's viewpoint, these bonds offer higher coupons and they are riskier than normal convertible bonds, but safer than common stocks.

The bond valuation is given by the value of an option-free bond less than the value of the embedded put option (Equation 9.15)[6]:

Value of a Reverse Convertible Bond =

Value of an Option-Free Bond − Value of the European Put Option   (9.15)

9.4.2   Dilution Effect

As illustrated above, the value of conversion option is determined as a call option of the underlying share. However, while the call option or warrant gives the right but not the obligation to acquire existing shares, the convertible bond gives the right but not the obligation to acquire new shares. The effect on existing shares for further new shares is known as *dilution*. Therefore, in order to take into account this characteristic, the price of a call option can be adjusted in this way:

$$C = \max \left[\left(\frac{S-X}{1+\lambda} \right), 0 \right]$$ (9.16)

where S is the stock price; X is the exercise price and λ is the dilution factor resulting from the exercise of the call option. This means that the price of a call option is the maximum of the diluted difference between the stock price and the exercise price and 0. However, this formula should be implemented when the convertible bond is deeply in the money. If the convertible bond is deeply out of the money, the dilution effect could be ignored.

9.4.3   Introducing Dividends into the Model

In previous examples, we have not considered dividend payments of the underlying asset. The dividend payments can be implemented into the model through an adjustment into the stock price tree. There are two main ways to include dividend payments:

- The first one, is to consider the dividend payment as a percentage above the stock price in each node i of the binomial tree as follows (Equation 9.17):

$$S_{i(\text{div.adj})} = S_i (1-\delta) \quad i = 1...j$$ (9.17)

where $S_{i(\text{div.adj})}$ is the dividend-adjusted stock price; S_i is the stock price in each node i before the dividend adjustment and δ is the dividend yield.
- The second one, is to consider the dividend in absolute terms in each node of the binomial tree as follows (Equation 9.18):

$$S_{i(\text{div.adj})} = S_i - D \quad i = 1...j$$ (9.18)

where D is the dividend amount per share.

---

6. The numbers of put options is defined by the conversion ratio.

The difference between the two approaches is that in the first one the dividend amount depends on the level of the stock price, while in the second one the dividend payment is fixed.

In both cases, the dividend adjustment reduces the growth of stock price tree and consequently the value of the convertible bond.

In the example shown in Section 9.3.1, we consider an underlying asset that does not pay dividends. We suppose now a stock that pays 1% of dividends in years 1, 2, 3, 4 and 5 in terms of dividend yield. As explained before, the introduction of dividends decreases the stock price tree. Therefore, at the end of the binomial tree, the stock price will be lower. For instance, as shown in Figure 9.26, the highest stock price tree without the inclusion of dividends is 11.51.

Differently, including dividends with a dividend yield of 1%, the highest stock price at year 5 is 10.95 (Figure 9.27).

With a dividend yield of 1%, the value of a convertible bond decreases from 107.5 to 105.2. This lower value is due to the lower stock price tree and value of conversion option (Figure 9.28).

0	1	2	3	4	5
					11.51
				8.11	
			5.72		5.72
		4.03		4.03	
	2.84		2.84		2.84
2.00		2.00		2.00	
	1.41		1.41		1.41
		0.99		0.99	
			0.70		0.70
				0.49	
					0.35

FIGURE 9.26 Binomial stock price tree without dividend payments.

0	1	2	3	4	5
					10.95
				7.79	
			5.55		5.44
		3.95		3.87	
	2.81		2.75		2.70
2.00		1.96		1.92	
	1.40		1.37		1.34
		0.97		0.95	
			0.68		0.67
				0.47	
					0.33

FIGURE 9.27 Binomial stock price tree with dividend payments.

Results from convertible pricing model

	Without dividends		With dividends
Value of conversion option	17.8		15.5
Value of an option free bond	89.7		89.7
Value of a convertible bond	107.5		105.2

FIGURE 9.28   The value of a convertible bond with and without dividend payments.

9.4.4   Reset Features

Sometimes convertible instruments are issued with the possibility to change conversion terms and conditions, allowing to 'reset' the initial conversion price. The conversion ratio increases in the case of stock price depreciations, 'downward reset', or decreases in the case of stock price appreciations, 'upward reset', on certain dates. Downward reset clauses allow to reduce the conversion price at a specified date if the stock price is lower than a specified price level. After that, the investor will obtain a greater conversion ratio or more underlying shares. The new conversion price will reflect, therefore, the new target price of the underlying asset. Otherwise, in the case of upward reset clauses, the conversion price is increased if the stock price has been increased above a certain level. In this case, the investor will obtain fewer shares. For example, consider a convertible bond with a nominal value of €100, a conversion price of €4 and the current share price is €3. The conversion ratio is €100/4, or 25 shares for each bond exchanged. If the share price is below the limit, the new conversion price is reset to €3.8. With this conversion price the conversion ratio is €100/3.8, or closed to 26. The lower conversion price highlights the advantage of the bondholder by which the investor obtains on conversion more shares. Therefore, as the conversion price is lower, the value of option increases. Note that both reset features, downward and upward, can have, respectively, floor and cap level.

9.5   CONVERTIBLE PRICE SENSITIVITIES

As introduced in Section 9.3.2, share price, volatility of underlying asset and interest rates are the main parameters affecting convertible bond price. The convertible bond price is, therefore, positively correlated with:

- *Share price*: The higher level of share price increases the equity component of convertible and the value of the convertible;
- *Volatility of the underlying stock*: The higher volatility level increases the value of the option element and consequently the value of the convertible;
- *Interest rates*: The higher level of interest rates makes the option element more valuable.

The convertible bond price is negatively correlated with:

- *Stock dividends*: As exposed in Section 9.4.3, the introduction of dividend payments into the model limits the growth of stock price tree, making the value of the convertible bond lower;

- *Interest rates and credit spread*: A greater level of interest rates decreases the value of the option-free bond or bond floor. Because the credit spread is applied only into the bond floor valuation, a greater credit quality decreases the credit spread and interest rate, and increases the value of the option-free bond. Conversely, higher is the interest rates and credit spread, lower is the value of an option-free bond.

9.5.1 The Greeks

The value of an option is sensitive to many inputs than other financial instruments. This makes the valuation more complex. For each main variable described above, there is a derivate known as *Greek*.

9.5.1.1 Delta

The most important Greek for convertible bond valuation is the *delta*. Delta measures the sensitivity of the option price to changes in the price of the underlying share price as follows (Equation 9.19):

$$\delta = \frac{\Delta C}{\Delta S} \tag{9.19}$$

or, the delta is simply the partial derivate of the option premium above the underlying share price, as follows (Equation 9.20):

$$\delta = \frac{\partial P}{\partial S} \tag{9.20}$$

In convertible bonds, delta indicates the sensitivity between the convertible bond price and parity. It is given by Equation (9.21):

$$\delta = \frac{\Delta CB}{\Delta \text{Parity}} \tag{9.21}$$

For example, if an option has a delta of 50%, this means that if the share price or parity increases by one point, the option price or convertible bond price will rise by 0.5 points.

The delta is also defined *hedge ratio*. In this case, the hedge ratio allows to adjust the interest rate by taking into account when the convertible bond trades as an equity component (share price greater than conversion price) or as bond floor (share price lower than conversion price). Conventionally, in the first case, the convertible bond in the binomial path should be discounted with a risk-free rate. Conversely, if the option is deeply out of the money, the risk of default is high and should be favourable applies a risky rate. In practice, the hedge ratio determines the weight of the adjustment. The adjusted risky rate is given by Equation (9.22):

$$r_{\text{adj}} = \delta r_{\text{f}} + (1 - \delta) \text{ credit adjustment} \tag{9.22}$$

Therefore, the discount rate is a risk-free rate r_{f} or risky rate depending on the hedge ratio:

- If the hedge ratio is 1, we have a risk-free rate. In this point, the position of the investor is long above the underlying share price and also receiving a coupon. At a hedge ratio of 1, the option will move identically to the underlying asset.

$$r_{adj} = r_f \qquad (9.23)$$

- If the hedge ratio is 0, according to formula (9.22) we obtain a risky rate. At a hedge ratio of 0, the option does not follow the moves of underlying share price.
- If the hedge ratio stays in the middle, the discount rate is still a risky rate.

For instance, consider the case in which the convertible has a reference price of 2 and a conversion price of 2.6. We reduce the share price by 0.01, or 1.99 as shown in Figure 9.29.

The change in share price determines a change in the option value. For instance, at the highest value of the share price or 11.51 the option value is 8.91. If the share price changes to 11.45, the new option value is 8.85. Therefore, the hedge ratio for that node is equal to 1 as follows:

$$H_h = \frac{(11.51 - 11.45)}{(8.91 - 8.85)} = 1 \qquad (9.24)$$

Conversely, at the lowest node, the hedge ratio is 0 because the option is out of money or 0. This means that in the first case the bond trade like the equity, while in the second case like a conventional bond. Therefore when the share price increases the delta approaches unity, implying that the option is deeply in the money. In contrast, when the share price is low relative to the conversion price, the sensitivity of the convertible and therefore of the embedded option is low.

0	1	2	3	4	5
					11.51
				8.11	
			5.72		5.72
		4.03		4.03	
	2.84		2.84		2.84
2.00		2.00		2.00	
	1.41		1.41		1.41
		0.99		0.99	
			0.70		0.70
				0.49	
					0.35

0	1	2	3	4	5
					11.45
				8.07	
			5.69		5.69
		4.01		4.01	
	2.82		2.82		2.82
1.99		1.99		1.99	
	1.40		1.40		1.40
		0.99		0.99	
			0.70		0.70
				0.49	
					0.35

FIGURE 9.29 Share price sensitivity.

0	1	2	3	4	5
					1.00
				1.00	
			1.00		1.00
		0.94		1.00	
	0.82		0.84		1.00
0.68		0.65		0.60	
	0.48		0.36		0.00
		0.22		0.00	
			0.00		0.00
				0.00	
					0.00

FIGURE 9.30   Hedge ratio at each node.

0	1	2	3	4	5
					1.04%
				1.04%	
			1.04%		1.04%
		1.48%		1.04%	
	2.29%		2.15%		1.04%
3.25%		3.49%		3.83%	
	4.70%		5.51%		8.04%
		6.52%		8.04%	
			8.04%		8.04%
				8.04%	
					8.04%

FIGURE 9.31   The discount rate.

In the first case the right discount rate to apply is the risk-free rate equal to 1.04%, while in the second case is the risky rate equal to 8.04%. Figure 9.30 shows the hedge ratio at each node.

Depending on the hedge ratio, the discount rate changes according to the formula (9.22). This is shown in Figure 9.31.

9.5.1.2 Gamma

The second important Greek is *gamma*. Gamma measures the rate of change of delta to the change of the underlying share price. Gamma is given by Equation (9.25):

$$\gamma = \frac{\Delta\delta}{\Delta S} \tag{9.25}$$

or the second partial derivative of the option price with respect to the underlying share price as follows (Equation 9.26):

$$\gamma = \frac{\partial^2 C}{\partial S^2} \tag{9.26}$$

In convertible bonds, gamma refers to the change of delta by the change of parity. Gamma reflects how the bond price is sensitive from the underlying share price. If the bond is deeply out of the money, that is when the share price is highly less than conversion price, the gamma is less sensitive or not significant. In rising share prices, the convertible is more sensitive.

9.5.1.3 Vega

The *Vega* reflects how much the option price changes to the changes in volatility of the underlying asset. It is given by Equation (9.27):

$$v = \frac{\Delta C}{\Delta \sigma} \tag{9.27}$$

The convertible bond will be more sensitive with the change of volatility when the option is at the money, or the share price is closed to the conversion price.

9.5.1.4 Rho

The *rho* of an option measures the change of the option value with the change of movements of interest rates. Mathematically it is expressed as follows (Equation 9.28):

$$\rho = \frac{\Delta C}{\Delta r} \tag{9.28}$$

For convertible bonds, rho reflects the sensitivity of convertible bond value to change in interest rates. The value of rho increases when the parity decreases. When the bond is deeply out of the money, the instrument is more sensitive to the change of interests, trading like a straight bond.

9.5.1.5 Theta

Theta measures the change of the option value to the change of time to maturity.

$$\theta = \frac{\Delta C}{\Delta T} \tag{9.29}$$

Therefore, theta measures the time decay of an option. For a bondholder, when the convertible approaches to maturity the option element tends to decrease its value decreasing theta value.

9.6   WEB SITE MODELS

The Web site associated with this book contains an Excel spreadsheet demonstrating the valuation of convertible bonds. The reader may use the spreadsheet undertake this form of valuation using his or her own parameter inputs.

Details of how to access the Web site are contained in the preface.

Issuer Name	Sector	Ticker	Issue Date	Maturity Date	Coupon %	Yld to Mty (Mid)	Maturity Type	Conversion Premium at Issue	Implied Premium after Issue
Safilo Group SpA	Consumer Discretionary	SFLIM	5/22/2014	5/22/2019	1.25	1.1533017	Convertible	40%	46%
Beni Stabili SpA	Financials	BNSIM	10/17/2013	4/17/2019	2.625	0.0769865	Convertible	37%	15%
Sogefi SpA	Consumer Discretionary	SOIM	5/21/2014	5/21/2021		2.076467	Convertible	38%	57%
Prysmian SpA	Industrials	PRYIM	3/8/2013	3/8/2018	1.25	0.0389555	Convertible	34%	49%
Maire Tecnimont SpA	Industrials	MTIM	2/20/2014	2/20/2019	5.75	2.7402217	Convertible	35%	20%
Eni SpA	Energy	ENIIM	1/18/2013	1/18/2016	0.625	−4.4582549	Convertible	20%	8%
Eni SpA	Energy	ENIIM	11/30/2012	11/30/2015	0.25	−1.3726116	Convertible	35%	23%
Astaldi SpA	Industrials	ASTIM	1/31/2013	1/31/2019	4.5	0.6328391	Convertible	35%	22%
Beni Stabili SpA	Financials	BNSIM	4/23/2010	4/23/2015	3.875	−0.5224704	Convertible	30%	36%
Gruppo Editoriale L'Espresso SpA	Communications	ESIM	4/9/2014	4/9/2019	2.625	4.3341811	Convertible	30%	65%
Beni Stabili SpA	Financials	BNSIM	1/17/2013	1/17/2018	3.375	−1.997204	Convertible	32%	11%
Schematrentaquattro SpA	Consumer Discretionary	EDIZIM	11/29/2013	11/29/2016	0.25	−0.7736328	Convertible	25%	26%
Buzzi Unicem SpA	Materials	BZUIM	7/17/2013	7/17/2019	1.375	−0.6368203	Convertible	35%	44%
Azimut Holding SpA	Financials	AZMIM	11/25/2013	11/25/2020	2.125	0.1525947	Convertible	30%	46%
Cam 2012 SpA	Energy	CAMFIN	10/26/2012	10/26/2017	5.625	−0.346996311	Convertible	30%	21%

Data source: Bloomberg.

SELECTED BIBLIOGRAPHY AND REFERENCES

Black, F., Scholes, M., 1973. The pricing of options and corporate liabilities. J. Polit. Econ. 81 (3), 637–654.

Brennan, M.J., Schwartz, E.S., 1977. Convertible bonds: valuation and optimal strategies for call and conversion. J. Financ. 32 (5), 1699–1715.

Choudhry, M., Moskovic, D., Wong, M., 2014. Fixed Income Markets: Management, Trading and Hedging, second ed. John Wiley & Sons, Singapore.

Connolly, K.B., 1998. Pricing Convertible Bonds. John Wiley & Sons, England.

Cox, J.C., Ross, S.A., Rubinstein, M., 1979. Option pricing: A simplified approach. J. Financ. Econ. 7 (3), 229–263.

Damodaran, A., 2006. Damodaran on Valuation: Security Analysis for Investment and Corporate Finance, second ed. John Wiley & Sons, Hoboken, N.J, 2004.

Davenport, C., 2003. Convertible Bonds—A Guide. Citigroup.

Eales, B., 2004. A primer on convertible bonds. YieldCurve.com.

Eckmann, A., 2013. Convertible Bonds: A Defensive Way to Build Equity Exposure. UBS Global Asset Management.

Klein, W.A., 1975. The convertible bond: a peculiar package. Univ. Pennsylvania Law Rev. 123, 547–573.

Kovalov, P., Linetsky, V., 2008. Valuing convertible bonds with stock price, volatility, interest rate, and default risk. Working Paper No. 2008–02, FDIC Center for Financial Research.

Lintner, J., 1965. The Valuation of Risk and the Selection of Risky Investments in Stock Portfolios and Capital Budgets. Rev. Econ. Stat. 47 (1), 13–37.

Merton, R.C., 1973. Theory of rational option pricing. Bell J. Econ. Manag. Sci. 4 (1), 141–183.

Philips, G.A., 1997. Convertible Bonds Markets. Macmillan Business, Houndmills, Basingstoke, Hampshire.

Ranaldo, A., Eckmann, A., 2004. Convertible Bonds: Characteristics of an Asset Class. UBS Global Asset Management.

Schwartz, E.S., 1975. Generalized Option Pricing Models: Numerical Solutions and the Pricing of a New Life Insurance Contract, Unpublished Ph. D. Dissertation, University of British Columbia.

Sharpe, W.F., 1964. Capital Asset Prices: A Theory of Market Equilibrium under Conditions of Risk. J. Financ. 19 (3), 425–442.

Chapter 10

Floating-Rate Notes

Chapter Contents

In this chapter, we describe the analysis of floating-rate notes. This type of bonds has increased in popularity since the crash because of investors' desire to minimize interest-rate risk. 'Floaters' are issued by both governments and corporate participants. In fact, increasing interest rate volatility has led in bond markets to develop this security and transfer this risk to market participants. The price of a floating-rate note is in theory more stable than that of a fixed-rate bond. Floaters reduce transaction costs of a roll-over strategy. In fact, as an alternative to an issue of floating-rate notes, bond's issuers can roll over the short-term debt at regular intervals. However, this leads to high transaction costs. Thus, this chapter introduces the basis of floating-rate analysis by illustrating the particularity compared to conventional debt instruments.

10.1 MAIN FEATURES OF FLOATERS

A fixed-rate bond pays fixed coupons during the bond's life known with certainty. Conversely, a floating-rate note or *floater* pays variable coupons linked to a reference rate. This makes the coupon payments uncertain. The main purpose of this debt instrument is to hedge the risk of rising interest rates. Although the financial crisis and liquidity provided by central banks have decreased the level of interest rates, they will at some point of course rise in future years.

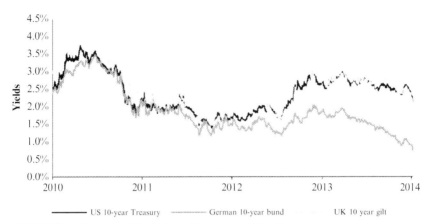

FIGURE 10.1 Government bond yields. *(Data source: Bloomberg.)*

In addition, market turmoil has created concern about the volatility in bond markets from the investor's viewpoint. Figure 10.1 shows the yield trend of the main government bonds in recent years.

Therefore, the potential benefits are:

- *Interest-rate protection and stable prices*: In particular, conventional bonds are affected by the price sensitivity to interest rates. This cannot happen with floaters because their price is stable during market periods of high volatility, by fluctuating less than a fixed-rate bond. Figure 10.2 shows the prices of fixed and floating Italy government bonds. As illustrated, the price of the floating-rate note remains stable while the one of the fixed-rate bond changes during the bond's life.

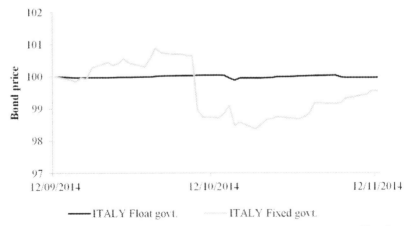

FIGURE 10.2 The price trend of Italy floating and fixed-rate bonds. *(Data source: Bloomberg.)*

- *Potential return*: Floaters can have higher returns if the economy's recession goes to end, by rising interest rates;
- *Portfolio risk management*: These bonds assure the price protection to portfolios by changes in interest rates. Moreover, they show a low correlation with other asset classes, including bonds.

The potential risks are:

- *Interest-rate risk*: Floating-rate notes are not completely covered by the change of interest rates because it depends on the reset frequency. Since coupons change only at reset dates, if the interest rate changes between the reset date the bond will temporarily trade at discount or premium. This is known as *reset risk*. Moreover, although floating-rate notes offer protection for rising interest rates, if interest rates fall the value of coupon payments will decrease;
- *Unpredictable cash flows*: While in fixed-rate securities the coupon payments are known with certainty, with floaters we cannot predict future cash flows;
- *Credit risk*: Fixed and floating-rate bonds are both subject to changes of credit risk.

10.2   THE STRUCTURE

The coupon payment is determined by two main components, the *reference rate* and the *quoted margin* and is given by (10.1):

$$\text{Coupon rate} = \text{reference rate} + \text{quoted margin} \qquad (10.1)$$

where the reference rate is the interest rate or index benchmark and the quoted margin is the spread added to the reference rate in order to compensate the credit and liquidity risk.

10.2.1   Coupon Payment

The coupons reset periodically in order to reflect the market interest rate. The frequency can be daily, monthly, quarterly and annually and usually the reset date coincides with the coupon's payment date. Most of the floating-rate notes in major domestic markets pay coupons on quarterly basis. As exposed before, the floaters have low price volatility because the coupon or its reference rate resets periodically. Therefore, if the *required margin* or *discount margin* applied into the discount rate is equal to the quoted margin, the floaters are priced at par. Otherwise, if the required margin is greater than quoted margin, the bond prices at discount, and if the required margin is less than quoted margin, the bond prices at premium. Between coupon payments, the bond trades at discount or premium depending on whether the reference rate will go up or down. At each reset date, the reference rate resets and the bond trades at par, unless demand and supply effect.

10.2.2 Reference Rate

As introduced, the reference rate represents the interest rate or index used to obtain the linkage. In the European market, the major parts of floating-rate note issuances are linked to the Euribor and the remaining to the constant maturity swap. In the US and UK markets, they are tied to the Libor and short-term treasury bonds.

10.2.3 Day Count Conventions

The most common day conventions used for floaters are actual/360 and actual/365. The first one is the most popular for euro- and dollar-denominated bonds while for sterling-denominated bonds, the convention is actual/365.

10.3 THE VALUATION

10.3.1 Theoretical Pricing Models

Conversely to a conventional bond, future coupon payments are not known with certainty. Therefore, the heart of the bond's valuation is the correct estimation of the interest rate term structure. Authors as Cox et al. (1980, 1985) and Ramaswamy and Sundaresan (1986) implemented a model for valuing floating-rate notes studying the effect of lags in coupon payments, special contractual features as callability, convertibility, restriction on coupon payments and the issuer's credit risk. They give emphasis on coupon estimation in which the value of a floater strictly depends on the interest rate term structure and the floater pays coupons in continuous time through a mean reverting stochastic process.[1]

In Chapter 8, we described several models to measure the term structure of credit spread and we introduced the model proposed by Longstaff and Schwartz (1995) for pricing fixed-rate debt. The authors propose also a model to valuing floating-rate notes. The equation derived for pricing floating-rate bonds is given by (10.2):

$$F(X, r, \tau, T) = P(X, r, T)R(r, \tau, T) + wD(r, T)G(X, r, \tau, T) \qquad (10.2)$$

where $F(X,r,\tau,T)$ is the price of a floating-rate note. The first term in the equation defines the price of a risky discount bond times the expected value of the interest rate r and time τ. The second term takes into account the correlation between the risk-free rate r and default risk value of X.

The authors find that conversely to the price of a fixed-rate coupon payment, which is a decreasing function of the maturity T, with floating-rate notes, the value depends on the level of interest rates. In fact, when the interest rate is below the long-run average value, the increase of T reduces the value of the floater and vice versa. In addition, the price of a floating-rate note increases with rising risk-free interest rates.

---

1. See Chapter 3 for an explanation of the CIR model.

10.3.2   The Pricing

The pricing of a floating-rate note at issue does not differ from a conventional bond. In fact, it is the present value of coupon payments and principal repayment and is given by (10.3):

$$P = \sum_{t=1}^{t=N} \frac{C_t}{(1+r)^t} + \frac{F}{(1+r)^N} = \sum_{t=1}^{t=N} \frac{(re+QM) \times F}{[1+(re+RM)]^t} + \frac{F}{[1+(re+RM)]^N} \quad (10.3)$$

where P is the fair price of a bond; C_t is the annual coupon payment; r is the discount rate; re is the reference rate; F is the face value of the bond, or principal, or par value; QM is the quoted margin and RM is the required margin.

10.3.3   Simple and Discounted Margin

There are many ways to calculate the return of a floating-rate note relative to an indicator. One of these is the *simple margin*. It compares the average return of the floater during its life with the reference rate. The calculation is divided into two parts: the first one is the average annual capital gain or loss, calculated as the difference of the face value and full price over the bond's time to maturity; the second one is the quoted margin applied over the reference rates. The equation is given by (10.4):

$$SM = \frac{F - P_f}{100 \times (T-t) + QM} \quad (10.4)$$

where SM is the simple margin; P_f is the full or dirty price; T-t is the number of years from settlement date to maturity; QM is the quoted margin and F is the face value.

A positive simple margin indicates that the floater has a higher return than that of the indicator chosen.

Another way to calculate the yield return is the *discounted margin*. It differs from the simple margin because the first one amortizes the bond's premium or discount at a constantly compounded rate. The main disadvantage of this method is that it requires estimation of the reference rate over the bond's life. Assuming a bond paying semi-annual coupons, the discounted margin is given by (10.5):

$$P_f = \left\{ \frac{1}{\left[1 + \frac{1}{2}(re+DM)\right]^{\frac{days}{years}}} \right\} \times \left\{ \frac{C}{2} + \sum_{t=1}^{N-1} \frac{\frac{(re^*+QM)}{2} \times F}{\left[1 + \frac{1}{2}(re^*+DM)\right]^t} + \frac{QM}{\left[1 + \frac{1}{2}(re^*+DM)\right]^{N-1}} \right\}$$

$$(10.5)$$

where P_f is the full or dirty price; DM is the discounted margin; QM is the quoted margin; F is the face value; re is the reference rate and re^* is the expected reference rate over the remaining bond's life.

Therefore, the discount rate is the one that equals the bond's price to the present value of all its cash flows. As explained above, if the quoted margin is equal to the discount margin, the bond trades at par.

Figure 10.3 shows the Bloomberg YAS page for BP Capital Markets bond 2018. The bond has a simple margin (in Bloomberg called *spread for life*) of 57.19 and a discounted margin of 57.32 basis points. The screen shows also other two types of margins. The first one is called *adjusted simple margin*. This margin takes into account for one time the cost of carry effect, in the case of floating-rate bond being bought by leveraged financing. As shown by Fabozzi and Mann (2000), the adjusted simple margin is given by (10.6)

$$ASM = \left[\frac{F \times (F - P_{adj})}{T - t} + QM \right] \times \frac{F}{P_{adj}} \qquad (10.6)$$

where ASM is the adjusted simple margin; F is the face value or par value; P_{adj} is the adjusted price of a floating-rate note; QM is the quoted margin in basis points and $T\text{-}t$ is the time to maturity.

The adjusted simple margin for BP is 60.02 basis points and is derived from the adjusted price of 100.12. The other one is known as *adjusted total margin*

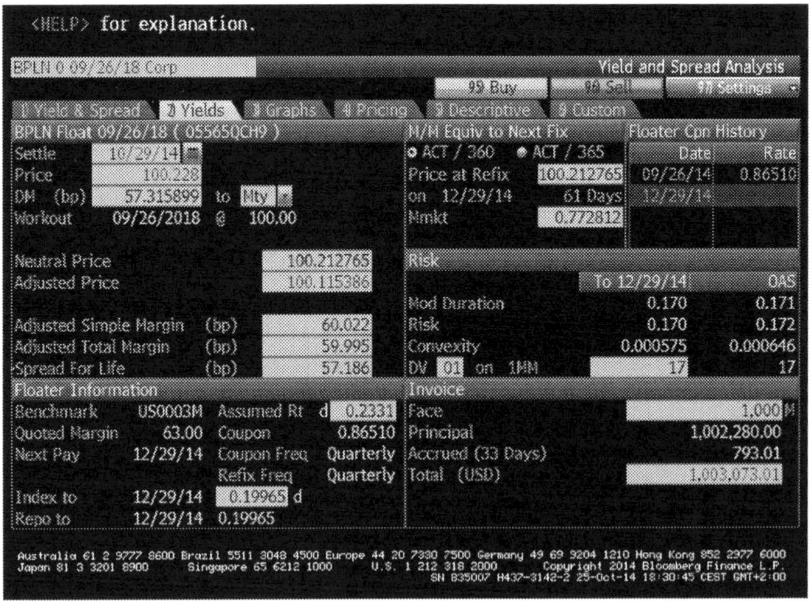

FIGURE 10.3 Bloomberg YAS page for BP Capital Markets bond. Used with permission of Bloomberg L.P. *(Copyright© 2014. All rights reserved.)*

which is a modified version of the adjusted simple margin. In fact, it is the adjusted simple margin plus the interest income obtained by investing the difference between the face value and adjusted price at reference rate chosen. The formula (10.6) may be reproduced as follows:

$$\text{ATM} = \left[\frac{F \times (F - P_{\text{adj}})}{T - t} + \text{QM} + F \times (F - P_{\text{adj}}) \times re_{\text{avg}} \right] \times \frac{F}{P_{\text{adj}}} \qquad (10.7)$$

where ATM is the adjusted total margin and re_{avg} is the average value of the reference rate.

The adjusted total margin for BP is 59.995 basis points.

10.3.4   Take the Position in Floating-Rate Note Market

Chapter 8 shows several spread measures that can be used to compare fixed-rate bonds. Conventionally for floating-rate notes, traders use the discounted margin. To analyse a floating-rate note with a fixed-rate note, one method is to compare the discounted margin of a floater with the asset swap spread of fixed-rate bonds.

Another approach is to compare the floating-rate note with a derived yield of a fixed-rate bond by using an interest rate swap curve matched with floater coupons. Figure 10.4 shows the Bloomberg YASN screen for Mediobanca float

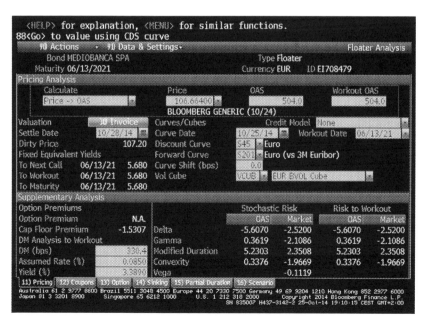

FIGURE 10.4   Bloomberg YASN page for Mediobanca float bond. Used with permission of Bloomberg L.P. *(Copyright© 2014. All rights reserved.)*

2021 as on 25 October 2014. The bond has a fixed equivalent yield of 5.68%, and this is compared to a floating yield of 3.389%, which is the sum of Euribor (0.085%) and discounted margin (3.304%).

10.4 OTHER FEATURES OF FLOATING-RATE NOTES

10.4.1 Duration

Duration is the price sensitivity to changes of interest rates. As understood, floaters have a shorter duration due to the variable coupon payment. There are two main duration measures:

- *Index duration*: Measuring the price sensitivity to change of reference rate only;
- *Spread duration*: Measuring the price sensitivity to change of quoted margin, maintaining a fixed reference rate.

Index duration is usually equal to the time until the next reset date, whereas spread duration is equal to a modified duration of a bond paying fixed coupon, with same coupon payments and time to maturity. Therefore, conventionally floaters have lower index duration and higher spread duration.

Moreover, duration will be influenced by the floater's structure. In fact, the choice of the reference rate affects the duration depending on how much volatile the index is. The lower the frequency of coupon payments, the greater the price sensitivity between reset dates. Thus, while floating-rate notes have a lower price sensitivity to a change of the reference rate, fixed and floating-rate notes both have a price sensitivity to changes of credit spread reflecting the issuer's creditworthiness. A shift of the credit term structure will determine the decline of the bond's price.

10.4.2 Special Contract Features

Floating-rate notes can include additional features. One example is the inclusion of *cap*, *floor* and *collar* clauses. A floater with cap feature means that the reference rate cannot overcome the threshold rate defined in the indenture. Usually the threshold is expressed in terms of coupon, that is after a coupon threshold (e.g. 6%, reference rate plus quoted margin) the investor receives at maximum the cap level. In this case, the floater is not completely covered by rising interest rates, in which after the threshold the floater trades as a conventional bond. In contrast, a floater with a floor feature represents the minimum coupon level that an investor can receive, hedging to the downside risk of interest rates. If the bond includes both cap and floor, this feature is known as collar or collared floating-rate note. The bond can include also a *drop-lock* feature that after a threshold it ceases to float.

Like other fixed-income bonds, floaters can include embedded options, as call and put provisions. The floater with a call option, or *callable* floater, gives the right to the issuer to redeem the bond in the case of decreasing interest rates, in terms of reference rate or required margin. The inclusion of this feature will compensate the investor with higher quoted margin. With a put provision, the bondholder can give back the bond to the issuer at put price.

10.4.3   Inverse Floaters

An inverse floating-rate note pays coupons that increase if the reference rate decreases. Therefore, this bond gives a benefit at investors with a negative yield curve. The coupon structure of inverse floaters usually is determined as a fixed interest rate less a variable interest rate linked to a reference index. Moreover, they can include floor provisions.

A particular structured finance operation involving inverse floaters is a *Tender Option Bond* program (TOP). In practice, in a tender option bond program, an institutional investor purchases a longer maturity fixed-rate bond in which is placed in a *Tender Option Bond Trust*. Consequently, the trust issues two types of securities. The first one is a floating-rate note, which is typically sold in a money market mutual fund with daily or weekly interest rate resets. The second one is an inverse floating-rate note. This longer maturity security is held by the institutional investor. Adopting a tender option bond strategy allows the closed-end fund to borrow from the money market and use the money to purchase long-term fixed-rate bonds, with a greater yield than floaters.

BIBLIOGRAPHY

Bomfim, A.N., 2004. Understanding Credit Derivates and Related Instruments, first ed. Academic Press.

Choudhry, M., Moskovic, D., Wong, M., 2014. Fixed Income Markets: Management, Trading and Hedging, second ed. John Wiley & Sons.

Cox, J., Ingersoll, J., Ross, S., 1980. An analysis of variable rate loan contract. J. Financ. 35 (2), 389–403.

Cox, J., Ingersoll, J., Ross, S., 1985. A theory of the term structure of interest rates. Econometrica 53 (2), 385–407.

Fabozzi, F., Mann, S.V., 2000. Floating-Rate Securities, first ed. John Wiley & Sons.

Longstaff, F.A., Schwartz, E.S., July 1995. A simple approach to valuing risky fixed and floating rate debt. J. Financ. 50 (3), 789–819.

Ramaswamy, K., Sundaresan, S., December 1986. The valuation of floating-rate instruments: theory and evidence. J. Financ. Econ. 17 (2), 251–272.

Chapter 11

Bonds with Embedded Options

Chapter Contents

Bonds with embedded options are debt instruments that give the right to redeem the bond before maturity. As we know, the yield to maturity represents the key measure of bond's return (although, of course, it is an *anticipated* return that is seldom realised in practice). The calculation of the return is particularly easy for conventional bonds because the redemption date is known with certainty, as their value. In contrast, for callable bonds, but also for other bonds such as *putable* and *sinking fund* bonds, the redemption date is not known with certainty because the bonds can be redeemed before maturity. If we want to calculate the yield to maturity for this type of bonds, we must assume a redemption date and determine the yield to this date.

As introduced in Chapter 8, the most suitable measure of return for bonds with embedded options is known as *option-adjusted spread* or OAS. In this chapter, we show the analysis of bonds with embedded options, with particular focus on pricing methodology.

11.1 THE ANALYSIS OF BONDS WITH EMBEDDED OPTIONS

Bonds with embedded options are instruments that give the option holder the right to redeem the bond before its maturity date. For callable bonds, this right is held by the issuer. The main reason for an issuer to issue these debt instruments is to get protection from the decline of interest rates or improvement of issuer's credit quality. In other words, if interest rates fall or credit quality enhances, the issuer has convenience to retire the bond from the market in order to issue again another bond with lower interest rates.

In contrast, for putable bonds, the right to exercise the option is held by the bondholder. In fact, putable bonds allow the bondholder to sell the bond back before maturity. Conversely to callable bonds, this happens when interest rates go up (risk-free rate increases, or the issuer's credit quality decreases). In fact, the bondholders may have the advantage to sell the bond and buy another one with higher coupon payments.

Therefore, the main variable for these bonds is the estimation of the interest rate path. We illustrate this in the pricing section of this chapter.

11.1.1 Price and Yield Sensitivity

While a conventional bond shows a positive convexity, callable bonds exhibit a *negative convexity*. This means that the price appreciation of a callable bond will be less than the fall in price for a given change in interest rates. Figure 11.1 shows the changes of prices of an option-free bond and a callable bond by the change of the interest rate. The evidence is that if interest rates go below the interest threshold, the price shows a negative convexity, that is the price is limited to the redemption values illustrated in the indenture. Otherwise, if the interest rates are equal or higher than interest threshold, the callable bond exhibits the same convexity of a conventional bond. The difference between the price of an option free and callable bond represents the value of the embedded option.

Putable bonds exhibit a positive convexity, although lower than a conventional bond, above all with rising interest rates. Figure 11.2 shows the changes of prices according to the interest rate. If the interest rates decrease, option free and putable bonds have the same convexity. If the interest rates rise, putable bonds become more valuable.

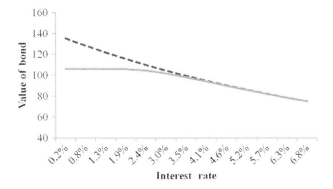

FIGURE 11.1   The prices of an option free and callable bond.

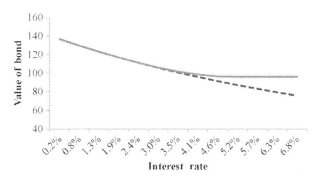

FIGURE 11.2   The prices of an option free and putable bond.

To calculate the internal rate of return of a bond with embedded option, we can have three main measures:

- *Yield to maturity*: This measure assumes that the bond is not called until the maturity date. Therefore, it is calculated as the yield of a straight bond;
- *Yield to call*: This method calculates the yield for the next available call date. The yield to call is determined assuming the coupon payment until the call date and the principal repayment at the call date. For instance, the *yield to first call* is the rate of return calculated assuming cash flow payments until first call date. When interest rates are less than the ones at issue, the yield to call is useful because most probably the bond will be called at next call date;

- *Yield to worst*: This represents the most conservative yield measure. This is the minimum between the yield to maturity and yield to call for any date.

11.1.2 Effective Duration and Convexity

The duration shows the bond's price sensitivity to its yield to maturity. The change in bond's price is plotted in a curve in which the duration represents the slope of the tangent at any point of the curve. Conversely, the effective duration, or also known as *curve duration*, shows the price sensitivity to the change of the benchmark yield curve or market yield curve. This duration is more suitable than Macaulay or modified duration for bonds with embedded options because the latter ones have not a well-defined yield to maturity. The effective duration is given by (11.1):

$$D_{\text{Effective}} = \frac{P_- - P_+}{2 \times P_0 \times \Delta BY} \qquad (11.1)$$

where P_0 is the initial price of the bond; P_- is the bond's price when the yield falls by ΔBY; P_+ is the bond's price when the yield increases by ΔBY and ΔBY is the change in the benchmark yield of the bond.

To calculate the effective duration using equation (11.1), we adopt the following steps:

- Determine the OAS for the bond;
- Determine the price of a callable bond with the current market yield curve;
- Change the benchmark yield curve with a downward parallel shift;
- Use the new current yield curve to obtain the price P_-;
- Change the benchmark yield curve with an upward parallel shift;
- Use the new current yield curve to obtain the price P_+;
- Apply Formula (11.1).

For instance, consider a hypothetical case in which a callable bond has a price equal to 103.78. Suppose that the benchmark yield curve changes by 1 basis point. For a downward parallel shift, the price obtained is 103.83, while for an upward shift the price is 103.73. Therefore, applying Formula (11.1) the bond's effective duration is around 4.93.

The convexity is a more correct measure of the price sensitivity. It measures the curvature of the price-yield relationship and the degree in which it diverges from the straight-line estimation. Like the duration, the standard measure of convexity does not consider the changes of market interest rates on bond's prices. Therefore, the conventional measure of price sensitivity used for bonds with embedded options is the *effective convexity*. It is given by (11.2):

$$CV_{\text{Effective}} = \frac{P_+ + P_- - 2 \times P_0}{P_0 \times (\Delta BY)^2} \qquad (11.2)$$

with the same elements used in Formula (11.1).

11.1.3 Option-Adjusted Spread (OAS)

The *option-adjusted spread* (OAS) is the most important measure of risk for bonds with embedded options. It is the average spread required over the yield curve in order to take into account the embedded option element. This is, therefore, the difference between the yield of a bond with embedded option and a government benchmark bond. The spread incorporates the future views of interest rates and it can be determined with an iterative procedure in which the market price obtained by the pricing model is equal to expected cash flow payments (coupons and principal). Also a Monte Carlo simulation may be implemented in order to generate an interest rate path. Note that the option-adjusted spread is influenced by the parameters implemented into the valuation model as the yield curve, but above all by the volatility level assumed. This is referred to *volatility dependent*. The higher the volatility, the lower the option-adjusted spread for a callable bond and the higher for a putable bond.

Consider also that because the OAS is applied over the risk-free yield curve, it includes the credit risk and liquidity risk between defaultable and default-free bonds. Figure 11.3 shows an example of the OAS Bloomberg screen for Mittel's callable bond.

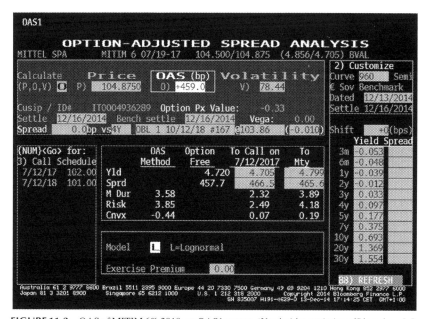

FIGURE 11.3 OAS of MITIM 6% 2019, on OAS1 screen. *(Used with permission of Bloomberg L.P. Copyright© 2014. All rights reserved.)*

EXAMPLE 11.1 OAS Analysis for Treasury, Conventional and Callable Bonds

Consider the following example. We assume to have two hypothetical bonds, a treasury bond and a callable bond. Both bonds have the same maturity of 5 years and pay semiannual coupons, respectively, of 2.4% and 5.5%. We perform a valuation in which we assume a credit spread of 300 basis points and an OAS spread of 400 basis points above the yield curve. Table 11.1 illustrates the prices of a treasury bond, conventional bond and callable bond. In particular, considering only the credit spread we find the price of a conventional bond or option-free bond. Its price is 106.81. To pricing a callable bond, we add the OAS spread over the risk-free yield curve. The price of this last bond is 99.02. We can now see that the OAS spread underlines the embedded call option of the callable bond. It is equal to 106.81-99.02, or 7.79. In Section 11.2.3, we will explain the pricing of a callable bond with the OAS methodology adopting a binomial tree.

11.2 CALLABLE BOND PRICING

11.2.1 Bond Structure

In this section, we illustrate the pricing of bonds with embedded options. The price of a callable bond is essentially formed by an option-free bond and an embedded option. In fact, it is given by the difference between the value of an option-free bond and a call option as follows:

$$P_{\text{callable bond}} = P_{\text{option free bond}} - P_{\text{call option}} \qquad (11.3)$$

The value of a callable bond, and therefore of a call option, depends on the interest rate path. Thus, a callable bond has a lower price than the one of a conventional bond due to the embedded option. If the value of a call option increases, the value of a callable bond decreases and vice versa. This happens when interest rates are lower than the ones at issue.

We can have three main call features:

- *European call option*: For which the issuer can recall the bond only once on the call date;
- *American call option*: The bond can be called on the call date and any time thereafter;
- *Bermudan call option*: The bond is callable only on specified call dates.

The value of a putable bond is the sum of an option-free bond and an embedded put option. It is attractive for investors because it works as a floor. Thus, greater the value of the option, greater the value of the putable bond. It is given by Formula (11.4):

$$P_{\text{putable bond}} = P_{\text{option free bond}} + P_{\text{put option}} \qquad (11.4)$$

TABLE 11.1 OAS analysis for a Treasury Bond, Conventional Bond and Callable Bond

| Period | Date | Treasury Bond | | | Conventional Bond | | | Callable Bond | |
		Spot Rate	Cash Flows	Present Value	Spot Rate + Credit Spread	Cash Flows	Present Value	Spot Rate + OAS spread	Present Value
0	02/01/2015	1.00%			4.00%			5.00%	
1	08/01/2015	1.06%	2.4	2.37	4.06%	5.5	5.29	5.06%	5.24
2	02/01/2016	1.20%	2.4	2.34	4.20%	5.5	5.07	5.20%	4.97
3	08/01/2016	1.26%	2.4	2.31	4.26%	5.5	4.85	5.26%	4.72
4	02/01/2017	1.32%	2.4	2.28	4.32%	5.5	4.64	5.32%	4.47
5	08/01/2017	1.39%	2.4	2.24	4.39%	5.5	4.44	5.39%	4.23
6	02/01/2018	1.41%	2.4	2.21	4.41%	5.5	4.25	5.41%	4.01
7	08/01/2018	1.46%	2.4	2.17	4.46%	5.5	4.05	5.46%	3.79
8	02/01/2019	1.55%	2.4	2.12	4.55%	5.5	3.85	5.55%	3.57
9	08/01/2019	1.61%	2.4	2.08	4.61%	5.5	3.67	5.61%	3.37
10	08/01/2020	1.69%	102.4	86.60	4.69%	105.5	66.71	5.69%	60.66
Price				106.72			106.81		99.02

11.2.2 Binomial Tree Model

To calculate the value of these bonds, it is preferable to use the binomial tree model. The value of a straight bond is determined as the present values of expected cash flows in terms of coupon payments and principal repayment. For bonds with embedded options, since the main variable that drives their values is the interest rate, the binomial tree is the most suitable pricing model.

In order to find a fair value of the embedded option, the Black & Scholes model is not suitable for the following reasons:

- *Constant interest rate*: The main reason for which B&S misprices the embedded option is that the model does not take into account the interest rate path;
- *Constant volatility*: Another reason is that the model considers a constant volatility. Conversely, this debt instrument tends to have a decreasing volatility as the bond approaches maturity. Consider also the type of the underlying asset, in fact while the B&S model assumes that the asset prices are lognormal distributes, therefore without having negative values, for bonds with embedded option the underlying asset or interest rate may become negative;
- *European option*: B&S is not very useful because it assumes the exercise of the option at maturity only, while it does not consider the possibility of exercising for several dates;
- *Call or put price*: Moreover, since some bonds have more call or put dates, consequently they can have different prices. This is not performed with B&S.

In the next section, we will show that the bond's value is estimated by assessing the value of the option-free bond and the value of the embedded option using the binomial tree. The same factors that are implemented into B&S formula are used for the binomial tree. They are:

- The strike price of the option;
- The underlying bond's price;
- The time to expiration;
- The risk-free rate;
- The expected volatility during the bond's life.

The binomial tree model evaluates the return of a bond with embedded option by adding a spread to the risk-free yield curve. Generally, the price obtained by the model is compared to the one exchanged in the market. If the theoretical price is different, the model can be calibrated with three key elements. The first ones are the volatility and drift factor. They allow to calibrate the model interest rate path in order to obtain the equality with the market yield curve. The third one is the spread applied over the yield curve. Generally, when volatility and drift are correctly calibrated, the last element to select in order to obtain the market parity is the spread. Conventionally, banks define it in the following way:

- The binomial tree determines the theoretical bond's price;
- The theoretical bond's price is compared with the market price;
- If the two values differ and volatility and drift are already calibrated, the interest rates used in the binomial model are adjusted with a further spread. The spread is found with an iterative procedure;
- The new theoretical price is compared with the market one;
- The procedure is repeated until the theoretical bond's price is equal to the market price.

11.2.3   Valuing Callable Bonds

The proposed methodology determines the value of a callable bond using the binomial tree. The example assumes a 5-year callable bond with the following conditions (Table 11.2):

Moreover, the callable bond can be called according to the following call schedule (Table 11.3):

The value is estimated with the following steps:

- Determine the interest rate path;
- Determine the value of an option-free bond;
- Determine the value of an embedded call option;
- Determine the value of a callable bond.

TABLE 11.2 Callable Bond Inputs

Coupon:	8%
Maturity:	5 years
Frequency:	semiannual
Credit spread:	580 bps
Face value:	100

TABLE 11.3 Call Schedule

year 0.5	year 1	year 1.5	year 2	year 2.5	year 3	year 3.5	year 4	year 4.5	year 5
106	105	103	103	102	102	101	101	100	100

11.2.3.1 Determine the Interest Rate Path

In the first step, we determine the interest rate path in which we create a risk-neutral recombining lattice with the evolution of the 6-month interest rate. Therefore, the nodes of the binomial tree are for each 6-month interval, and the probability of an upward and downward movement is equal. The analysis of the interest rate evolution has a great relevance in callable bond pricing. We assume that the interest rate follows the path shown in Figure 11.4. In this example, we assume for simplicity a 2-year interest rate. We suppose that the interest rate starts at time t_0 and can go up and down following the geometric random walk for each period. The interest rate r_0 at time t_0 changes due to two main variables:

- The first one, is the volatility that determines the width of the binomial tree. Higher the volatility, greater the up and down movements from the prior nodes;
- The second one, is known as *drift* factor which defines the direction of the interest rate path. If we think that interest rates can be higher in the future, we can assume a positive drift factor. For instance, if at time t_0 we have an interest rate of 6% and we assume a drift factor greater than 0%, this means that the interest rate at time t_2 will be higher than 6%. If the drift factor is equal to 0%, then the interest rate at time t_2 will be equal than the one at time t_0. This parameter is useful if we want to fit the model yield curve to the one observed in the market. If the market foresees an upward yield curve, we can calibrate the model with the market values at time of issue.

Coming back with our hypothetical callable bond, the 6-month interest rate has the path illustrated in Figure 11.5. In the example, we assume a volatility of the period equal to 11%. Assuming a drift factor equal to 0%, the interest rate of 2.96% at time t_0 can reach at time t_5 a maximum value of 8.56% and a minimum value of 1.03%. In this case, the yield curve is flat and the interest rates in the base scenario at time t_0, t_1, t_2, t_3, t_4 and t_5 are always equal (2.96%).

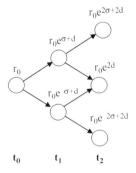

FIGURE 11.4 The binomial interest rate tree.

0	0.5	1	1.5	2	2.5	3	3.5	4	4.5	5
										8.56%
									7.70%	
								6.92%		6.92%
							6.23%		6.23%	
						5.60%		5.60%		5.60%
					5.04%		5.04%		5.04%	
				4.53%		4.53%		4.53%		4.53%
			4.07%		4.07%		4.07%		4.07%	
		3.66%		3.66%		3.66%		3.66%		3.66%
	3.29%		3.29%		3.29%		3.29%		3.29%	
2.96%		2.96%		2.96%		2.96%		2.96%		2.96%
	2.67%		2.67%		2.67%		2.67%		2.67%	
		2.40%		2.40%		2.40%		2.40%		2.40%
			2.16%		2.16%		2.16%		2.16%	
				1.94%		1.94%		1.94%		1.94%
					1.74%		1.74%		1.74%	
						1.57%		1.57%		1.57%
							1.41%		1.41%	
								1.27%		1.27%
									1.14%	
										1.03%

FIGURE 11.5   The binomial interest rate tree.

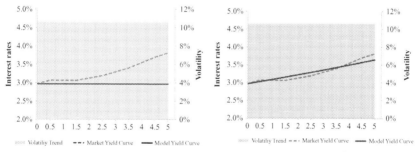

FIGURE 11.6   The interest rate drift factor.

Alternatively, if we think that interest rates will be higher in the future, we can assume a drift factor greater than 0%. In this case, we can calibrate the model yield curve with market yield curve. In other words, we adopt an iterative procedure in which we set the pricing error between the model and market yield curve equal to 0 by changing the drift factor.

Figure 11.6 shows the model yield curve before and after interest rate calibration.

After drift adjustment, the new binomial tree is plotted in Figure 11.7. Increasing the slope of the model yield curve, all interest rates are greater than before. The maximum interest at time t_5 is now 10.52%.

As exposed before, the volatility level implemented in the model is constant and assumed equal to 11%. However, in reality, the volatility tends to decrease as the bond approaches expiration. The main reason is that the probability of the issuer to call the bond back decreases in the last years of the instrument, until the

0	0.5	1	1.5	2	2.5	3	3.5	4	4.5	5
										10.52%
									9.26%	8.51%
								8.16%	7.49%	6.88%
							7.19%	6.60%	6.06%	5.56%
						6.34%	5.82%	5.34%	4.90%	4.50%
					5.58%	5.13%	4.71%	4.32%	3.97%	3.64%
				4.92%	4.52%	4.15%	3.81%	3.49%	3.21%	2.94%
			4.33%	3.98%	3.65%	3.35%	3.08%	2.83%	2.59%	2.38%
		3.82%	3.50%	3.22%	2.95%	2.71%	2.49%	2.29%	2.10%	1.93%
	3.36%	3.09%	2.83%	2.60%	2.39%	2.19%	2.01%	1.85%	1.70%	1.56%
2.96%	2.72%	2.50%	2.29%	2.11%	1.93%	1.77%	1.63%	1.50%	1.37%	1.26%

FIGURE 11.7   The binomial interest rate tree after drift adjustment.

0	0.5	1	1.5	2	2.5	3	3.5	4	4.5	5
										7.95%
									7.37%	6.53%
								6.79%	6.05%	5.47%
							6.24%	5.58%	5.07%	4.68%
						5.69%	5.12%	4.68%	4.34%	4.09%
					5.17%	4.68%	4.29%	4.00%	3.79%	3.64%
				4.67%	4.25%	3.92%	3.67%	3.49%	3.36%	3.24%
			4.20%	3.84%	3.56%	3.35%	3.19%	3.05%	2.93%	2.83%
		3.76%	3.45%	3.22%	3.03%	2.87%	2.73%	2.61%	2.51%	2.42%
	3.35%	3.09%	2.88%	2.70%	2.54%	2.40%	2.29%	2.19%	2.10%	2.03%
2.96%	2.73%	2.54%	2.36%	2.22%	2.09%	1.97%	1.88%	1.80%	1.73%	1.67%

FIGURE 11.8   The binomial interest rate tree after drift adjustment and floating volatility.

bond is at maturity and there is no sense to do it. Therefore, we can assume a decreasing volatility from 11% to 5% during the bond's life. This reduces the width of the binomial tree. With this assumption, the maximum interest rate of the binomial tree at time t_5 is 7.95% (Figure 11.8).

11.2.3.2   Determine the Value of an Option-Free Bond

After determining the evolution of the interest rates, we calculate the value of the option-free bond. In this case, we develop a binomial tree by ignoring the call feature in which at maturity the value of bond is 100. Although the final value could be equal to 104 (principal plus coupons), we consider at maturity the bond's ex coupon value. In fact, at year 5 the bond's price is 100.

In other nodes, the fair value of the bond is calculated by using the discount rate determined before in Figure 11.8. For instance, at year 4.5, the bond's price

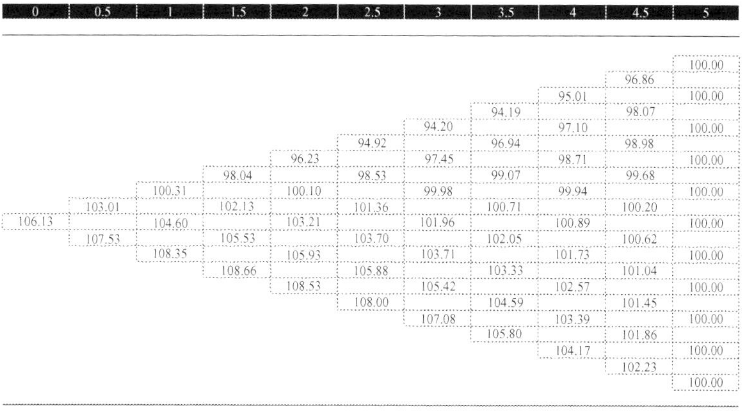

FIGURE 11.9   The binomial price tree for an option-free bond.

at the highest yield of 7.37% is given by Formula (11.5). The bond's price is 104 in the up- and downstate.

$$P_{\text{bond}} = \frac{0.5 \times 104 + 0.5 \times 104}{1 + 0.0737} = 96.86 \qquad (11.5)$$

We can perform the calculation for each node at year 4. At the highest yield for year 4 (6.79%), the price is given by (11.6):

$$P_{\text{bond}} = \frac{0.5 \times (96.86 + 4) + 0.5 \times (98.07 + 4)}{1 + 0.0679} = 95.01 \qquad (11.6)$$

The process is repeated until time t_0 for which the bond's price is 106.13. The binomial tree is shown in Figure 11.9.

11.2.3.3   Determine the Value of an Embedded Call Option

After determining the value of an option-free bond, we calculate the value of the option element. On the maturity, the value of the option is 0 because the bond's ex coupon value is 100 and equal to the strike price. In other nodes, the option has value if the strike price is less than bond's price. The strike price for each node is shown in Table 11.3. Consider also that the value of the option decreases as the bond approaches maturity due to the decreasing probability to redeem the bond. Figure 11.10 shows the value of a call option. The holder of the option has substantially the choice to exercise the option or wait a further period. Therefore, the value of the option if exercised is given by (11.7):

$$V_T^C = \max(0, P - S) \qquad (11.7)$$

where V_T^C is the value of the call option if exercised; P is the value of the bond at each node and S is the strike price according to the call schedule.

Conversely, if the option is held the value is discounted at each node at the risk-free rate of the binomial tree. It is given by (11.8):

0	0.5	1	1.5	2	2.5	3	3.5	4	4.5	5
										0.00
									0.00	0.00
								0.00	0.00	0.00
							0.00	0.00	0.00	0.00
						0.00	0.00	0.00	0.00	0.00
					0.01	0.00	0.00	0.00	0.00	0.00
				0.08	0.15	0.03	0.05	0.00	0.00	0.00
			0.23	0.38		0.27		0.10	0.00	0.00
		0.52	0.80		0.62		0.49		0.20	0.00
	1.10	1.69		1.23		0.96		0.89		0.00
2.31			2.58		1.84		1.31		0.62	0.00
	3.52	5.35		3.93		2.71		1.73		0.00
		5.66			3.88		2.33		1.04	0.00
			6.53			4.42		2.57		0.00
				6.00			3.59		1.45	0.00
					6.08			3.39		0.00
						4.80			1.86	0.00
							4.17			0.00
									2.23	0.00

FIGURE 11.10   The binomial price tree for a call option.

$$V_t^C = \frac{0.5 \times V_U + 0.5 \times V_D}{(1+r)} \qquad (11.8)$$

where V_t^C is the value of the option held for a further period; V_U is the value of the option in the upstate; V_D is the value of the option in the downstate and r is the discount rate.

Therefore, the value of the option is given by (11.9):

$$V^C = \max \left(V_T^C, V_t^C \right) \qquad (11.9)$$

Several factors affect the decision if exercising the option or not. The first one is the asymmetric profit-loss profile. The potential gain of the option holder is unlimited when the price of the underlying asset rises, and losing only the initial investment if the price decreases. The second one is the time of value. In fact, in callable bonds, usually the price decreases as the bond approaches maturity. This incentives the option holder to delay the exercise for a lower strike price. However, coupon payments with lower interest rates can favour the early exercise.

11.2.3.4   Determine the Value of a Callable Bond

Since the option is held by the issuer, the option element decreases the value of the bond. Therefore, the value of a callable bond is found as an option-free bond less the option element according to Formula (11.3). For the hypothetical bond, the price is 106.13–2.31 or 103.82. This is shown in Figure 11.11. The binomial tree shows that at maturity the option free and callable bond have the same price, or 100. Before the maturity, if the interest rates go down, the callable bond's values are less than an option-free bond, and in particular when the embedded option is deeply in the money, the callable values equal the strike price according to the call schedule. Conversely, when the interest rates go up, the option free and callable bonds have the same price.

0	0.5	1	1.5	2	2.5	3	3.5	4	4.5	5
										100.00
									96.86	
								95.01		100.00
							94.19		98.07	
						94.20		97.10		100.00
					94.90		96.94		98.98	
				96.14		97.43		98.71		100.00
			97.81		98.38		99.02		99.68	
		99.80		99.72		99.70		99.84		100.00
	101.91		101.33		100.74		100.22		100.00	
103.82		102.91		101.98		101.00		100.00		100.00
	104.02		102.95		101.86		100.75		100.00	
		103.00		102.00		101.00		100.00		100.00
			103.00		102.00		101.00		100.00	
				102.00		101.00		100.00		100.00
					102.00		101.00		100.00	
						101.00		100.00		100.00
							101.00		100.00	
								100.00		100.00
									100.00	
										100.00

FIGURE 11.11   The binomial price tree for a callable bond.

Consider also that the option element can be included in the interest rate. In Section 11.1.3, we explained the concept of option-adjusted spread. Given the bond's price, we can calculate the spread including the option element. This is performed with a binomial tree used for pricing an option-free bond.

In other words, if the callable bond price is 103.82, we set this price in the binomial tree shown in Figure 11.9 and through an iterative procedure, we find an option-adjusted spread that matches the price sought. In our case, the option-adjusted spread is around 630 bps over the risk-free yield curve (Figure 11.12).

11.2.4   Valuing Putable Bonds

The pricing of putable bonds is performed with the same methodology exposed before. As introduced, putable bonds give the bondholder the right to sell the bond back before maturity. This is usually done if the interest rates go up.

0	0.5	1	1.5	2	2.5	3	3.5	4	4.5	5
										100.00
									96.32	
								94.05		100.00
							92.90		97.61	
						92.65		96.28		100.00
					93.16		95.83		98.59	
				94.30		96.10		98.00		100.00
			95.99		96.99		98.10		99.34	
		98.15		98.40		98.79		99.32		100.00
	100.76		100.30		99.99		99.86		99.90	
103.82		102.67		101.70		100.91		100.33		100.00
	105.54		103.91		102.48		101.29		100.35	
		106.65		104.59		102.78		101.23		100.00
			107.24		104.81		102.65		100.80	
				107.37		104.61		102.14		100.00
					107.08		104.01		101.25	
						106.38		103.03		100.00
							105.31		101.69	
								103.87		100.00
									102.09	
										100.00

FIGURE 11.12   The binomial price tree with the option-adjusted spread.

TABLE 11.4 Put Schedule

year 0.5	year 1	year 1.5	year 2	year 2.5	year 3	year 3.5	year 4	year 4.5	year 5
96	96	97	97	98	98	99	99	100	100

To explain the pricing methodology, we suppose a putable bond with the same characteristics of the callable bond. The putable bond can be given back to the issuer with the following put schedule shown in Table 11.4.

The pricing of the conventional bond is the same than the one exposed for callable bonds in Figure 11.9. Therefore, the option-free bond is always equal to 106.13. The main difference consists in the estimation of the embedded option (put option rather than call option) and pricing of the putable bond. Thus, we illustrate these two steps:

- Determine the value of an embedded put option;
- Determine the value of a putable bond.

11.2.4.1   Determine the Value of an Embedded Put Option

Conversely to a callable bond, the embedded option of a putable bond is a put option. Therefore, the value is estimated as the maximum between 0 and the difference between the strike price and bond's price. The strike price is defined according to the put schedule, while the bond's price is the value of the option-free bond at each node as shown in Figure 11.9. The value at maturity of a putable option if exercised is given by Formula (11.10):

$$V_T^P = \max(0, S - P) \qquad (11.10)$$

Also for putable bonds, there is the choice of the option holder if exercising the option or wait a further period. Therefore, Formula (11.8) and (11.9) can be used also for putable bonds.

The embedded option has value when the interest rates go up. Figure 11.13 illustrates the value of a put option. As with callable bonds, the put option is worthless at maturity because the bond is given back in each case. Before the maturity, the put option decreases its value as the bond approaches maturity. The put option value is equal to 0.33.

An important consideration should be made. Both bonds, callable and putable, have been evaluated with an upward yield curve. In fact, as discussed in the previous section, the model yield curve is calibrated with the market yield curve, which has a positive slope. Therefore, the main rule is that increasing

0	0.5	1	1.5	2	2.5	3	3.5	4	4.5	5
										0.00
									3.14	
								4.99		0.00
							4.81		1.93	
						4.80		2.90		0.00
					3.17		2.09		1.02	
				2.07		1.55		1.29		0.00
			1.33		0.97		0.73		0.32	
		0.84		0.60		0.40		0.16		0.00
	0.53		0.36		0.22		0.08		0.00	
0.33		0.21		0.12		0.04		0.00		0.00
	0.12		0.07		0.04		0.00		0.00	
		0.04		0.02		0.00		0.00		0.00
			0.01		0.00		0.00		0.00	
				0.00		0.00		0.00		0.00
					0.00		0.00		0.00	
						0.00		0.00		0.00
							0.00		0.00	
								0.00		0.00
									0.00	
										0.00

FIGURE 11.13   The binomial price tree of a put option.

the slope of interest rates, the callable bond decreases the value. In contrast, for putable bond, an upward yield curve increases its value.

11.2.4.2   Determine the Value of a Putable Bond

As exposed in Formula (11.4), the value of a putable bond is the sum of an option-free bond and an embedded put option. Therefore, conversely to a callable bond, the embedded option increases the value of the bond. When the option is deeply in the money, the bond matches the values defined in the put schedule. When the option has no value, option free and putable bonds have the same price. The value of our hypothetical putable bond is $106.13 + 0.33$ or 106.45. This is illustrated in Figure 11.14.

0	0.5	1	1.5	2	2.5	3	3.5	4	4.5	5
										100.00
									100.00	
								100.00		100.00
							99.00		100.00	
						99.00		100.00		100.00
					98.09		99.80		100.00	
				98.30		100.38		100.10		100.00
			99.38		99.50		100.80		100.20	
		101.16		100.70		102.00		100.89		100.00
	103.54		102.49		101.58		102.05		100.62	
106.45		104.81		103.33		103.71		101.73		100.00
	107.66		105.60		103.72		103.33		101.04	
		108.38		105.94		105.42		102.57		100.00
			108.67		105.88		104.59		101.45	
				108.53				103.39		100.00
					108.00				101.86	
						107.08				100.00
							105.80			
								104.17		100.00
									102.23	
										100.00

FIGURE 11.14   The binomial price tree of a putable bond.

11.3 STEP-UP CALLABLE NOTES

Step-up callable notes are a particular type of structured fixed income products. These bonds offer a coupon payment that increase during the bond's life. Moreover, they include a call option, that as we discussed earlier, the issuer has the right to redeem the bond early. The question, whether a callable step-up note will be called or not always depends on the evolution of interests rates. Therefore, the inclusion of these two characteristics makes the bond attractive to investors with higher performance than a conventional bond. The added variable coupon element acts for an investor as cushion compared to a conventional callable bond. In fact, the increasing coupon payment increases the value of a callable bond. However, if interest rates go down and coupon payments increase, the incentive of the issuer to redeem the bond early is greater than a simple callable.

To explain this bond, we illustrate the same example shown before in which we include also a variable coupon payment with the time schedule shown in Table 11.5.

The first effect that we have is that the value of an option-free bond increases with rising coupon payments. The pricing of the conventional bond performed in Figure 11.9 is modified with the step-up coupon payment. The pricing is shown in Figure 11.15.

TABLE 11.5 Coupon payment Schedule

year 0.5	year 1	year 1.5	year 2	year 2.5	year 3	year 3.5	year 4	year 4.5	year 5
4	4	4.15	4.15	4.3	4.3	4.45	4.45	4.6	4.6

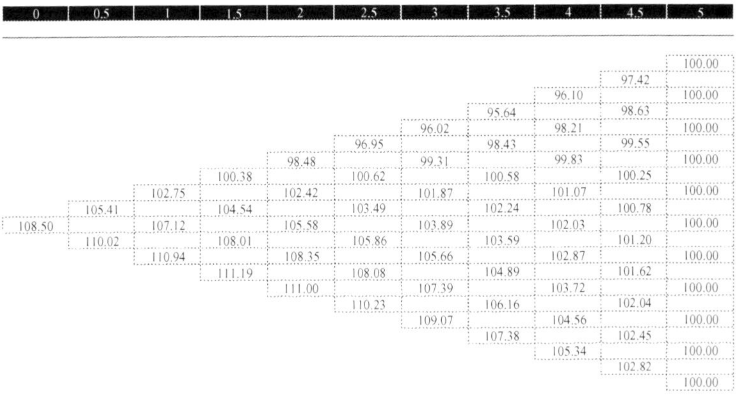

FIGURE 11.15 The binomial price tree of a conventional bond with step-up feature.

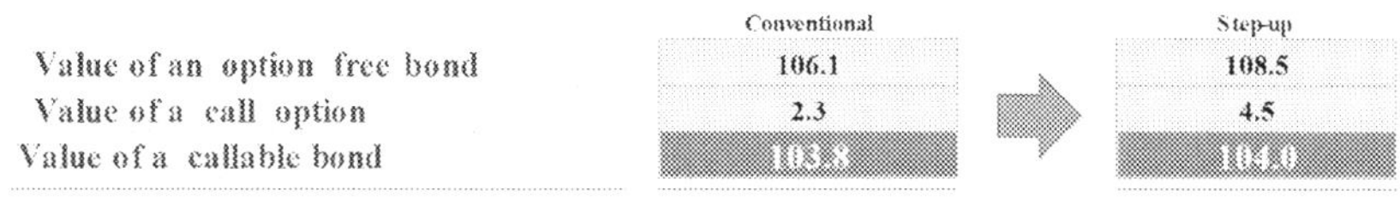

	Conventional		Step-up
Value of an option free bond	106.1		108.5
Value of a call option	2.3		4.5
Value of a callable bond	103.8		104.0

FIGURE 11.16   The binomial price tree of a callable bond with step-up feature.

As shown in Figure 11.15, the added step-up feature increases the value from 106.13 to 108.5. However, the inclusion of this feature affects also the values of the embedded call option and callable bond. In practice, increasing the value of the conventional bond at each node increases the value of the embedded option. The call option is now 4.5. As a conventional callable bond, the value of a call option is then subtracted to the one of an option-free bond. Figure 11.16 shows that the value of a step-up callable note is 104.

11.4   SINKING FUNDS

Sinking fund is a debt instrument that requires the issuer to redeem a part of the outstanding principal each year over the bond's life. The provision assures that the bond is periodically repaid, avoiding the large principal repayment at maturity. This characteristic decreases the yield compared to a conventional bond. The issuer can redeem the bond with two main methods:

- The first one, the issuer may purchase the bond in the open market and deliver it to the trustee for cancellation;
- The second one, it works as a callable bond and the issuer may call the bond back. This is, therefore, a *partial call*, in which only a part of the bond may be called.

Since in the second case the issuer redeems the bond only if interest rates drop, the choice of the method is affected by the level of interest rates. If the interest rates rise, the issuer will purchase the bond in the market. Alternatively, if the interest rates drop, the issuer will call the bond back. In the second case, the bond is evaluated using the same binomial tree method that we introduced earlier.

11.5   WEB SITE MODELS

The Web site associated with this book contains an Excel spreadsheet demonstrating the valuation of callable and putable bonds. The reader may use the spreadsheet to undertake such valuation analysis using his or her own parameter inputs.

Details of how to access the Web site are contained in the preface.

BIBLIOGRAPHY

Brennan, M.J., Schwartz, E.S., March 1977. Saving bonds, retractable bonds and callable bonds. J. Financ. Econ. 5 (1), 67–88.

Choudhry, M., 2003. The bond and money markets: strategy, trading, analysis, first ed. Butterworth-Heinemann.

Kalotay, A.J., Williams, G.O., Fabozzi, F.J., 1991. A model for the valuation of bonds and embedded options. Financial Analysts J. 49, 35–46, May-June.

Kish, R., Livingstone, M., 1992. The determinants of the call feature on corporate bonds. J. Banking Financ. 16, 687–703.

Windas, T., 1993. An introduction to option-adjusted spread analysis, first ed. Bloomberg Press.

Index

Note: Page numbers followed by *f* indicate figures.

real cash flows and yields, 132–133
  zero-coupon indexation, 128–129
Variable roughness penalty (VRP) method, 98
Vasicek model, 48–51
Volatility, 60, 185–188

W

Waggoner model, 95–98
Wiener process. *See* Brownian motion

Z

Zero-coupon bond, 47
Zero-coupon bond market, 101
Zero-coupon curve, 2
Zero-coupon indexation, 128–129
Zero-coupon yield curve, 146–147, 147*f*
Zero volatility spread, 157
Z-spread measure, 6